The Baby Book

The Baby Book

Dr David Harvey

CAVENDISH HOUSE

Acknowledgements
The publishers would like to thank the following:
Dr. J. S. Yu from the Royal Alexandra Hospital
for Children in Sydney for his advice on Australian
medical practice. J. M. Tanner and R. H. Whitehouse
of the University of London Institute of Child Health
for the use of the Height and Weight Standard Charts
reproduced on pages 138-141. The University of
London Audio-Visual Centre for the use of drawings
by Jennifer Webb reproduced on pages 9, 26, 59 and 60.
The chart on page 71 is taken from Sinsarian and
McLendon, 1942, Journal of Paediatrics, Vol. 20, p.93,
reproduced by kind permission of C. V. Mosby
Company, St. Louis, Missouri, USA.
We would also like to thank the staff of the
Paediatric Department at Queen Charlotte's Maternity
Hospital, London, for their patience and
co-operation during the preparation of this book.

Published by
Marshall Cavendish Books Limited
58 Old Compton Street
London W1V 5PA

© Marshall Cavendish Limited 1975-83

First printing 1975
Revised 1980
Third printing 1983
Printed in Hong Kong

ISBN 0 85685 897 8

Editor's note
Square brackets denote Australian terminology
and medical practice.

A note about this book

I have set out to make this book as straightforward as possible. My aim has been to give clear and ordinary information on medical and developmental matters to do with babies, from conception up to the age of three years. Throughout the book, I have described the baby as *he* or *him*. This is purely an expression of convenience; I hope that if you have a little girl you will not feel upset. It is just that I hate describing a baby as *it*, and there is no personal pronoun which will do for both sexes in English at present. I hope there will be one day.

The sort of information I have included about the growth and development comes from work described in scientific journals, mainly British or American. I hope that it is not too technical; I think it should help you to understand the enormous range of development in the under-threes, and to see how your child fits into the overall pattern.

This book is meant to explain some of the medical mysteries of childbirth and babies. I do not believe there is anything to be gained by doctors hiding what they think or do. I hope that the explanations are clear without being frightening.

If you have had a baby, you will already have ideas about baby care. You may disagree with me or have very definite views of your own. That is good, because you know your own baby: I haven't met him. Any thoughts about babies can only be very general; you, your husband and the baby will need to work out life between you.

As I am a paediatrician, or children's doctor, I was pleased to have assistance with the chapters on pregnancy and confinement from Miss Underhill, an obstetrician, and Miss Adams, a midwife, who have been most helpful. They have altered these chapters for the better. Dr. Fancourt, a paediatrician like me, has helped me with the whole book. I should also like to acknowledge all I have learnt from those paediatricians with whom I trained.

David Harvey, 1975

Contents

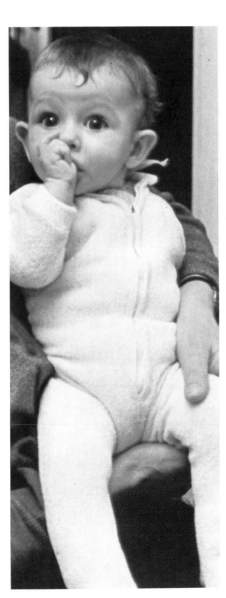

Conception & pregnancy

Conception

Below: in the middle of the menstrual cycle the mature ovum leaves the ovary (1). After fertilization (2), the ovum divides once (3), then into four (4): this takes about two days. Further cleavage occurs (5, 6) with the cell doubling each time. The dividing ovum travels into the uterus, forming an outer casing and an inner cell mass (7). Implantation (8) then takes place after about a week in all.

A book about babies should really start at the very beginning, as it helps to understand exactly what is happening to your body during pregnancy. A newborn baby may look small to you, but he was minute when he started life 40 weeks earlier when two cells joined. The sperm and the ovum (or egg) are far too small to be seen, except under a microscope. They join after a journey by the sperm which is beset by hazards, which could make one wonder how conception ever occurs.

A man is constantly producing sperms and is therefore capable of fathering a baby at any time from puberty, at about 13 years of age, until he dies; but a woman only produces an ovum once a month. She starts producing ova at puberty and continues until menstruation stops, a time called the menopause, at about 45 years of age. An ovum usually leaves the ovary about two

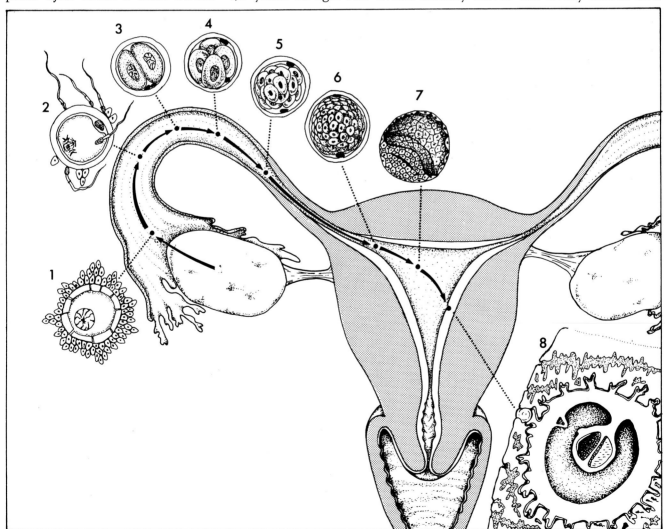

weeks after a menstrual period; if it does not meet a sperm within 48 hours, it cannot develop further and will be washed out of the uterus at the next menstrual period. The moment of ovulation, when the ovum leaves the ovary, is accompanied in a woman by some physical changes, of which the most easily recorded is a sudden jump in body temperature. This can be useful for a couple who wish to choose a time for sexual intercourse with the best chance of conception.

The diagram on the previous page shows the uterus (also called the womb), the Fallopian tubes, and the ovaries. The ovum is collected by the finger-like ends of the Fallopian tube nearest to it. It is then wafted slowly along the tube until it reaches the uterus after about four or five days.

Hundreds of millions of sperms are deposited in the vagina during sexual intercourse, but only a few hundred will reach the Fallopian tubes, and only one will fertilize the ovum. They have a long swim and a number of hazards on the way – the mucus in the cervix tends to block their passage and they have to swim against the current of the fluid on the lining of the uterus.

After the ovum has been fertilized, the cell divides into two within a single coat, then the two cells divide again and so on, until the millions of cells in the baby have been formed.

The developing ovum passes down the tube and settles in the lining of the uterus. Remarkable hormone changes are produced in the woman, so that the next menstrual period is prevented and the baby can develop – it is called an embryo at this stage.

Twins can be produced in two ways: the egg may split into two shortly after it has met the sperm, producing two babies who look exactly alike – identical twins; or the mother may produce two eggs which are fertilized by two different sperms, which will produce two babies who look like brothers or sisters, but are not identical. Twins are commoner in some families than others, but non-identical are the more usual type.

Inheritance

Opposite: The rules of inheritance do not always take account of mutations, accidental changes in the genes. This Indian boy's bright blue eyes are the result of such a mutation. Most people in India have brown eyes.

You may be wondering why a baby inherits certain features from the father and others from the mother. Each one of the cells of our body contains tiny worm-like structures called chromosomes. There are twenty-three pairs of chromosomes, including a pair called the sex chromosomes. Of every pair, one chromosome has come from the mother and one from the father. The chromosomes contain minute chemical substances which make our bodies produce the ordinary physical characteristics we recognize, such as blue eyes or black hair, as well as controlling the thousands upon thousands of chemical processes inside us. Each of us is an equal mixture of our parents.

These chemical substances of a chromosome are known as genes and each one is matched exactly by another gene on the other chromosome. They are therefore present in pairs. One gene may overpower the effect of the gene on the other chromosome and is then called dominant. The one which is overpowered is known as recessive.

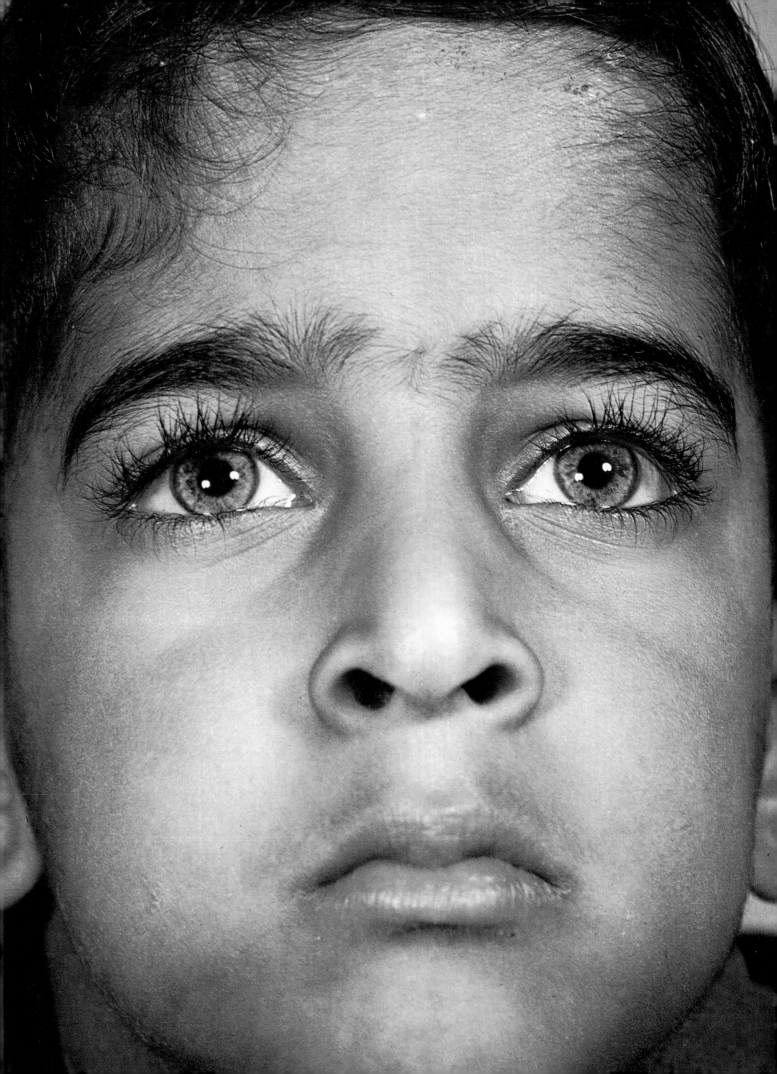

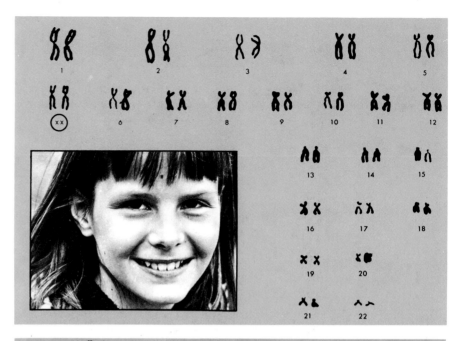

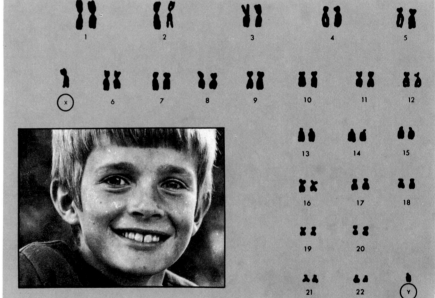

Every human cell contains 46 chromosomes, two of each kind, and these in turn all contain minute chemical substances called genes. Right: A girl has two large chromosomes, called the XX pair. Below: A boy, on the other hand, has only one X chromosome, plus a much smaller Y one. These determine their sex.

Some conditions are inherited with a dominant gene: an example is a small piece of skin joining the second and third toes: a feature which is common in some families. In this case a parent will have one gene for this condition on one of the two chromosomes; there will therefore by a one-in-two chance of passing the condition on to the baby. If a gene is recessive, it can be passed on to the baby but will have no effect unless it is matched by another recessive gene on the other chromosome. Babies can only have this double dose if both their parents are carrying a recessive gene. In this situation only one in four babies of such parents will show the feature, two of the other four will be carriers like their parents, and the fourth will be completely normal. There are a large number of conditions inherited in this way, including many illnesses of the body's chemistry such as phenylketonuria, for which the Guthrie Test is done at birth (see page 54). A normal feature which is inherited in this way is red hair.

The sex chromosomes are rather special because they are not the same size. A woman has two X chromosomes whereas a man has an X and a Y. A woman can thus only pass on an X chromosome to her child, whereas a man passes on an X or a Y. This means that it is the man who will determine the sex of a child. There are many stories in history of men who have divorced their wives for producing only female children — the men were the ones to blame!

The first signs of pregnancy

As soon as the growing embryo has settled comfortably into the uterus, hormone changes produce signs which will tell a woman that she is pregnant. These are:

1. **Amenorrhoea (or absence of periods).** The length of a pregnancy is usually dated from the first day of the last normal period which has occurred, that is usually about two weeks *before* conception has taken place. It is very important that the doctors should know the exact date of the last period; it is helpful for a woman to make a note of each period in a diary or on a calendar, so that the safe time for the baby's arrival can be calculated. It is safer for the baby to be born at about 40 weeks of pregnancy, and less safe earlier or later than this date.

2. **Changes in the breasts.** These are often noticed before anything else. The breasts get larger and may become tender. Later in pregnancy the nipple enlarges and the area of special skin around the nipple darkens. This area is called the areola.

3. **Morning sickness.** This is a traditional sign of pregnancy, but luckily not every woman has it. The feeling of sickness, or nausea, is usually in the morning but can be at any time of the day. It is not always accompanied by actual vomiting.

4. **Frequency in passing urine.** This is probably due to the enlarging uterus pressing on the bladder, which contains urine.

Apart from a missed period, these signs can often be very vague and a woman may therefore be in some doubt whether she really is pregnant. This can often happen in a woman with irregular periods. There are now some rapid chemical tests which will produce a result within a few hours from a specimen of urine. These tests are pretty reliable and can detect pregnancy about ten days after the first missed period, that is, about six weeks after the last period.

The growing embryo

During the first two months of pregnancy, the embryo grows rapidly from a tiny speck to a small animal which looks almost human. The shapes an embryo goes through are fascinating because they trace the history of our ancestors. At one stage the embryo has a tail which later shrinks. Blood vessels which were important to distant fish-like ancestors come and go. An analysis of all the changes in the embryo has been very important in mapping out the course of evolution. The developing baby is called an *embryo* for the first two months and then a *fetus* until birth. The chart on page 24 shows embryonic and fetal development during the full 40 weeks of pregnancy.

Care of your health in the first three months of pregnancy

About one pint of milk per day, plus iron supplements in tablet form, are important in pregnancy.

14

Morning sickness. One of the most annoying disorders which can occur in any pregnancy is sickness. It usually takes the form of a feeling of sickness (nausea), but can lead to distressing vomiting. You should consult your doctor if you find you are vomiting very frequently; he may be able to prescribe something to help you. Simple measures may alleviate nausea. Some biscuits beside your bed to take first thing in the morning may help, as may an early morning cup of tea. Fatty foods are particularly likely to make the nausea worse and you should therefore avoid fried foods and anything containing fat or grease. A short break from cooking often works wonders.

Vaginal bleeding. If you are quite certain that you are pregnant, you should report any bleeding from the vagina to your doctor; such bleeding may indicate that you could have a miscarriage. By the way, the proper name for a miscarriage is abortion, which is not only used as a term for those pregnancies which are interrupted early and deliberately.

Sex during pregnancy. Couples are often anxious to know if sex should be avoided during pregnancy. There seems to be no reason why sexual intercourse should not take place at any time during a normal pregnancy. However, it should not take place if there has been any vaginal bleeding, as this may indicate the beginning of a miscarriage and intercourse might make the miscarriage inevitable.

Diet. A pregnant woman should continue to take the diet she usually eats. It is, of course, very important that it should be balanced. This means that it should contain reasonable quantities of protein, fat and carbohydrate, as well as minerals and vitamins. Proteins are found in meat, milk and cheese; fats are present in cream and the fatty parts of meat; carbohydrates are the commonest foods, mostly eaten as bread, sugar and starchy vegetables such as potatoes. Green vegetables and fruit add important vitamins to your diet. If you put on too much weight during pregnancy, your doctor may suggest that you should cut down the carbohydrate in your diet.

Milk is a very useful food as it contains protein and other useful foods together with calcium which the baby needs for his bones and teeth. Try to drink one to two pints of milk a day, if you can. Some women are upset by milk; cheese and yoghurt are good substitutes.

Never go on a crash slimming diet during pregnancy. This used to be done in the past to try and reduce the baby's size at birth, but it is very unwise, both for yourself and the baby.

Cravings for unusual foods are very common during pregnancy. Usually this takes the form of a desire to eat something like bananas or drink orange-juice at all hours of the day, but some women have noticed most peculiar appetites which give them a desire for coal or mothballs! You should avoid eating things which are not usually regarded as food.

Drugs. Do not take any drugs at all during pregnancy, unless you have asked your doctor if it is safe to take them. Most

A good balanced diet is essential in pregnancy though it is not necessary to eat extra food: 'eating for two' is a popular delusion. Good, fresh meat, fish and vegetables, fruit, eggs and cheese, combined with a reasonable quantity of carbohydrate in foods like pasta, bread and potatoes: all these will give you the nourishment you need without upsetting the family budget.

medicines do not affect the fetus, but there are some which do.

Your doctor will give a supply of iron and vitamin tablets, if he thinks you need them during your pregnancy. Be very careful to keep iron tablets out of the reach of young children. The pills look like sweets, but are very dangerous if swallowed in large amounts.

Rubella. Try to avoid contact with any infections. Fortunately, most common illnesses do not affect the baby, but one exception is rubella or German measles. This virus causes a mild 'flu'-like illness and a rash. It does no harm to adults or children; once you have had German measles you, and your baby if you later become pregnant, will be protected from a further attack.

However, if the disease is contracted in early pregnancy it interferes with the development of many organs in the fetus, particularly the heart, eyes and ears.

A blood test can now be done to show if you have had recently been infected with the rubella virus. If you think that you have been in contact with rubella or are worried that you have the illness, you should contact your doctor at once.

It is now also possible to vaccinate a woman against rubella. The vaccine cannot be given during pregnancy as it too might interfere with the developing fetus, but it is usually given to all girls in their early teens and to mothers after the baby's birth. It is only given to those women who have never had rubella; in this way all their future pregnancies will be protected.

The first visit to the ante-natal clinic

To work out the date your baby is due pick out the date in the top line when your last period began. Immediately below is the approximate date of birth, about 40 weeks ahead.

It is very important indeed to visit the ante-natal clinic early in your pregnancy. Usually, your family doctor will give a letter to attend a hospital; they will arrange your first visit between two and three months after your last period. At that visit you will meet some of the midwives at the hospital and will be examined by a doctor. This visit is important because many of the basic tests and examinations are done at that time. For instance, your blood-pressure will be measured and any other blood-pressures taken later in pregnancy can be compared with it. Blood will be taken to test your blood group and to make certain you do not have any infection which can be passed on to the baby. Your

Obstetric chart

```
January    1  2  3  4  5  6  7  8  9 10 11 12 13 14 15 16 17 18 19 20 21 22 23 24 25 26 27 28 29 30 31   January
October    8  9 10 11 12 13 14 15 16 17 18 19 20 21 22 23 24 25 26 27 28 29 30 31  1  2  3  4  5  6  7   November

February   1  2  3  4  5  6  7  8  9 10 11 12 13 14 15 16 17 18 19 20 21 22 23 24 25 26 27 28            February
November   8  9 10 11 12 13 14 15 16 17 18 19 20 21 22 23 24 25 26 27 28 29 30  1  2  3  4  5            December

March      1  2  3  4  5  6  7  8  9 10 11 12 13 14 15 16 17 18 19 20 21 22 23 24 25 26 27 28 29 30 31   March
December   6  7  8  9 10 11 12 13 14 15 16 17 18 19 20 21 22 23 24 25 26 27 28 29 30 31  1  2  3  4  5   January

April      1  2  3  4  5  6  7  8  9 10 11 12 13 14 15 16 17 18 19 20 21 22 23 24 25 26 27 28 29 30      April
January    6  7  8  9 10 11 12 13 14 15 16 17 18 19 20 21 22 23 24 25 26 27 28 29 30 31  1  2  3  4      February

May        1  2  3  4  5  6  7  8  9 10 11 12 13 14 15 16 17 18 19 20 21 22 23 24 25 26 27 28 29 30 31   May
February   5  6  7  8  9 10 11 12 13 14 15 16 17 18 19 20 21 22 23 24 25 26 27 28  1  2  3  4  5  6  7   March

June       1  2  3  4  5  6  7  8  9 10 11 12 13 14 15 16 17 18 19 20 21 22 23 24 25 26 27 28 29 30      June
March      8  9 10 11 12 13 14 15 16 17 18 19 20 21 22 23 24 25 26 27 28 29 30 31  1  2  3  4  5  6      April

July       1  2  3  4  5  6  7  8  9 10 11 12 13 14 15 16 17 18 19 20 21 22 23 24 25 26 27 28 29 30 31   July
April      7  8  9 10 11 12 13 14 15 16 17 18 19 20 21 22 23 24 25 26 27 28 29 30  1  2  3  4  5  6  7   May

August     1  2  3  4  5  6  7  8  9 10 11 12 13 14 15 16 17 18 19 20 21 22 23 24 25 26 27 28 29 30 31   August
May        8  9 10 11 12 13 14 15 16 17 18 19 20 21 22 23 24 25 26 27 28 29 30 31  1  2  3  4  5  6  7   June

September  1  2  3  4  5  6  7  8  9 10 11 12 13 14 15 16 17 18 19 20 21 22 23 24 25 26 27 28 29 30      September
June       8  9 10 11 12 13 14 15 16 17 18 19 20 21 22 23 24 25 26 27 28 29 30  1  2  3  4  5  6  7      July

October    1  2  3  4  5  6  7  8  9 10 11 12 13 14 15 16 17 18 19 20 21 22 23 24 25 26 27 28 29 30 31   October
July       8  9 10 11 12 13 14 15 16 17 18 19 20 21 22 23 24 25 26 27 28 29 30 31  1  2  3  4  5  6  7   August

November   1  2  3  4  5  6  7  8  9 10 11 12 13 14 15 16 17 18 19 20 21 22 23 24 25 26 27 28 29 30      November
August     8  9 10 11 12 13 14 15 16 17 18 19 20 21 22 23 24 25 26 27 28 29 30 31  1  2  3  4  5  6      September

December   1  2  3  4  5  6  7  8  9 10 11 12 13 14 15 16 17 18 19 20 21 22 23 24 25 26 27 28 29 30 31   December
September  7  8  9 10 11 12 13 14 15 16 17 18 19 20 21 22 23 24 25 26 27 28 29 30  1  2  3  4  5  6  7   October
```

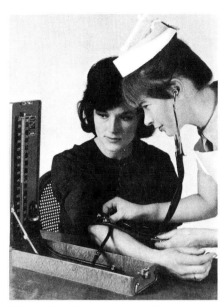

Your blood-pressure will be taken at every ante-natal check up.

The growing baby in the middle of pregnancy

urine will be tested for protein and sugar: this is to check you do not have kidney disease or diabetes. You will also be weighed.

Apart from all these things, the doctor will examine you carefully to make sure you are medically fit and to check on the stage of pregnancy you have reached. You can expect him to do a vaginal examination to estimate the size of the uterus; at about ten weeks of pregnancy, it is easy to feel its size and confirm the length of pregnancy by comparing it with the date of your last period. He will explain to you when the baby is due and why he thinks you should be delivered in hospital or at home.

You can work out when the baby is due by adding nine months and seven days on to the date of the first day of your last normal menstrual period. A pregnancy therefore usually lasts 40 weeks – the end of this time is called term.

The hospital will often arrange for your family doctor to do some of your ante-natal check-ups. You will be given a card, usually called a co-operation card, in which the doctors record what they have found. Keep it very carefully.

Pregnancy is usually divided into three trimesters, each of them lasting three months. At the beginning of the second trimester (12 weeks) the fetus is still very small and would not be able to survive by itself. Inside the uterus the fetus now looks like a miniature human, and is surrounded by a sac of fluid – this is known as the amniotic sac and contains the amniotic fluid. The sac serves to cushion the fetus so that it is not hurt by any minor accident that may occur to its mother.

The fetus receives all the food and oxygen it needs from the mother, and it is also able to get rid of any waste products back into her. Both the feeding and the elimination of waste products occurs through an organ called the placenta, or after-birth, so called because it leaves the uterus and is expelled from the vagina after the baby has been born. The embryo is at first completely enclosed in membranes which can obtain nourishment from the lining of the uterus. Gradually, part of the membranes thickens to become a pad (the placenta); the fetus is attached by the umbilical cord, which contains blood-vessels. The fetus pumps blood to the placenta to get rid of waste products and to receive supplies of food and oxygen in the blood returning along the same cord.

During the second trimester a woman becomes obviously pregnant. At twelve weeks after the last menstrual period, the uterus can just be felt by a doctor examining the abdomen but he will need to do a vaginal examination to estimate its size. Soon the uterus can easily be felt and the abdomen swells as the fetus gets bigger. A very important moment in the second trimester is when the fetus's movements are first strong enough to be felt. The fetus moves a lot, wriggling, kicking and somersaulting. The first fluttering movements in a woman expecting her first baby are felt about eighteen weeks after the last period, but may be felt earlier in somebody who is expecting her second baby. A

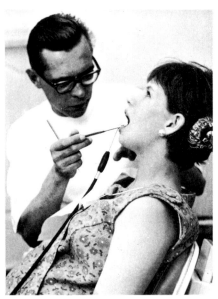

Regular dental check-ups are important during pregnancy. Combined with a good diet and effective brushing they help you avoid problems with your teeth.

Amniocentesis

Opposite: The position of the fetus in the sixth month (about 28 weeks) of pregnancy. This is a stylized view: in fact the fetus's blood vessels are much more prominent and the skin colour is redder. Premature babies retain this red skin tone, whereas babies born after term have very pale skin. The fetus is surrounded by a sac of fluid which cushions and protects it. The source of the amniotic fluid is not known for certain. At least a part of it is produced by the fetus passing urine into the sac. The volume of fluid is kept constant because the baby swallows some of it and some more passes across the placenta or the membranes into the mother. The placenta is connected to the fetus by the umbilical cord, through which the fetus obtains nourishment and can get rid of waste matter. At 28 weeks a fetus may well be in a breech position, but will probably turn later.

careful note should be made of the day when you feel movements, as the doctor may use them in calculating more accurately when the baby is due to arrive.

Smoking is known to decrease the growth of a fetus. We are not certain how it does this, but it may affect the amount of blood reaching the uterus or reduce the amount of oxygen carried in the mother's blood. As a result, the babies of smoking mothers are smaller at birth than those of non-smokers. It is also possible that mental growth is hampered.

It is important to reduce your smoking as much as possible during pregnancy; if at all possible, cut it out altogether. You should think of giving up smoking as soon as you are expecting a baby, but it is not too late to reduce it at any time.

Teeth. Visit the dentist at least twice during your pregnancy. Let him know that you are pregnant if it isn't obvious at the first visit, then he can take precautions if he thinks that x-rays are necessary. In Britain and some western countries mothers may be entitled to free treatment both during pregnancy and afterwards. Treatment is especially important if you are intending to breast-feed. It is worth being careful about brushing your teeth and avoiding sugary foods, a major cause of dental caries.

You may find that your doctor will recommend this procedure, especially if you are older than the average – for example over 40. I have mentioned that the baby is surrounded by amniotic fluid; it is possible to tap this fluid by passing a fine, hollow needle through the abdominal wall into the sac. The fluid contains chemicals that the fetus has passed out in urine, but more important it also contains cells which have been shed from the skin of the fetus. These cells can be grown in a laboratory and examined for some defects of the body's chemistry or to look at the chromosomes. One of the commonest reasons for doing this is to look for a condition where every cell in the body has an extra chromosome, so that there are 47 chromosomes in each cell instead of the usual 46. This condition is called Down's syndrome, or mongolism, which is a major cause of mental handicap today. It occurs more frequently in the children of older mothers; this is the reason for searching for it in someone over about 40. The cells in the fluid are cultured and the chromosomes counted to show whether the fetus is normal or not. In cases where a mongol fetus is found, termination of pregnancy might be offered if the parents felt that this was something they could accept.

Some rare disorders of the body's chemistry (called inborn errors of metabolism) can also be looked for in the growing cells. Unfortunately not all of them can be found in this way; your doctor will be able to advise you, if there is someone in your family who has such an illness.

The chemicals in the fluid can also be measured. The most usual reason for doing this is rhesus disease; the fluid becomes yellower than usual and the intensity of the colour shows whether

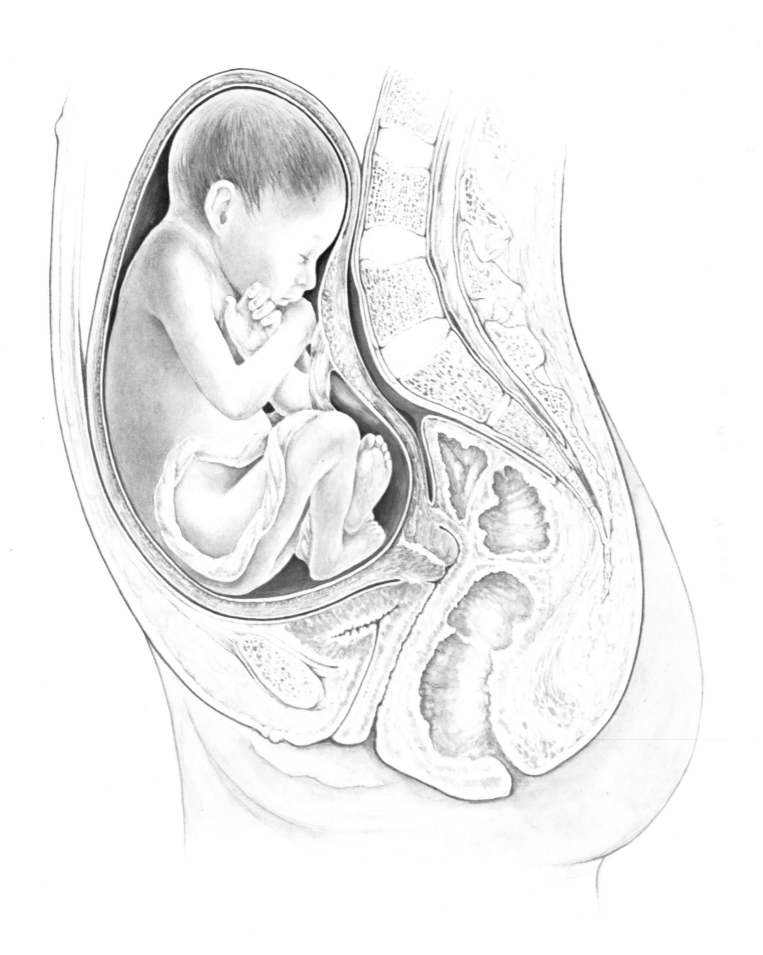

the fetus is affected or not. Another test can be used late in pregnancy to see whether the fetus's lungs have become mature enough for him to breath normally after birth. This may be done before induction to ensure a baby is ready to be born.

Rhesus disease

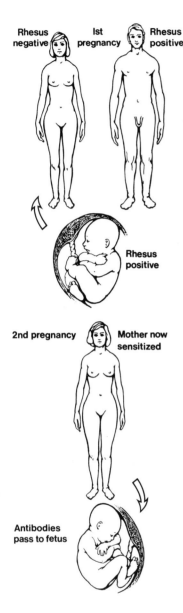

How rhesus disease can occur: 1st pregnancy – a rhesus-negative mother may conceive a rhesus positive fetus. Some of its cells pass across to the mother at birth. She may then produce antibodies to destroy them. 2nd pregnancy – the mother has been sensitized. Her antibodies cross back to a second rhesus positive fetus to destroy its red blood cells.

This is luckily an uncommon condition, but it is an important one because it can produce a serious illness in the fetus or new-born baby. In Britain and Australia about 15% of women have the rhesus-negative blood group, but in some other parts of the world it is extremely rare indeed. If a rhesus-negative woman has a rhesus-positive husband, it is possible for their baby to be rhesus-positive – this is when rhesus disease can occur. During the first pregnancy some of the baby's rhesus-positive red blood cells may get into the mother's blood-stream; this is particularly likely to happen just after the baby has been born. The mother reacts against these foreign cells by producing antibodies to destroy them. These antibodies have no effect on her but would affect another rhesus-positive fetus. Thus during a later pregnancy the antibodies may cross back through the placenta into the fetus to attack its red blood cells. This has two effects: there are not enough red blood cells in the fetus, a condition called anaemia; and severe jaundice occurs in the baby shortly after birth. Rhesus disease may be very mild but sometimes it is bad enough to make a fetus die before being born – one of the causes of stillbirth.

At the first visit to the ante-natal clinic, blood is taken from you to see whether you are rhesus-positive or negative, and at the same time tests are done to see if there are any antibodies in the blood. If you are rhesus-negative, further blood tests will be done at other visits to see if antibodies appear or are increasing. If the antibody level is high an amniocentesis may be performed to estimate the amount of jaundice in the fluid and thus indicate how badly affected the fetus is.

Where there is a serious risk of the fetus dying before being born, three or four blood transfusions may be given to it. This is an exciting advance in medicine, because it means that some babies can be saved from dying before birth. In any case, a baby with rhesus disease is usually born early; labour is started artificially about a month before term.

There is now another exciting advance: rhesus disease can be prevented altogether by giving an injection after the birth of the first rhesus-positive baby. The substance injected, called Anti-D, is the very same antibody that produces so much havoc inside a fetus. When given to a mother shortly after delivery it will destroy any of the baby's red blood cells that have crossed into her blood, before she has any time to produce antibodies of her own against them. It is very important that a rhesus-negative woman should have this injection after delivery or an abortion; otherwise antibodies develop, and her body has a permanent memory for rhesus-positive cells, and all subsequent pregnancies would have to be monitored.

Visits to the ante-natal clinic during the last part of pregnancy

Your doctor will ask you to attend the clinic more frequently as you get nearer to term, when the baby is due. In the last month, you must expect to go to the clinic every week. At every visit your blood pressure will be taken and your urine tested. The purpose of these checks is to make certain that you do not have toxaemia of pregnancy (also called pre-eclampsia), which is common in late pregnancy. It is a combination of high blood-pressure, protein in the urine, and excess fluid in the body causing swelling of the ankles, hands and face (known as oede-ma). If you should develop this condition it will be necessary for you to rest, perhaps in hospital, and labour may have to be started early.

Although the clinic visits often seem tedious and irritating, they are very important. You must make sure that you attend every appointment and be sure to ring the hospital if you are unable to go. The appointments secretary will always try and help you find a time which is convenient for you.

Right: Towards the end of pregnancy the doctor will listen to the fetal heart-beat at every ante-natal check-up.

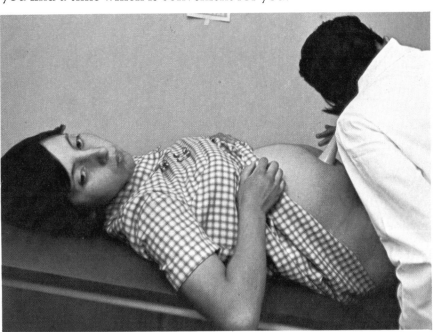

X-rays and ultrasound

X-rays. The doctors will sometimes want to examine you or the baby by x-rays. When this is necessary, it is usually done late in pregnancy when it is safer for the baby.

The bones of a fetus show up on x-rays and help to indicate how old it is. X-rays of your pelvis may also be necessary. Your pelvis is the bony basin inside the hips; if the cavity of the pelvis through which the baby has to pass is too small, then delivery may be very difficult and it may be better to arrange an opera-tion – a caesarian section. An x-ray of the pelvis will help the doctors to assess its size accurately and will help them to decide the safest method of delivery. A vaginal examination is also necessary to work out the size of the birth-canal, which can be assessed by feeling the bones surrounding the vagina; such an examination is often done during the last weeks of pregnancy.

One further reason for taking an x-ray is to see the position of the baby. Most babies lie head-down and it is therefore usual

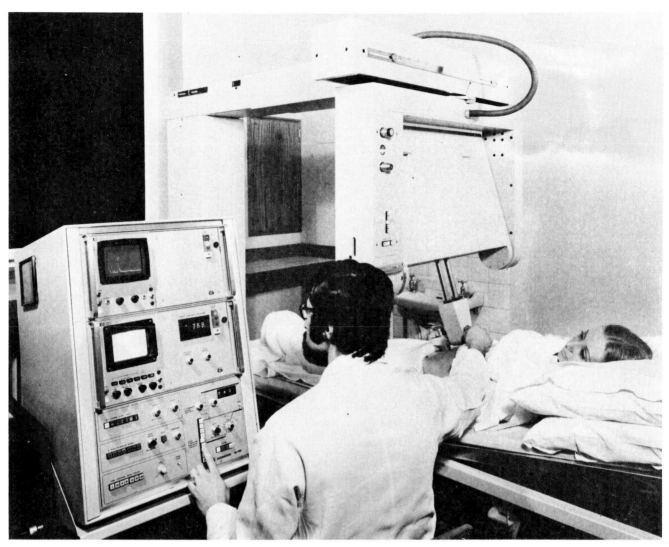

The ultrasound machine looks imposing but it gives the doctor useful information about the fetus. The operator passes the arm of the machine backwards and forwards across the mother's abdomen, and watches the ultrasound 'picture' build up on the small screen in front of him.

for a baby to be born head-first. Sometimes the baby lies with his bottom downwards, this is called breech presentation. One can usually tell by feeling the abdomen whether the fetus is lying head-down or not, but it may be necessary to decide its position by taking an x-ray. It is important, because there is a little more risk for the baby if he is born bottom first and the doctors need to consider carefully which way to deliver him.

If your baby is a 'breech', your doctor may turn him round, but if he will not turn comfortably he can be born safely provided an x-ray of your pelvic bones shows plenty of room.

Ultrasound is an exciting new method of examining the fetus and his growth. A beam of sound waves, at much too high a pitch to be heard, is passed through the abdomen and uterus. The sound bounces off the bones and other organs in the fetus. It is therefore possible to obtain a picture of a cross section of the fetus on a screen which looks rather like a radar screen. The size of the head can also be measured; this means that the growth of the fetus can be followed very accurately, by measuring the size of his head and the rate at which it grows. It is one of the most accurate methods of telling the age of the fetus; and in addition, it gives a warning if the fetus is not growing well and may need to be born early. In that case, the doctors will induce it.

The last few weeks of pregnancy

During most of pregnancy the cervix (or neck) of the uterus projects down a little into the vagina and is tightly closed. In the last few weeks of pregnancy the cervix flattens out, it is usually said that the cervix is 'taken up' so that the opening becomes ready to dilate. During these few weeks the baby's head sinks down into the pelvis; this is called *engagement* of the head. It is important for the doctor to find this because it indicates that your pelvis is big enough to allow the baby to pass through. It occurs earlier in women expecting their first baby than in the second or subsequent babies. When engagement happens you may feel more comfortable, the baby seems less of a heavy load.

Many women are able to continue working until the baby is almost due to be born. In Britain you may be eligible for a maternity allowance which can also make a difference to the time you give up work. Check with the hospital or your local welfare office. In Britain and Australia you could check whether there is a provision for paid maternity or paternity leave at your own or your husband's place of work. You may find that you feel more tired during the last few weeks; it is important that you take sufficient rest when you do feel tired. Many people do not

The last few weeks of pregnancy can be a trying time as the weight of the fetus can make the mother very tired. Try to put your feet up once a day and keep yourself occupied with sedentary jobs like sewing or knitting.

like to lie and sleep during the afternoon, but it is wise to sit down and rest several times a day. The length of time you can keep on working will depend largely on you; if you find that the baby is very heavy, then give up work several weeks before term.

If toxaemia should occur, with high blood-pressure and swelling of the ankles, the doctor may order you to rest strictly at home or even in hospital. Discuss the situation with your employer and decide a time between you when to give up work.

If your waters should break at any time or if you have any bleeding from the vagina, you must report this at once to your doctor or the hospital. Remember that labour sometimes starts before term, so be prepared to go into hospital if necessary two or three weeks before the baby is due.

Time since last period	Time since conception	Approximate length	Stage of development	
4 weeks	2 weeks	½ mm	Embedded in lining of uterus. Embryo is still only a plate of cells – a tiny speck.	
6 weeks	4 weeks	1 cm	Head forming; buds of arms and legs are visible. The heart is beating already.	
8 weeks	6 weeks	1½ cm	Nose, fingers and toes can be seen. The mouth is present and the eyes are forming.	
10 weeks	8 weeks	3 cm	Eyes and eyelids. Fingers clearly separated. Looks human for the first time, but head is big compared to body.	
12 weeks	10 weeks	6 cm	Major parts of the brain are present. Eyelids have closed. Blood cells forming inside bones; joints present.	
16 weeks	14 weeks	12 cm	Lungs formed, but not ready for breathing yet. Skin transparent. The tail has disappeared. External sex organs can be seen. Nail and hair forming.	
20 weeks	18 weeks	20 cm	Movements can be felt. Palate complete. The tiny bones inside the ear are finished.	
24 weeks	22 weeks	30 cm	Average weight 600 grams. Almost ready for independent life, but another 3 months in the uterus for full development. Hair appears on head.	
28 weeks	26 weeks	35 cm	1.1 kg (2½ lbs)	Eyes reopen. Teeth forming. Lungs almost fully formed.
32 weeks	30 weeks	40 cm	1.9 kg (4¼ lbs)	Fine hair over body. Red skin and soft ears.
36 weeks	34 weeks	45 cm	2.75 kg (6 lbs)	Testes descended. White greasy vernix on skin. Creases forming on soles of feet.
40 weeks	38 weeks	50 cm	3.7 kg (7½ lbs)	Skin thicker and paler. Breasts formed. Cartilage present in ears.

Labour & birth

The place of delivery

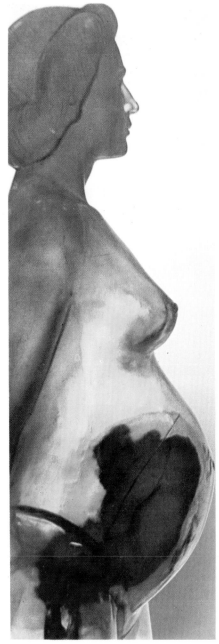

A model showing the position of the fetus near term.

At one time it was usual for every baby to be born at home. Now, most babies are born in hospital and the proportion who are born there is increasing every year. Many of us feel sad that babies are not born at home any longer, but there are very good medical reasons for arranging deliveries in hospital. Many of the unusual emergencies, that occur during labour and need treatment for the sake of either the mother or the baby, appear very suddenly and often cannot be predicted. In hospital it is possible to take immediate emergency action which is not possible at home. It is also possible to improve care during labour by using sophisticated machinery to control the length of labour and to monitor the health of the baby.

Of course some things are lost when a baby is born in hospital. One would like it to be a family event so that the new baby can be introduced to brothers and sisters and grandparents in a family house rather than in the strange atmosphere of a hospital. The individual care that a doctor and midwife might give would be more pleasant than the more impersonal feeling of a hospital. It is not as easy in a hospital to keep a mother and her baby close together. However, hospitals are aware of the problems and are doing their best to make your stay more pleasant; if you have any practical suggestions for the improvement of maternity care, you should send them to your local Family Health Centre.

There are many experimental schemes being started at the moment. Many hospitals run an early discharge system so that you can go home at 48 hours or, in Britain, even much earlier, at about six hours after the birth. This has to be arranged before delivery, so ask the ante-natal clinic if you want to leave hospital early. Sometimes there will be reasons to keep you in hospital – such as a caesarian section or jaundice in the baby – so do not bank on everything going absolutely without a hitch.

Remember that there are practical reasons for arranging your delivery in hospital, because it is safer for you and the baby. This is particularly important when the doctor feels that you are more likely to have a complication than another woman; he may then insist that you should be delivered in hospital. It is sensible to ask the doctor the reasons for a hospital delivery, but it is important to realize that it is all in the interests of both of you.

The start of labour

If this is your first baby, you must expect labour to last at least 12 hours before the baby is born. This means that you should have plenty of time to get to the hospital when labour has started. If you have already had one baby, your labour may be

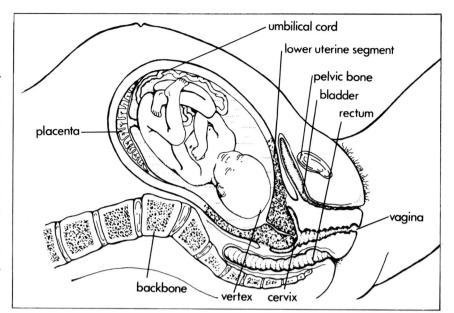

This diagram shows the fetus in the womb, indicating the position of the main organs of the mother and fetus. During the first stage of labour, the muscles in the lower uterine segment begin to contract all round, which can cause backache as well as pains in the lower abdomen. The cervix begins to stretch, causing mucus and a few streaks of blood to be lost from the vagina, known as a 'show'. During the second stage the whole uterus contracts rhythmically, pushing the fetus down the birth canal.

shorter the next time and it is advisable to go to the hospital as soon as you think you are in labour. If you are uncertain whether to go in or wait, telephone the labour ward for advice.

There are several signs that labour is about to start:

1. The water may break. The sac of amniotic fluid that surrounds the baby often breaks at the beginning, of labour so that a fluid like water suddenly gushes from the vagina. Even if you do not feel any pain, it is important to go to hospital because the doctors will want to examine you and to take precautions to avoid the baby becoming infected.

2. A show. As the neck of the womb stretches at the beginning of labour, a small amount of bleeding may take place. The few streaks of blood and mucus that you may lose from the vagina are often called a show. If there is more blood than these few streaks, enough to soak a pad, you must report this to a doctor at once because it could be serious.

3. Labour pains. You get a pain when the muscles in the wall of the uterus contract. These contractions of muscles slowly open the neck of the womb and push the baby out. When a pain occurs you will be able to feel the contraction in the uterus, because you will be able to feel the uterus become hard when you place a hand on your abdomen. You may be able to feel irregular contractions from time to time many weeks before term, but they are painless. When the contractions are regular and accompanied by pain or backache this means that labour is starting.

Often the pains start with an ache in the lower part of the back. The pains, similar to period pains, are then felt in the lower part of the abdomen; each becomes more intense and then fades away. When these pains occur regularly, every five or ten minutes, you are in labour and must contact your doctor or go to the hospital.

What to expect in hospital

You should take advantage of all the teaching classes arranged for mothers during pregnancy. The hospital or community centre will give you simple lectures on the reasons for ante-natal care, breast-feeding and what you must expect to happen in labour. One of the advantages of going to the classes is that you are able to ask the midwives about labour and what to expect. All hospitals differ a little in their arrangements and it is nice to know the local circumstances. A tour of the hospital, and in particular, the labour ward, may be arranged for you. If you have seen the ward, it will seem much less frightening to you. A labour ward is a much calmer and quieter place these days, because methods of relieving pain are generally so much better.

When you arrive at the hospital the midwife – or doctor – will examine your abdomen to find out the position of the baby and to see if his head is going down into your pelvis. Your blood-pressure will also be taken, your urine examined, and they will check the case-notes of your pregnancy so that they fully understand any problems you have. You may have a vaginal examination, because the doctor or midwife will want to know if the neck of the uterus, the cervix, has started to open. They will be able to tell you how far labour has already progressed by the size of the opening.

Once you are in labour, you will be checked constantly by the doctor and midwife. They can reassure you that labour is progressing satisfactorily, as this scene in a Danish maternity hospital shows.

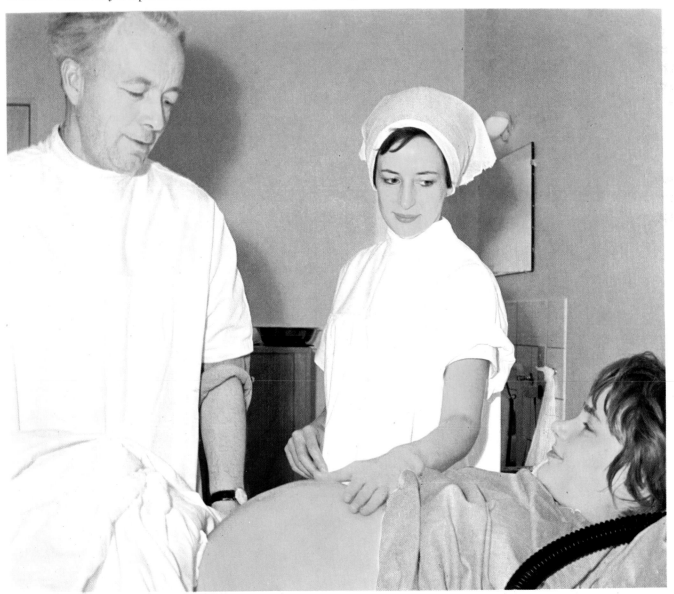

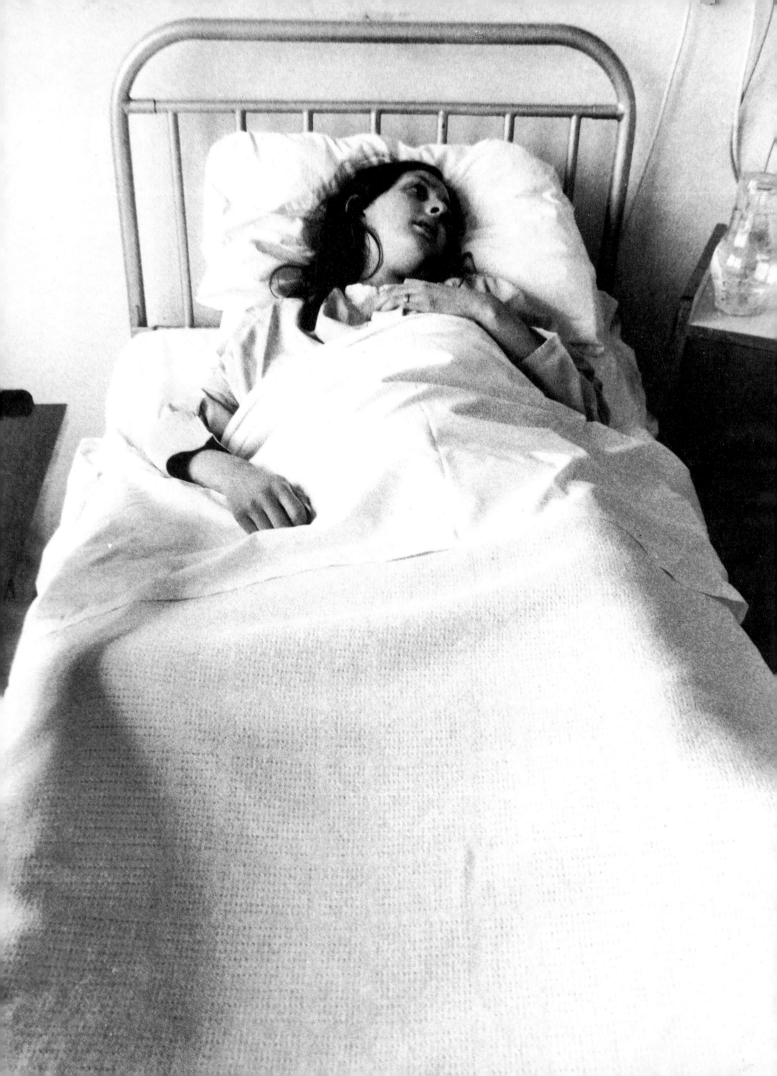

The stages of labour

Labour is usually divided into three stages: during the first, the uterus is contracting steadily to open up the cervix; in the second the cervix is fully open and the baby is pushed through the vagina and out into the world; in the third stage, the placenta, which is no longer needed to feed and give oxygen to the baby, separates from the wall of the uterus and is pushed out.

The first stage. The cervix opens steadily during labour and it is possible to tell how labour is getting on by feeling the size of the opening and how quickly it gets wider. At the very beginning the doctor can only get the tip of one or two fingers through the cervix, but afterwards he usually estimates the diameter of the opening in centimetres. The cervix is fully opened, or dilated, when it is about ten centimetres in diameter. During the examination of the size of the opening, the doctor or midwife can also feel the position of the baby's head. The bones of the head are not joined together until many months after birth so it is possible to feel the separation between them. There are two places on the baby's skull where the bones do not meet. In the front is a diamond-shaped place where there are no bones, this is called the anterior fontanelle or 'soft spot', and a triangular area at the back called the posterior fontanelle. When an examination is made through the cervix it is possible to tell whether the baby's face is pointing towards your spine or towards the front – this may be important during delivery. A vaginal examination will also show if there is plenty of room for the baby to come through the birth canal.

The first stage is the longest stage of labour, but it is shorter if you have already had a baby; even during your first labour it is very unusual for it to last longer than 24 hours these days; in most cases it is over within 12 hours.

The opening in the top of the pelvis is an oval with the wider part of the opening extending from one hip to another. The baby's head enters the cavity with the face to one side; as it descends it swivels so that the head usually faces your spine and the shoulders can enter the pelvis.

The second stage. As soon as the cervix has opened fully, the uterus pushes the baby's head downwards into the vagina. At this stage the pressure of the baby's head gives you the feeling that you wish to push down and push the baby out. It is the same sort of feeling as straining to open your bowels, if you are rather constipated. During a push you will need to take a big breath, hold it, strain down, and push. It is very important that this should happen at the same time as a contraction of the uterus; the midwife will help you to time your pushing. It is during this stage that the baby swivels; the lower opening of the pelvis is another oval with a widest diameter from front to back. The baby's head fills this, facing towards your back. A vaginal examination by the doctor will help him to assess that the baby has turned into the correct position.

The vagina expands to accept first the baby's head and then his shoulders. The crown, usually called the vertex, of the

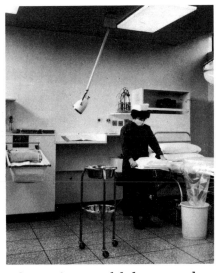

Above: A typical labour ward.
Left: This mother is relaxing in the early part of the first stage of labour. For her, the hard work is still to come. Use this period to rest (and sleep if possible) to prepare yourself for the actual birth.

At the beginning of the second stage the cervix is fully dilated and the baby's head passes sideways through the upper part of the pelvic basin.

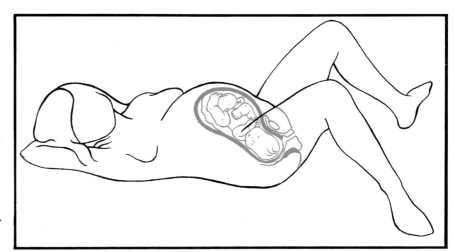

The baby swivels so the head faces towards the mother's back, allowing it to pass through the lower opening of the pelvis. The vagina expands to accept the vertex of the baby's head.

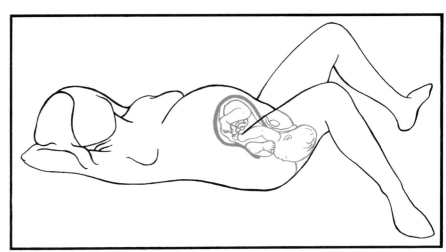

The head is completely born. The bones of the head are flexible, allowing it to pass through the vagina more easily.

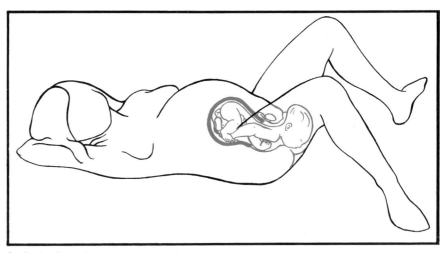

baby's head appears at the entrance of the vagina and steadily expands the entrance. Sometimes the vaginal entrance is a bit too small to allow the baby's head to pass through easily. If this is so, the midwife will 'freeze' the area with an injection of local anaesthetic and then make a small cut, called an episiotomy, to let the baby's head emerge. This cut is sewn up when the baby is born.

The head comes through the entrance of the vagina, then the baby rotates again so that his face is sideways and each shoulder is towards the front or back. The shoulder that is towards your front is born first followed by the other shoulder and then the rest of the body, which usually slips out easily. The hardest parts of the

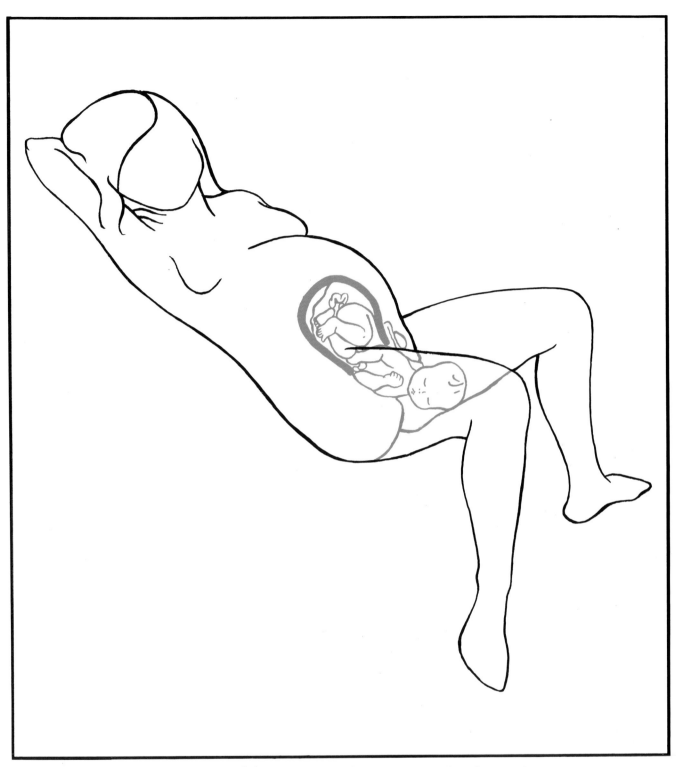

The baby rotates sideways once the head is born. The shoulder towards the mother's front is born first, followed by the other. The rest of the baby follows easily.

delivery are the birth of the head and shoulders.

The third stage. As soon as the baby has been completely born, the third stage begins. The uterus no longer contains a bulky baby and the whole organ contracts. When this happens the placenta, or after-birth, is sheared from the inside wall of the uterus.

These days a contraction is often produced routinely by a drug called ergometrine which is injected into one of your veins or a muscle as the baby is born. The uterus pushes the placenta into the vagina and you may have another feeling of wanting to bear down. You can push the placenta out, but the doctor or midwife will usually pull it out by the umbilical cord.

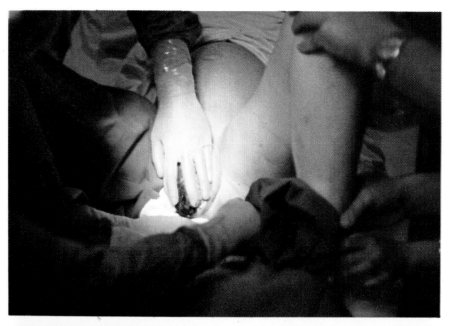

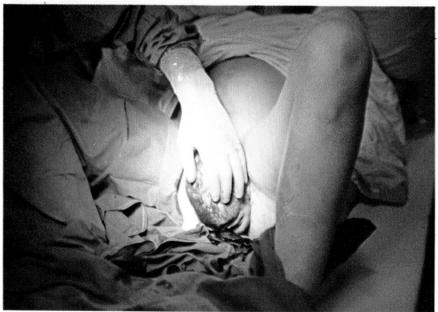

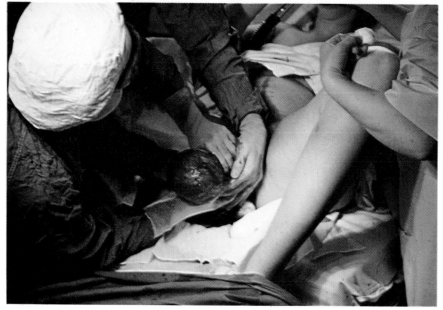

The birth of a baby is a very intense experience, both for the mother and father, if he is lucky enough to be present. Under the expert guidance of the midwife and nurses the baby begins to emerge quite quickly once the second stage has begun. The midwife helps the mother to time her pushes to the contractions of the uterus and each contraction forces the baby's head down the birth canal and through the vagina until it is born completely. Then the midwife helps to rotate the

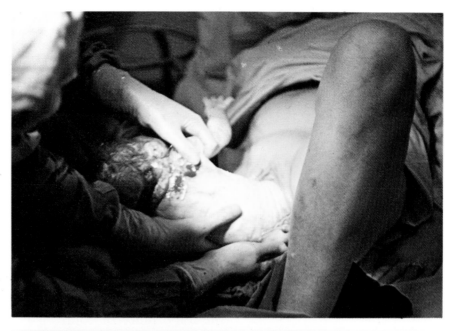

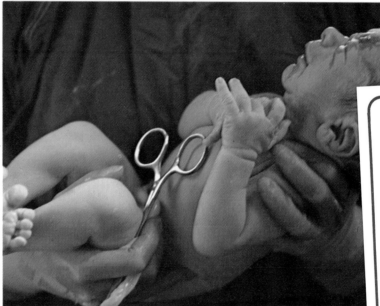

baby before the shoulders are born. Once the shoulders are born, it is a fairly simple matter for the midwife to lift the baby clear and lay him between the mother's legs. Mucus and fluid is cleared from his nose and throat and usually he cries for the first time at this point. The umbilical cord is clamped in two places then cut painlessly between them, separating the baby finally from the mother. The baby is then wiped gently and presented to the mother properly for the first time.

Relaxation and breathing

It is very important that you should understand what happens during labour and be prepared for what may happen. The benefit you may gain from attending relaxation classes may be the increased understanding you have of labour and delivery. It is also very nice for women to be shown simple physical exercises which will keep them active and comfortable during pregnancy. In addition, you will enjoy meeting and being with other women going through the experience of childbirth. It is a very happy time for you, but if you are apprehensive it is encouraging to share it with others.

It is difficult to be certain that relaxation classes make any actual difference to the physical ease with which you will go through labour. Some doctors feel that they are able to control the process of labour more effectively than in the past and relaxation classes may not always be necessary. Many systems have been devised to help women, including some which stress the importance of controlled breathing during a contraction. If you have something definite to do while you have a labour pain it may take your mind off it and therefore make it easier to bear. However, some forms of breathing may not help you and could make labour more difficult for the baby; overbreathing for a long time, that is rapid deep breaths, may cut down the amount of oxygen the baby gets, and should not be used.

Remember however, that childbirth cannot always be natural. In the past, many women and babies died because childbirth was permitted to be natural too often. Obstetricians have been able to make labour very safe for women and much safer for the baby; they have only done this by careful interference with the 'natural' process of childbirth. Do not feel sad, therefore, if you have to have a special delivery by forceps or caesarian section, it is being done for your benefit and to give you a healthier baby. Do not hesitate to discuss any worried or problems with the doctor or the midwife.

Relief of pain

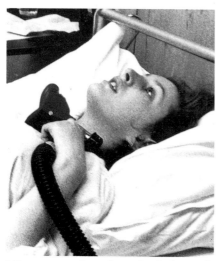

Nitrous oxide is breathed through a special mask.

Labour is an uncomfortable experience and unless it is very short you will need something to help you when you have a contraction. Pain is always more frightening when you are in a strange place and feel very lonely. Therefore contractions are likely to feel better if you are accompanied by someone you know, preferably your husband, and you know what to expect. There are many useful drugs which are now used to make labour much more comfortable. It is now very rare to hear women crying out in pain in a labour ward; to me they are much quieter, calmer places than when I was a medical student.

Pain-relieving drugs. There are many drugs which can be given by injection into a muscle or, to act more quickly, into a vein. Some of them also have a sedative action, so that they make you sleepy and less anxious. The midwife, or a doctor, will give you one of these drugs if you find the pain very unpleasant. Some of them have an effect on the baby's breathing at birth and so may have to be used less towards the end of labour.

Nitrous oxide. This is a gas which you can breathe when you have

34

Right: A patient being prepared for delivery by the midwives. She is obtaining pain relief by breathing nitrous oxide mixed with oxygen.

Below: When the doctor feels it is important to watch the progress of labour very closely, he may decide to monitor the fetal heartrate, and compare it to the rate of contractions at the same time. With this type of monitoring apparatus, electrodes are fixed to the mother's abdomen which record the contractions and fetal heartrate, feeding the information into the machine, which produces a simultaneous trace for the doctor to check. At the same time, the drug which controls the contractions is administered automatically by a pump.

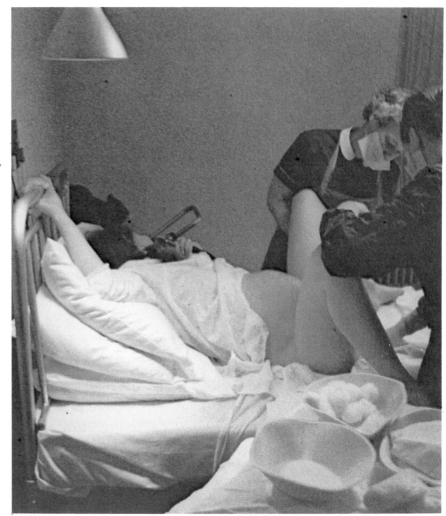

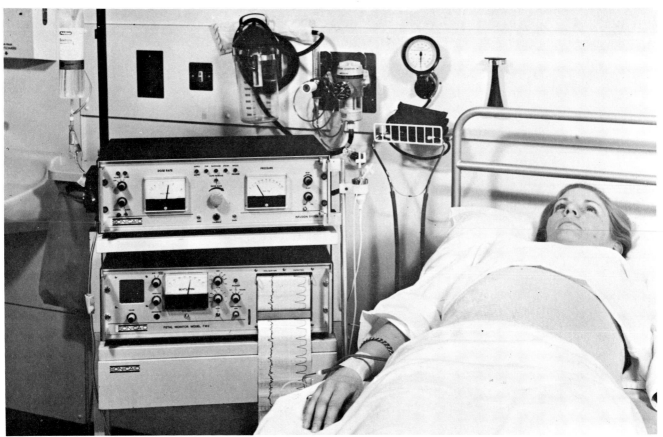

a pain. It is given in a mixture with oxygen and acts very quickly giving you immediate relief during a pain; it passes off rapidly afterwards but may leave you light-headed for a little time. The midwife will show you how to use a mask to breathe the gas and she will also tell you when to use it. It does not affect the baby's breathing at birth and so can be used late in labour.

Epidural anaesthesia. This is a modern method of relieving the pain of labour. An injection can be made into your back around the nerves which come from the uterus and the vagina. The local anaesthetic used is similar to the drug you are given to prevent pain when having a tooth filled. It will therefore relieve pain completely, but it often means that you will lose the ability to feel things, such as the pressure of the baby's head in the vagina.

A needle is passed into the back, between two of the bones, to introduce a fine tube outside the coverings of the spinal cord. Repeated injections of the drug can be made into this tube as often as necessary during labour, to give prolonged, complete pain relief.

It is undoubtedly a very useful way of giving you as comfortable a labour as possible. One of the advantages is that you will not need other drugs and can be quite conscious when the baby is born. Many hospitals now have facilities for this type of pain relief, so you may ask for it if you wish. There are some problems with epidural anaesthesia: for instance, you do not always know when to push and you will need to feel your abdomen to see when you have a contraction. You occasionally get a headache afterwards, but this is very uncommon.

Fathers in the labour ward

It is often a great comfort for some women to have their husbands with them during labour and delivery. This, of course, must be an individual decision for you and your husband; both of you must decide whether he should be there or not. Some men find the whole business of labour very upsetting and you should not dragoon him into being present, if you feel he is really frightened by it all. Many hospitals, these days, are very keen to encourage fathers; there may be a class in the ante-natal clinic to which you can take him, so that he will understand what will happen. It is particularly important for him to be with you during the long hours of the first stage of labour. There is often a special room for fathers on the labour ward; he can rest there or watch the television if you are asleep. During the second stage of labour he will be able to encourage you and it will be exciting for you both to see your baby born.

Some variations of labour

Induction. This means that the doctor begins labour artificially. It is very common and there are a variety of reasons for it. Amongst the most common are high blood-pressure or that labour has not started two weeks after term. In both these situations, and in others, there would be an increased risk to the baby if pregnancy continued, so it is safer to start labour.

The doctor usually ruptures the membranes, so that the

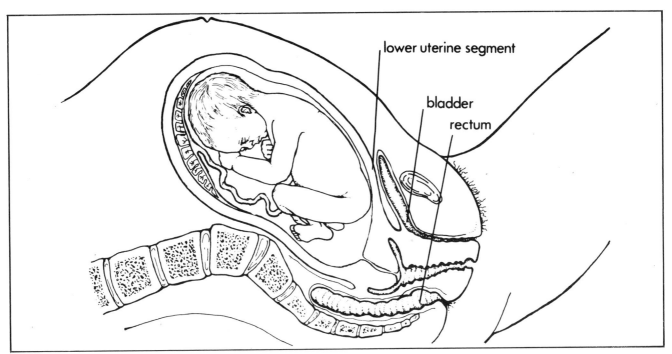

lower uterine segment

bladder

rectum

This diagram shows one of the form's of breech presentation, known as a 'flexed' breech. A breech delivery is always done in hospital.

amniotic fluid escapes, combining this with a drug which will make the uterus contract. The drug is called Syntocinon. It is given into a vein in a 'drip' or slow injection.

Breech delivery. This means that the baby is born bottom first, as opposed to a vertex delivery when he is born head first. When the baby is in a breech position the doctors may try and turn him so that his head is down – this will be done if it would be safer for the baby to be born head first. A breech birth is always undertaken in hospital and a doctor usually does the delivery. It occurs about five times out of a hundred.

Forceps delivery. Obstetric forceps are simple metal instruments which can hold and cradle the baby's head. They can be used to help in delivery when there is delay during the second stage – the second stage should never continue longer than one hour, it is often much shorter than that. Forceps delivery is now a very simple and safe procedure; there is no need to worry that the baby may be injured. The forceps will be used just to lift the baby's head out and speed things on; it is often a much safer way of delivering a baby than allowing him to be pushed out with difficulty.

Caesarian section. This is an operation to deliver the baby without the necessity of going through labour. It gets its name from a law in Roman times. The doctors may use this method of delivering you before labour if they think that there will be some danger to the baby in the process of labour, or if they think that the bones of your pelvis are too small to let the baby through. It is also used during labour if the first stage becomes too long or if there is any worry about the baby's health, so that he must be born as soon as possible. The operation is usually done under general anaesthetic, with the woman completely asleep, but it is sometimes possible to do it with an epidural anaesthetic – the woman is then able to see the baby immediately after birth and to hear his first cry.

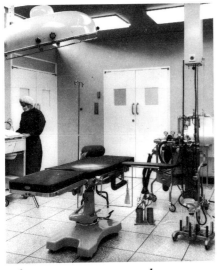

Above: an operating theatre prepared for caesarian section.

It is a comparatively simple operation although it does take some time. The abdomen is opened, the lower part of the uterus opened cross-wise, and the baby is then quickly delivered. After the placenta has been removed, the muscle wall is carefully sewn up, as is the wall of the abdomen. It is this which is the most time consuming part of the operation.

Accelerated labour. The drug Syntocinon is often used to speed up labour, because a long labour is known to be more risky for the baby and is very tiring for the mother. Doctors have therefore developed methods of shortening labour when necessary. This can be done by giving a very dilute solution of Syntocinon into the mother's vein as a drip or slow injection. The number of contractions can be counted and the injection slowed or made faster to produce one every two or three minutes. There are some machines which will do this automatically by controlling the injection according to the number of contractions.

The safety of the baby during labour

The fetus receives all the food he needs through the placenta from his mother's blood. One of the signs that the placenta is not working well is a fetus that is growing slowly – this slow growth may be found by feeling the size of the uterus or by ultrasound examination. From minute to minute the fetus also needs a vital supply of oxygen from his mother. If he did not get that oxygen he would soon die. Much of the care of the baby during the modern management of labour is devoted to a careful watch of his oxygen supply. Usually the baby's heart beats 120 to 140 times a minute, but it may get faster or slower if he runs short of oxygen. Midwives are therefore trained to listen to the baby's heart-rate frequently as labour progresses; if she hears a change she will tell the doctor.

This is very satisfactory for the ordinary management of labour, but if the doctors feel there is a very high risk of the baby

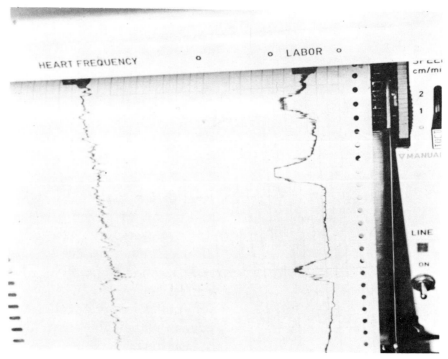

This is a typical normal trace showing the fetal heart-beat and the contractions of the uterus. With this machine, a tiny clip is attached to the baby's scalp and an electrode to the mother's abdomen, giving a very accurate record of the progress of labour.

losing his oxygen supply, such as the baby who has stopped growing, a more sophisticated method of watching the baby is needed. It is now possible to attach a tiny clip to the baby's scalp with a wire joining a special heart-rate recorder placed beside the mother; the recorder produces a continuous record of the baby's heart-rate. The contraction of the uterus is also recorded by another device which is attached to the mother's abdomen. A very fast heart-rate or marked slowing of the rate during or just after a contraction are both signs that the baby may have very little oxygen and needs immediate delivery. In addition a small blood sample can be taken from the head of the baby; the baby's scalp is pricked and a few drops of blood are allowed to run into a tube. The blood can be analyzed to see if it is acid – very acid blood is produced when the baby lacks oxygen.

These new methods mean that there is more machinery around the mother in the labour ward, but it enables the doctors to keep a close eye on the baby and deliver him quickly if necessary.

The 'puerperium'

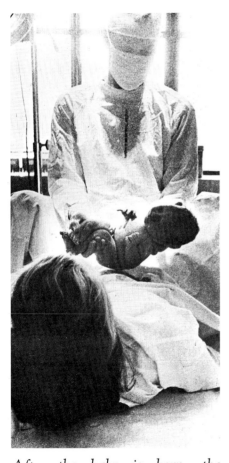

After the baby is born, the mother's body readjusts, with hormone changes which can lead to feelings of depression.

This is the period from the birth of the baby until your body has returned completely to normal. When labour has finished you will find that your womb is still quite big. If you feel your abdomen you will feel the uterus almost up to the level of your navel, about the size it was at four months of pregnancy. It continues to contract from time to time, in order to remove the remains of the lining. You may feel some cramp-like 'after' pains during the first three or four days after delivery; they sometimes happen while you are breast-feeding, because a hormone is released into your blood at that time and it causes a contraction. Do not be worried about these pains, they are helping your uterus to return to normal quickly.

You will notice a blood-stained discharge from the vagina – this is called the lochia. At first, it will be almost pure blood but it will become progressively browner and finally disappear about two weeks after your delivery. If you should ever notice a gush of blood or if bright blood should return, you must report this at once to the doctor. Very occasionally, a small amount of placenta is left in the womb and will cause some bleeding; the doctor will know whether anything needs to be done about it.

Depression. The first few days of the puerperium can be a trying time for you. You will feel physically exhausted after the labour and will probably sleep for many hours. The care of the baby, and learning how to feed him, takes up a lot of your time. It is very easy to get upset and worried at this time particularly about the baby. Part of the feeling may be an emotional let-down after all the excitement of labour; but the hormone changes in your body, which occur in every woman after delivery, also lead to a feeling of depression. Do not be surprised if you feel weepy or miserable, but rely on the staff and your husband for their help.

Use the time in hospital to get as much rest as you can. Try and be with your baby as much as possible, to understand the meaning of his cries and to learn to love him – or her.

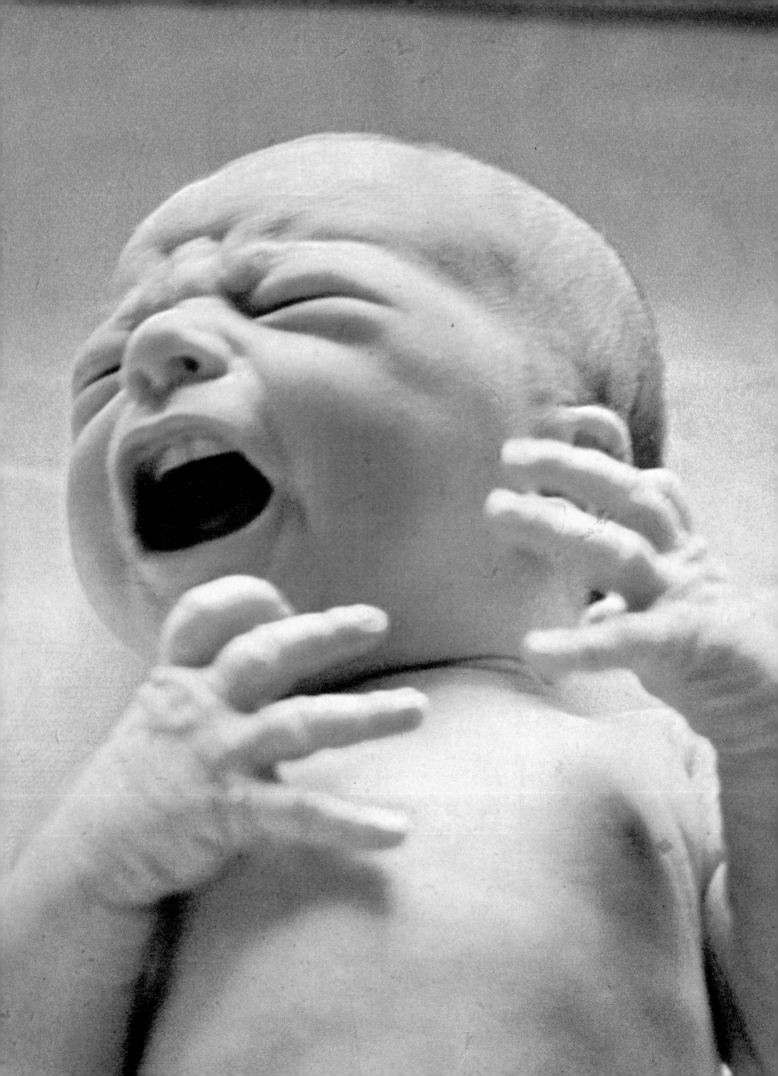

The newborn baby

Immediately after delivery

That long-awaited baby has arrived. The first few days will be a time of getting to know one another. You will find there is a lot to learn about a baby; he or she is an individual just like you.

The first time you see the baby will probably be when he is held up by the doctor or midwife immediately after delivery. He might look rather messy at that moment, as he will be blood-stained and very wet. The doctor's first act will be to divide the umbilical cord that has been his life-line for the past nine months. The traditional way of tying the cord is with a piece of string near to the baby's abdomen, but today it is more common to use an elastic band or a special plastic clip. These clips and bands prevent any bleeding from the vessels inside the cord. The baby will then be taken away for a moment to be assessed and examined.

The first cry

This is probably the most important event in anyone's life. At the moment of birth the baby can no longer get any oxygen from the mother and has to gasp to obtain oxygen from the air for the first time. A newborn baby usually takes his first breath as soon as he has been born and then starts crying as a reflex action, probably to open up his lungs more efficiently and fill them with air – before birth, they are filled with fluid. The midwife or doctor will clear all the fluid from his throat by sucking it out to make certain that he has a clear passage to breathe air into his lungs. At one minute of age, and usually at five minutes as well, the baby is assessed by a system known as the 'Apgar score'. This is named after an American doctor. It works on a scale which gives a baby ten points if he is in absolutely tip-top condition. The record of the Apgar score is useful for the doctor to assess any lack of oxygen at the moment of birth and will also guide him in deciding whether any treatment is necessary. The two most important parts of the score are heart-rate, which will be very low if the baby lacks oxygen, and breathing, which may be absent.

If the baby does not take a breath immediately, it may be necessary to blow some air into his lungs so that oxygen reaches the blood. This can be done quite simply by passing a tube into the windpipe, which is known medically as the trachea. The doctor has a special torch which helps him to see the entrance to the trachea at the back of the tongue and he will put a tube into it. It is then possible for him to blow air gently down the tube until the baby is completely pink, is breathing regularly and has a strong heartbeat. Then the tube will be taken out.

The sound that every parent hears with relief: the cry of a newborn baby. It is a reflex action which helps to fill the baby's lungs with air and send the all-important oxygen round his body. Many babies do not cry as soon as they are born: sometimes it is a minute or two before they do, even though they may be breathing quite well.

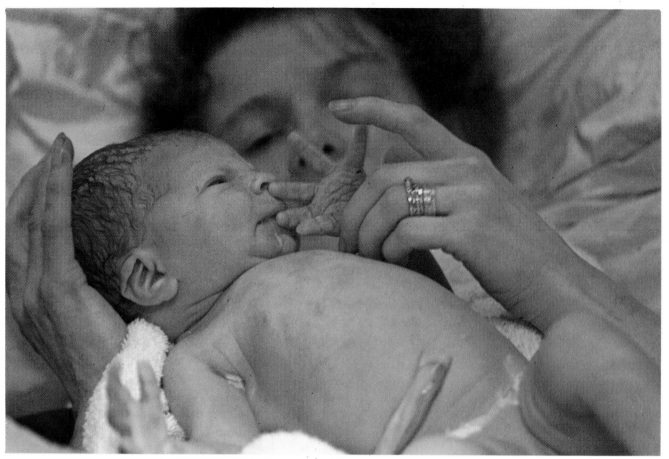

It is important to see the baby as soon as possible after the birth, perhaps to hold or even to give a breast-feed. You will then be satisfied that all is well even if the baby is to be taken away to a nursery or special care unit for a while after the birth.

Getting to know the baby

Mothers are often anxious if they do not hear the baby cry at once. Remember that it is very common for a baby to take a minute or two before crying, even if he is breathing quite well. Also, the baby may not be able to cry because the doctor has put the tube into the trachea; but the baby will be quite safe.

After the midwife is satisfied that the baby is breathing properly, a quick general examination will be carried out to make certain that he is normal. It is then important to dry the baby completely and wrap him up in a warm towel or blanket. The staff see to all this as a matter of course. At this stage, probably when he is only a minute or two old, he will be brought to you.

At this time, the placenta may not be delivered yet and the doctor may need to give you some stitches, to repair the entrance of the vagina. You probably won't have very much time to look at the baby but make sure that you do see him all over – slip your hand underneath the blanket so that you can feel his body and limbs. Your husband will probably want to hold him as well. In many hospitals it is the policy to give a breast-feed while the mother is still in the labour-room. This has the advantage of stimulating the production of milk in the breast as early as possible and it also releases hormones into the woman's blood which trigger off the process which returns the uterus to normal. After that, the baby will be put, well wrapped-up, in a cot and left in a warm room. The baby is not bathed soon after birth because it might cool him too much; instead, his face will just be wiped to make him look presentable.

Back in the post-natal ward

When the baby is with you in the post-natal ward you will be able to start learning his or her special ways within a few hours of the birth. But if you are very tired or unwell don't be ashamed to let the nurses remove the baby to a separate nursery to allow you to get some rest.

When you get to the ward, it is pleasant to have your baby with you as much as possible. You can watch him as he begins to open his eyes to look around, and as he screws up his face. If he is near you, you will know when he needs to be fed – he will start to cry. You can then pick him up to put him to the breast or give him a bottle. Studies on production of milk have shown that the breast flushes with blood as soon as the baby starts to cry and before he has started to suck on the nipple. The sound of his crying actually triggers a response in your brain which will help your breast to start producing milk. The cry of a baby is very individual and mothers are able to recognize their own baby's cry at three days of age.

If you are unwell or very tired, the nurses may have a small nursery where they can put the baby and look after him until you have recovered. They will always be at hand to help you if you have any worries and will show you the best way to handle your baby, how to dress and change him and, of course, help you both through the first few feeds (see page 59).

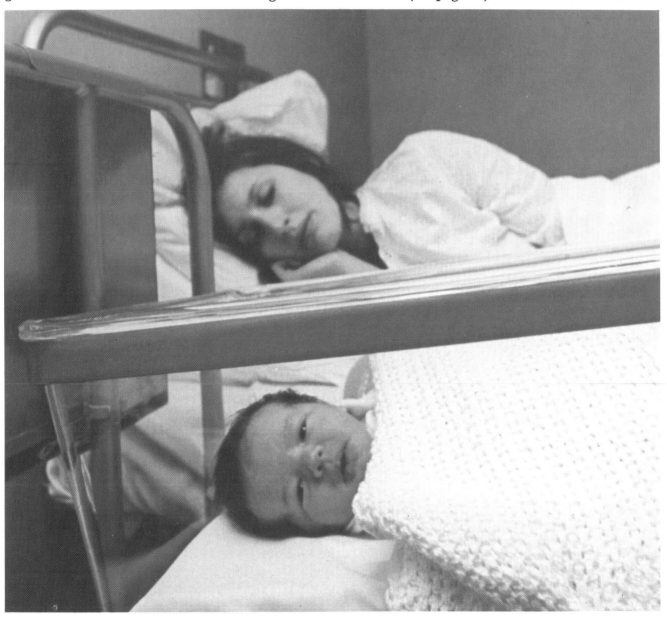

Examination of the newborn baby

The baby is examined at birth according to the Apgar score, but a much more detailed examination will be made at some time during his stay in hospital. In some hospitals it is done during the first day or two, in others just before he leaves to go home.

If possible, be present when the doctor does the examination; he will be able to ask you things about your family's medical history which may be important and you will be able to ask him any questions or tell him about things that worry you. All women have worries about their babies during the first week; but as always, don't be afraid to voice your fears: it is likely that there is nothing to worry about at all and that your baby is quite normal, but the doctor will be able to set your mind at rest. An example of something which might easily worry you is the moulding of the baby's head. In passing through the pelvis, the head is squeezed gently and becomes long instead of round. It takes a day or two for the head to return to its round shape, and may look odd at birth, but it is quite normal.

The full examination begins by looking at the baby and watching his movements. His clothes are taken off so that he is completely naked – if the examination is done in the first two days you may not have seen him completely stripped before.

The heart is listened to through a stethoscope to make certain there are no unusual noises, usually called murmurs, which may indicate that there is an abnormality in the structure of the heart.

The baby's breathing is also checked: it is important to make certain that it is not rapid or difficult.

A general examination will follow: the doctor will look at the baby's eyes, into his mouth to make sure that his palate is not cleft and that his tongue is normal, he will count the fingers and toes, and carefully feel the abdomen to make sure that the organs, especially the kidneys, are not enlarged.

The genitalia – or sex organs – will be looked at carefully as well. The most important item in a boy is to be certain that both testes have descended into the sac which is known as the scrotum. The testes usually descend during the last few weeks of life *in utero*. When they are undescended at birth the doctor will arrange to see the baby again later, because they usually descend within a few weeks; if not, an undescended testis may be the reason for an operation at about five or six years.

The legs are another important point of examination. Sometimes the hips are out of joint – dislocated – at birth. This is particularly common if the baby was in the breech position before birth. The doctor can tell if the hip is out of joint by moving the leg; he will feel a judder as the top of the thigh-bone slips in and out of its socket. It is vital to look for this in a newborn baby because very simple methods of treatment will enable the hip-joint to grow normally. But if the dislocation persists without early treatment it is very much more difficult to put it back into joint later, and usually means several operations.

The feet are sometimes turned in, and might look like club feet. In most of these cases it is possible to push the foot up above the

A newborn infant has a strong 'grasp' reflex. If a pen or finger is placed in the baby's palm he will fix his fingers round it tightly.

44

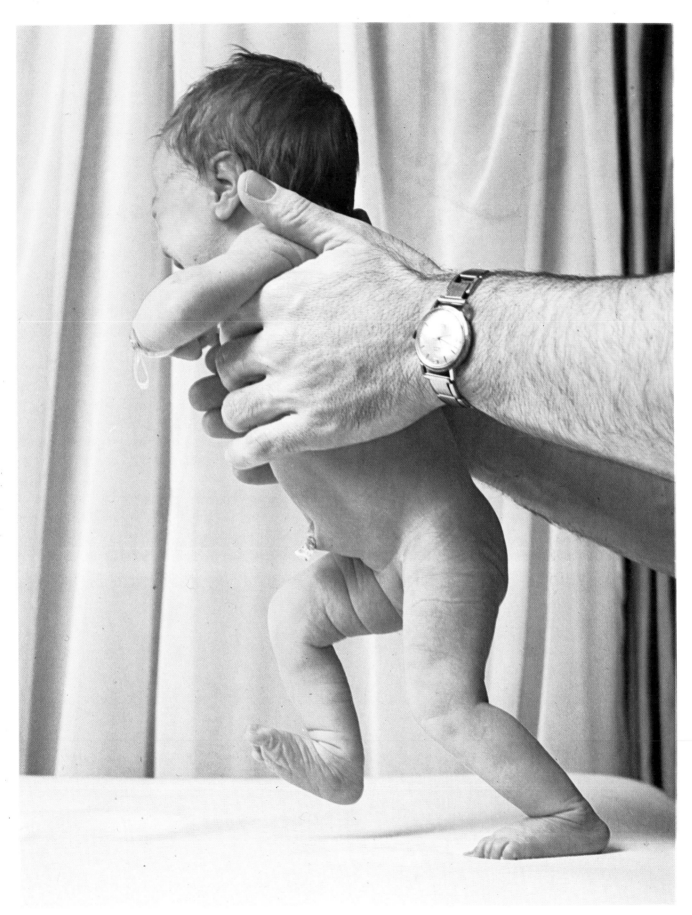

Many of a newborn baby's reflexes are tested during the first few days in hospital, sometimes as early as 24 hours after the birth. This picture shows the automatic walking reflex. If an infant is held upright on a flat surface she or he will march steadily forward.

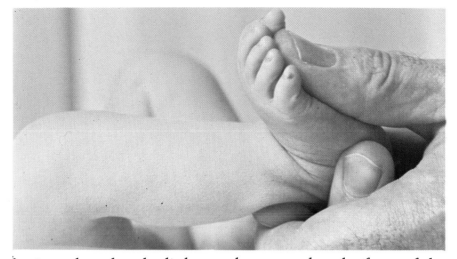

To check whether a baby's foot is normal the foot is pushed back towards the shin. This shows that all is well and that the baby does not have a club foot.

horizontal so that the little toe almost touches the front of the shin; if this is possible you need have no worry about club feet.

The baby's reflexes can be tested by the doctor to tell him that the baby's brain and muscles are working well. The 'Moro response' is rather like an embrace and occurs when the baby is suddenly upset or startled. The baby's arms and legs come forward as if for a sort of embrace. It is believed to have originated in man's monkey-like ancestors to help the baby to cling on to its mother's fur. A similar response is the grasp in the hands; if one puts a finger into a baby's hand the baby will grasp it fiercely and automatically. This response is even more marked when a baby is born early – in fact one can often pick a baby up by allowing him to grasp one's fingers. The newborn baby also shows automatic walking; he will march steadily forward if held upright on a flat surface, responses which disappear in three to four months.

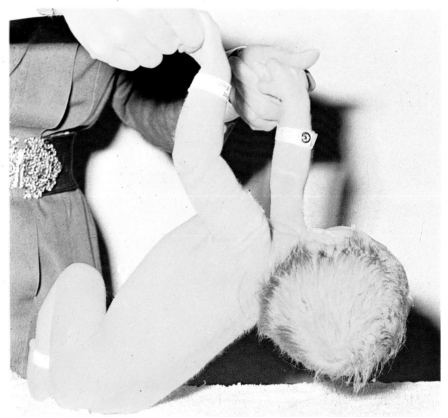

The grasp reflex is so strong in babies born before term that it is possible to lift them bodily as they grip two fingers.

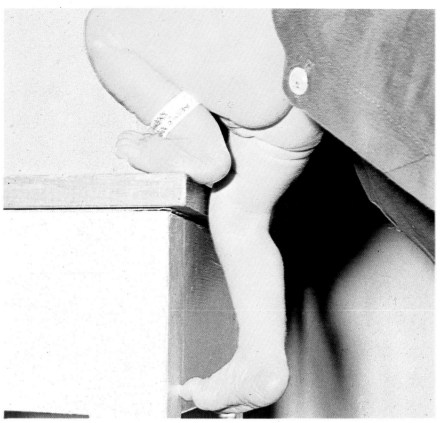

Another reflex of newborn babies is a stepping reflex. If the feet are touched against the underneath of a ledge, the baby will automatically lift his foot on to the surface like a step.

The doctor tests these reflexes to see if the baby's brain and nervous system are functioning properly. Unfortunately, it is still very difficult to pick out babies with an abnormality by testing the reflexes. This means that several checks over the first three years are necessary to be certain that a baby is developing normally.

Size at birth

Weight. A newborn baby has an average weight of about 3.4 kilograms (about 7½ pounds) but boys are usually a little heavier than girls. There is, of course, a very wide range of weight at birth and it is common for babies to weigh anything between 2.5 kilograms (5½ pounds) and 4.5 kilograms (10 pounds).

Small babies will need special care, because they often have difficulty in feeding at first and may need to be kept very warm. A baby weighing less than 2.5 kilograms (5½ pounds) is known as 'a baby of low birth weight'. Usually the baby is small because he has been born early (a pre-term or premature baby), but sometimes he is much smaller than one would expect for a baby who has spent 40 weeks in the uterus. These babies are called 'small for dates' and have usually grown slowly before birth. They are often more vigorous than other small babies.

Length. A baby's length at birth is about 50 centimetres (about 20 inches) or a little more. The circumference of the head is also measured at birth because it can be used later as a rough measure of how well the brain is growing. At birth it is usually about 35 centimetres (13½ inches), but may be anything between 30 and 38 centimetres (12-15 inches).

Weight loss. You must expect the baby to lose some weight during the first week; the loss of up to ten per cent of the birthweight is quite normal; after about five or six days the baby

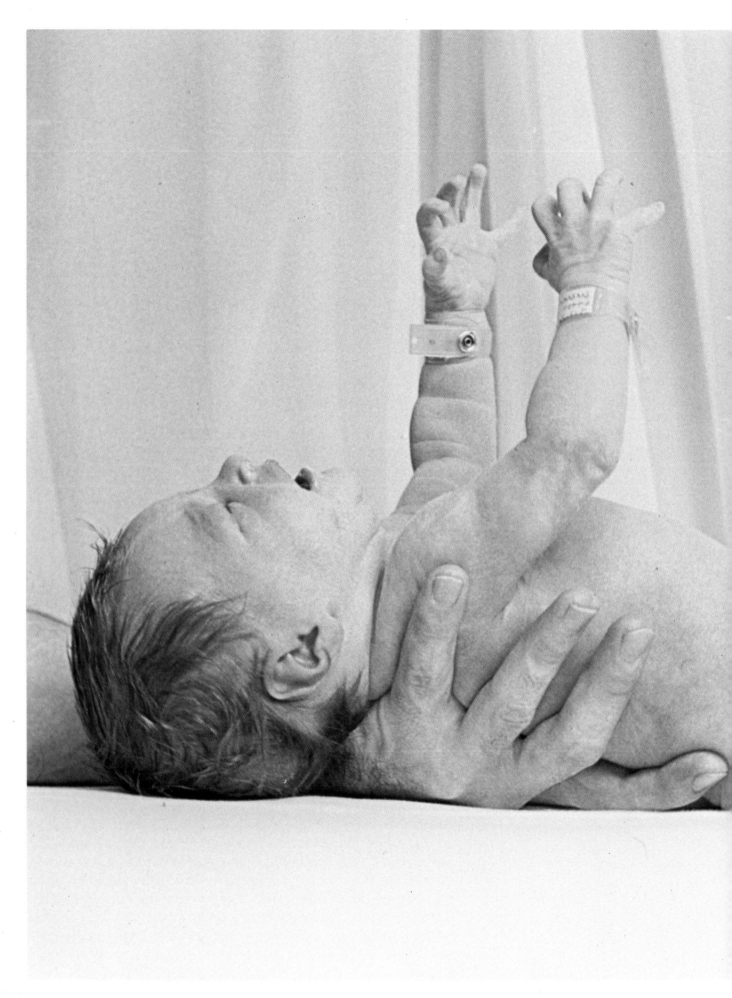

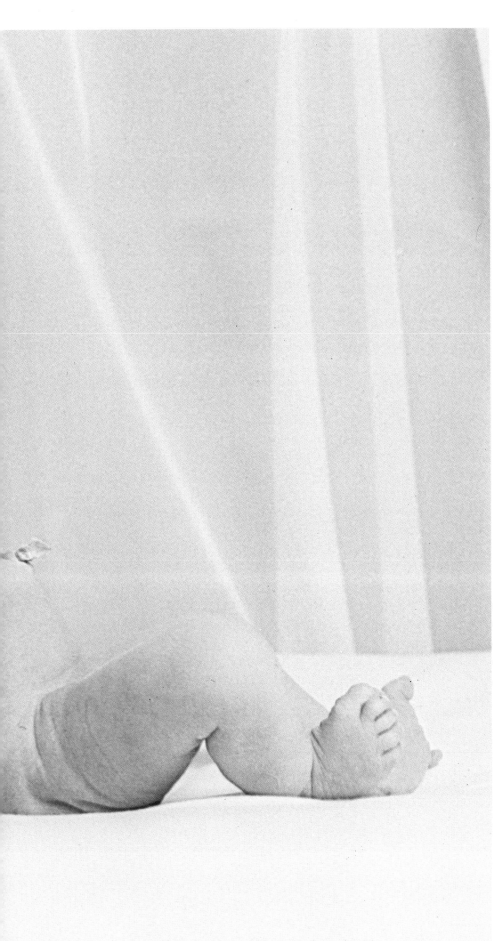

One of the most fascinating of the newborn reflexes is the Moro response. This response gets its name from E. Moro (1874-1951), a German paediatrician from Heidelberg, who first described the phenomenon, and pointed to its probable significance. When startled – for instance, when the head is allowed to drop back suddenly – the baby's arms and legs will be raised, with the fingers bent as if to clutch at something. It is thought that this is a legacy from man's ape-like ancestors: enabling their young to cling on to their mothers' fur in times of danger.

Babies don't enjoy the reflex very much so it is not necessary to look for it in a routine examination.

49

usually begins to gain weight again, but may not regain the birth-weight until about two weeks of age.

Meconium and urine

The baby's bowel contains a dark-green sticky material which is called meconium. The midwife will carefully record the first time he passes this, to make certain there is no obstruction at the bottom of his bowel. After a few days the dark-green colour of the meconium changes to yellow as milk reaches the end of the bowel. A baby's stool is quite soft, particularly if he is breast-fed, and looks like mustard. If he should develop diarrhoea – frequent stools like yellow water – you must report it at once to a nurse because it could be dangerous for the baby. A normal baby opens his bowels whenever he is fed; you should expect to change his nappy after almost every feed.

The baby usually passes urine just after birth, but then may not urinate again for 24 or 36 hours. After that you will find the nappy wet many times a day: every three hours is common.

Common problems with newborn babies

Babies in the first weeks often have minor problems, which may seem alarming to you, but will clear up without difficulty.

The skin. Babies who are born after term often have a very dry skin. It will soon begin to peel leaving a soft smooth skin underneath. You may notice cracking, particularly around the feet and ankles. There is no need to do anything about this peeling but you can rub oil, such as olive oil or baby oil, into the skin after a bath if you wish. Babies who are born early often have a red skin, while those who are born after term have a very pale one.

'Stork bite' is a harmless birthmark on the forehead and eyelids. It usually looks like a 'V' from the hair down to the root of the nose; the name 'stork bite' arises from the legend that it is the mark produced by the beak of the stork when he brought the baby. It is red, and is often accompanied by similar marks along the upper eyelids and the very back of the neck. The marks on the face fade slowly and have gone by the end of the first year. The red marks on the neck are permanent, but do not matter because they will be covered by hair. You can amuse yourself by looking for them on the next person who sits in front of you on a bus!

Rashes. Babies often have several types of harmless rash. The nose and cheeks is covered by little white spots often called 'milk spots' which are enlarged glands in the skin and disappear as the baby gets older. There is one special rash which is peculiar to newborn babies; it occurs all over the body, but particularly on the trunk and limbs, and looks like pale pimples surrounded by a red flush. It has many names, including eosinophil rash and neonatal urticaria. Sometimes it is called 'heat' rash, but this is a misleading name as it is not caused by heat, although it is more obvious, like most rashes, when the baby is warm. It is quite harmless and will go away eventually.

Hair. There is usually a good crop of hair at birth, but most of this falls out leaving the baby with only fine hair after a few weeks.

Bruises. It is not surprising that a baby may have a few small bruises on his skin after birth. Often it is possible to see a tiny bright red fleck on the white of the eye. This is also a tiny bruise which will disappear and does not mean that the eye has been damaged. There may be a collection of blood underneath one of the coverings of the bones of the head, usually the ones on each side of the crown. This collection of blood is called a cephalhaematoma; it will disappear gradually within three weeks. The only problem that may follow from all these bruises is that the baby can become more jaundiced than usual.

Sneezing and hiccups. These are very common and quite normal. Sneezing may be very frequent and does not necessarily mean that the baby has a cold. Many babies are snuffly for quite a few weeks after birth. Hiccups are common after a feed. It is normal to see a baby lying peacefully after a feed, hiccupping gently.

Swellings are very common. A hard lump just underneath the skin over the cheek or elbow is usually 'fat necrosis'. This means that a small amount of fat under the skin has become hard; it will become soft again after a few weeks.

Both boys and girls may have an enlargement of the breasts and produce milk. Be careful not to express the milk from the breast as it is thought that this may cause an infection. The swelling will disappear slowly, but sometimes lasts for many months or even a year; ask your doctor about it if it does not go away. A boy sometimes has fluid round his testis, called a 'hydrocele'.

Many young babies have 'milk spots' – enlarged glands in the skin. These are quite harmless and disappear after a few weeks.

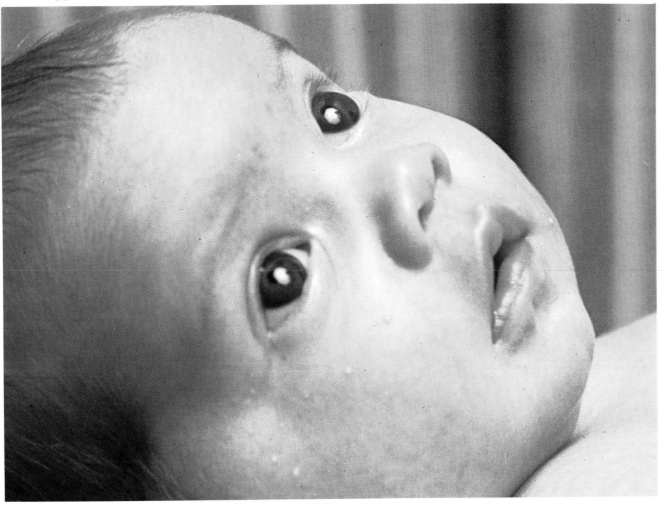

A newborn baby can be worrying: especially to the first-time mother. Jaundice is a common problem, and can cause a lot of anxiety since the baby's yellow-pigmented skin is instantly recognizable. However in many cases the jaundice clears by itself without the necessity for treatment.

Jaundice

This is one of the commonest problems in the newborn period. The baby's liver finds it difficult to excrete all the yellow colour (called bilirubin) which is produced in the first few days after birth. Before the birth the fetus gets rid of bilirubin by passing it across the placenta into the mother. The baby's liver is therefore not accustomed to excreting bilirubin and it may build up in the body after birth; the skin becomes stained with this yellow pigment and the condition is called jaundice.

The most severe variety of jaundice follows rhesus disease. The baby may have had treatment for this before birth, and it is likely that labour will have been induced early. At birth the baby may have anaemia and rapidly becomes severely jaundiced. The jaundice could affect the brain if it became very severe, but this brain damage is prevented by doing a blood transfusion. This is called an exchange transfusion because blood is withdrawn from the baby and replaced by normal rhesus-negative blood. About twice the amount of blood that is in the baby's body is given in exchange for the same amount taken out. The whole procedure lasts one to two hours and is done very gradually. It is often carried out shortly after birth to correct anaemia and may be repeated many times if the jaundice becomes severe.

The level of jaundice is estimated by measuring the bilirubin in the baby's blood by frequent tests. Blood samples are usually taken by pricking the baby's heel; this may be done one or more times a day when jaundice is present.

There are other causes of jaundice apart from rhesus disease. It is common if a baby is born early, has been bruised or has an infection. However in many cases doctors cannot find a cause.

The jaundice can be controlled in some cases by shining a strong light on to the skin. This is called phototherapy. The baby is nursed naked and blindfold under a special warm light. The light will bleach the biliburin in the baby's skin and thus improve the jaundice. The doctors will only arrange this if they think it is necessary after obtaining the results of the bilirubin in the blood. Exchange transfusions may occasionally be necessary for any type of jaundice, if the bilirubin level becomes high.

Circumcision

This means the removal of the foreskin of the penis, that is the part that covers the sensitive 'glans' at the tip of the penis. Many communities, notably the Jews and Muslims, arrange for all male babies to be circumcised. It is probably more convenient and less unpleasant for the boy if it is done when he is a tiny baby, rather than when he is older and likely to be upset.

However, there is no good medical reason for routine circumcision. It is not cleaner or more hygienic to remove the foreskin; it is naturally stuck down over the glans for the first four years. Later it can be eased back so that the glans can be cleaned quite simply. The foreskin protects the penis while the baby is still in nappies; an uncomfortable ulcer can be caused by the glans rubbing on the nappy if it does not have this protection.

At one time it was thought that cancer of the cervix of the

uterus was less common in the wives of men who had been circumcised. This was thought to be a good reason for the routine circumcision of boys. Recent research suggest that this is not true. If you feel it must be done for personal or religious reasons, it is easier to do it in the newborn period. In the past, the foreskin had to be cut off by a surgical operation, but there is now a much simpler type of circumcision using a plastic 'bell'. The bell is put inside the foreskin and a thread is tied around the skin on to a groove in the bell. This cuts off the blood supply to the foreskin which will fall off quite cleanly, with the bell, after four or five days.

The Guthrie test

There are a number of inherited illnesses which can cause mental retardation, which means that the baby's mental development is very slow. They are very rare conditions and are caused by a block in the body's chemistry so that a poisonous substance builds up in the baby's body and causes brain damage. The commonest of these conditions is phenylketonuria (often called PKU), which occurs in about 1 in 10,000 babies. A simple blood test can be done to detect this. On the sixth day or after [third to sixth day in Australia], the baby's heel is pricked to produce some drops of blood which are put on a special card of blotting paper. This is the Guthrie test; it is very important that your baby should have it. If one of these rare conditions is found, it is possible to give the baby a special diet so that he will grow up normally without any mental handicap.

The navel

The umbilicus, or navel, is the place on the baby's body where the umbilical cord was attached. The cord, which was tied at birth and then clamped, leaves a stump which quickly dries up. This dry, scab-like stump falls off the navel after several days. It is usual to put antiseptic or antibiotic in liquid or powder form on the cord stump to prevent infection. In this case the cord may take well over a week to fall off. You can expect the stump to come off at any time between four days and three weeks. At the time it drops off there is often a tiny amount of bleeding; this should not cause you any worry, but if the bleeding is more than a few specks or goes on for several days you should show it to your health visitor or doctor. Sometimes an infection occurs in the navel; you should consult your doctor if the skin is very red or if there is a discharge of pus.

The Special Care Unit

Maternity hospitals often have a special, or intensive, care unit where they can look after babies who are not very well. Most of the babies who have to go to such a unit have been born early and are therefore small. They need special nursing care; an incubator to keep them warm, and a fine tube through the nose down into the stomach to feed them as they are often unable to suck well. Any baby who has had a difficult delivery may go to such a unit for several hours after birth even if he has gone to full term and has a good birth weight. The purpose of these

Prematurity is one of the main reasons for special care of the newborn. A baby born several weeks before term is looked after in the controlled environment of the incubator. Heat, oxygen and humidity can be regulated and close attention is paid to maintaining a sterile atmosphere to avoid the risk of infection. At first, feeding is done – little and often – sometimes through a tube which is passed through one of the baby's nostrils, since many premature babies take several weeks to learn to suck. With modern technology a premature baby has every chance of growing into a normal healthy person and even babies of very low birth weights thrive well in modern hospital intensive care. Once the baby is beginning to grow and maintain temperature satisfactorily he will be moved out of the incubator and into a cot, but will stay under the careful supervision of the Unit until he is about 2.2kg (5lb) in weight.

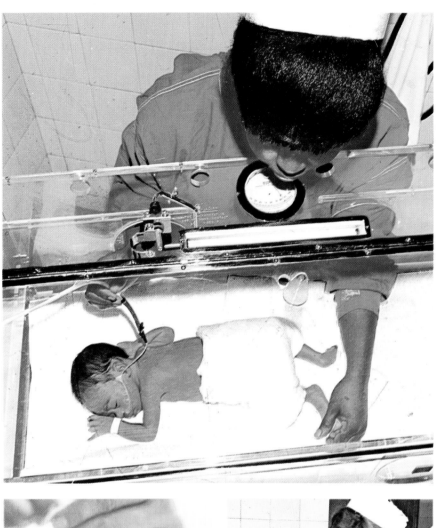

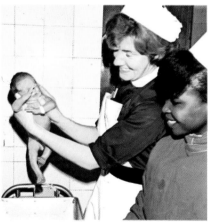

units is to make sure that the baby receives the expert nursing care he needs; it does not necessarily mean that he is very ill, only that he needs to be carefully watched. Do not hesitate to go and visit your baby as soon as possible if he is in such a unit. You will find that the nurses and doctors can explain the baby's problems to you; do not hesitate to ask questions.

Many people find that their minds go a complete blank when they are talking to a doctor on his rounds. It is a good idea to jot down any questions you have on a bit of paper as they occur to you. You will then be able to remember them when the doctor comes to talk to you. Do not feel embarrassed if you have a lot of questions and some of them seem minor; the doctor will understand: it is his job to answer any worries you have.

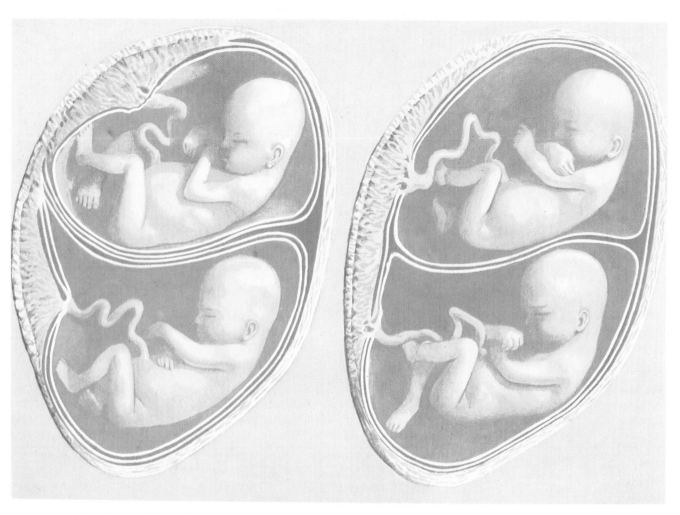

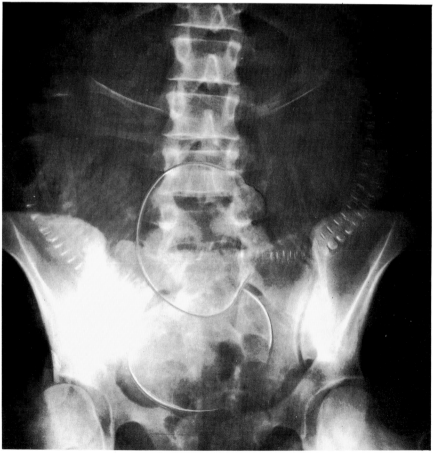

Multiple births

Top left: Non-identical twins in the uterus, with separate placentas. Right: Identical twins share the placenta. Left: An X-ray showing the presence of twins. They can also be detected with ultrasound. Above: Though it can be hard work at first, bringing up twins is a uniquely rewarding experience.

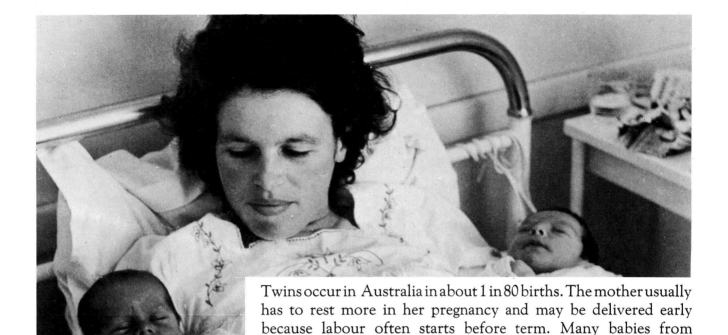

After the birth of twins, take advantage of your time in hospital to get as much rest as possible.

Twins occur in Australia in about 1 in 80 births. The mother usually has to rest more in her pregnancy and may be delivered early because labour often starts before term. Many babies from multiple births have to spend time in Special Care Nurseries.

If you have twins, make sure you take plenty of rest in the first week after giving birth. Feeding two babies needs more patience than feeding one. You can breast-feed by putting one baby to the breast after the other – at each feed you can use one breast for each baby. Alternatively, both babies can be fed at the same time. Some people combine breast and bottle-feeding. If you decide to bottle-feed both babies save time by making up enough bottles for at least three feeds (see page 82). Your husband's help will be invaluable, especially with night and early morning feeds. Dummies are particularly useful too: when you are on your own you will probably have to feed one baby at a time, and it helps to pacify a hungry baby waiting his or her turn to be fed. This may not be such a problem as one twin may well be more passive than the other.

Contraception

When you have had a baby, it is advisable to think at once about the timing of further children, if you want to add to your family. Remember that a woman can become fertile again within a couple of months, even before she has returned to regular periods. Unless you and your husband feel you want to have another child soon after the first one, it is a good idea to use some form of contraception immediately after the birth. Bear in mind that a toddler is very demanding; unless you are very well organized, you may find it hard to cope with a newborn baby as well, both physically and mentally.

There are many forms of contraception. If you have already had experience of a satisfactory method before conceiving your first child, you will probably want to return to it after the baby. However if you have no previous experience or want to change to a different method, there are several people you can turn to for advice. The doctor in the hospital where your baby was born, your family doctor or your local family planning clinic will be able to help you decide which is best.

Breast feeding

Learning to breast-feed

People are inclined to think that a baby does nothing but eat and sleep. Of course one only has to watch babies to see that their lives are much more interesting than that, even in the first few days. However, feeding is very important both for you and the baby. It is worth persevering with it in the newborn period and using your time in hospital to learn from the Sister and nurses on the ward. It is easy to get worried that feeding is not going well at about three or four days after delivery; try to take things as calmly as possible and to be patient with a maddening baby who does not take to it easily.

Breast or bottle-feeding

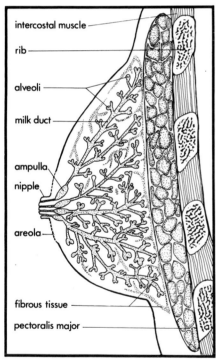

The decision about breast-feeding does not have to be made till you have been delivered and can actually hold your own baby. You may then feel that you want to put him to the breast or that the bottle is more convenient for you. It is a good idea, though, to think about the different ways before the baby has arrived.

There are very good reasons for thinking that breast-milk is the best food for a baby during the first few months of his life. Each animal has its own special milk, evolved over many centuries to provide food for that particular baby animal. This milk differs widely from one species to another. You can immediately see the difference between human milk and cow's milk: human milk looks rather watery compared to that in the bottle left by the milkman. It is wrong to think that your own milk is not good enough for a newborn baby because it does not look as rich as cow's milk. On the contrary, it is easier for the baby's immature stomach to digest and is more nutritious.

Cow's milk contains a lot of protein, but much of it is curd which will clot in the baby's stomach. The protein in human milk is much finer and more easily digestible. As you will notice from many bottles of milk the amount of fat in cow's milk varies a great deal. It is for this reason that some cow's milk [or milk-based feedings] are partially skimmed. The amount of lactose or milk-sugar is about the same in both milks, but the minerals are very different. Cow's milk contains a lot more sodium, usually present as common salt, and this may cause many problems if the baby is feverish or has diarrhoea. There is also a lot of phosphorous in cow's milk; this may lower the amount of calcium in the blood and can sometimes cause convulsions in the newborn baby.

There are several substances in breast-milk which are of major importance to a baby because they counteract infection. There are anti-bodies and other compounds in the milk which appear to stop germs from entering the baby's body through the gut

Left: Breast-feeding a baby can be one of the most rewarding aspects of motherhood. As well as providing a convenient and perfectly balanced diet, it protects the baby from infection and disease.

Above: Diagram of the structure of the lactating breast, showing the nipple, areola, ampulla (milk sacs) and alveoli (tiny sacs which first receive the milk made by the cells lining the sac).

These tables compare the relative nutritional content of human and cow's milk. The shaded areas refer to human milk. Table A shows that the total amount of solids in both milks is roughly the same, giving about 67 calories per 100ml of milk. However, as shown in Table B, cow's milk contains about twice as much protein as human milk, much of it a protein called casein which forms tough curds in the baby's stomach, (Table C). Fat is present in equal quantities (Table B), but cow's milk contains saturated fat which is more difficult for a baby to digest than the unsaturated fats of human milk. There is proportionately more calcium, sodium and phosphorus in cow's milk (Table D). The large quantity of phosphorus can cause poor calcium absorption; the extra sodium (salt) makes it difficult if he is losing fluid from vomiting or diarrhoea. All in all, it is true to say that human milk is better-suited to babies than cow's milk.

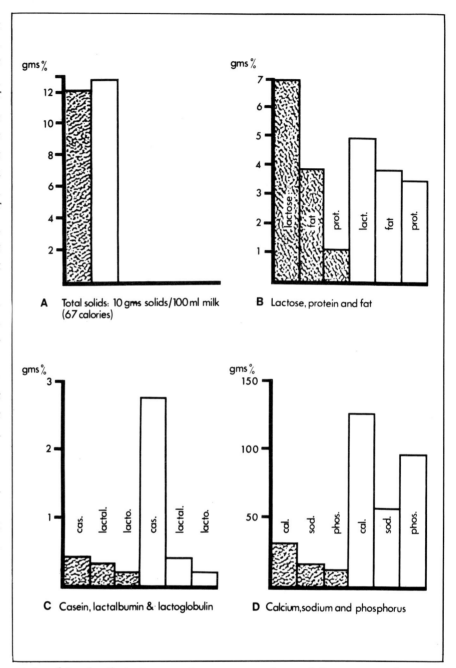

A Total solids: 10 gms solids/100 ml milk (67 calories)

B Lactose, protein and fat

C Casein, lactalbumin & lactoglobulin

D Calcium, sodium and phosphorus

giving him built-in immunity to a number of dangerous diseases.

Very occasionally, babies die during the first year of life and many of these deaths occur quite tragically and suddenly. These deaths are less frequent in breast-fed babies than in those that have been bottle-fed. We do not yet know the cause of these tragedies, but it is likely that many of them are due to sudden infection which may be prevented by breast-feeding.

You will see that in breast-feeding there are many advantages for the baby: the milk contains all the necessary foods in the right proportions and easily digestible forms, there is less salt and other minerals in the milk, and it will help to prevent an infection early in life.

Choosing to breast-feed

The choice is yours. For your own good, it is important that you should breast-feed only if you feel you wish to. Do not feel guilty if you really feel that you cannot face the whole idea.

Breast-feeding is very convenient and most mothers find that their babies are feeding well within a few days of the birth. It is important to start as soon as possible: since colostrum – the liquid that precedes actual milk – contains important antibodies which protect the baby from disease.

Feeding at the breast can continue for as little as two weeks or as much as a year – either way both mother and baby will have benefited from the experience.

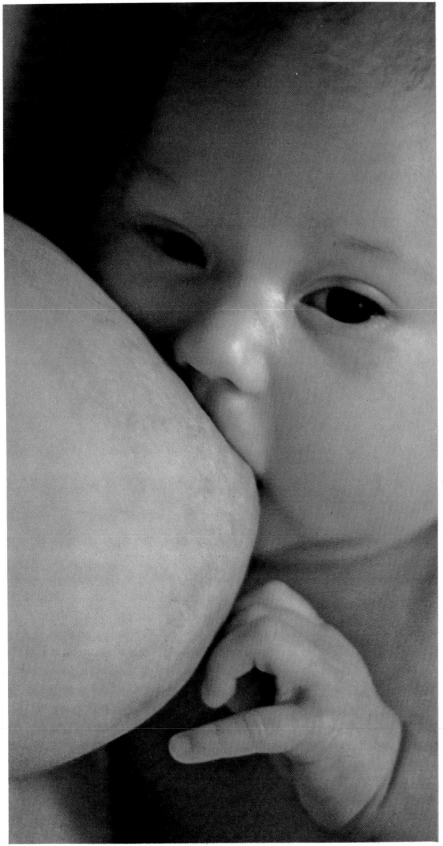

There are women who find the idea of breast-feeding unpleasant and, since bottle-feeding is quite satisfactory, there is no reason why they should breast-feed. The choice of feeding method must remain an entirely personal one.

Convenience. If you are undecided but not unhappy about the idea of breast-feeding, it is probably a good idea to try the

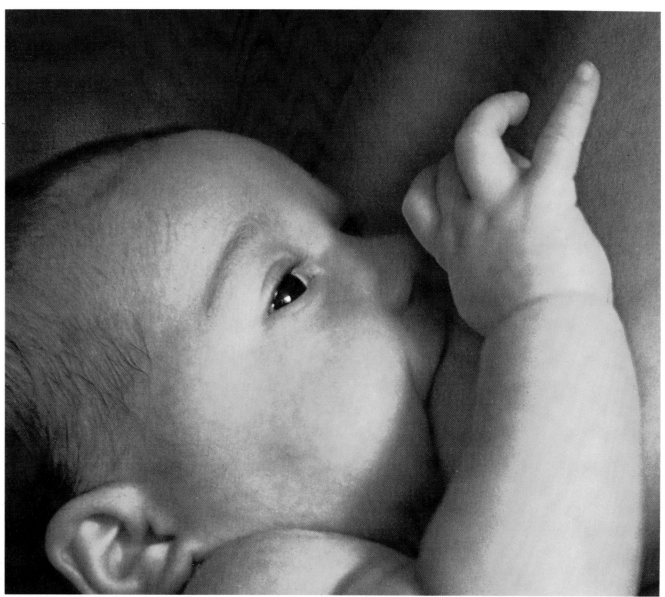

A small baby derives a great deal of pleasure from feeding. Hunger is actually painful to a baby's immature stomach, so a feed will naturally relieve this; but in addition babies seem to enjoy the act of sucking especially combined with the warmth and security given by close proximity to their mothers. Within a few days of the birth a baby may start to stare fixedly at his mother while feeding, focusing his eyes for the first time on her face.

baby on the breast first, since you may find it very enjoyable and convenient. The breast is always ready with milk after the first few days: in fact it is a prepackaged convenience food of the best sort. When the baby cries in the night it is not necessary to fiddle around with bottles and teats – the baby can be fed at once. Breast-feeding is particularly good for a journey in a car because you do not have to take any paraphernalia with you and the milk does not have to be warmed.

Inconvenience. Of course there are some disadvantages in breast-feeding: sometimes it can be very inconvenient. It is easy to go out now and then for the evening and leave the baby with a bottle, but it is much more difficult if you want to go away for the weekend and leave the baby with relatives. At first your breasts may leak and can sometimes make your clothes messy if you do not wear a heavy pad inside your brassiere. Many women wish to return to work only a few weeks after delivery and, unfortunately, there are very few factories or offices which have nurseries or can arrange their work to suit the irregular hours of the feeding baby. Feeding also inevitably becomes only the mother's occupation and her husband is not able to help her in the night,

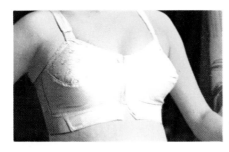

This special bra is designed to support lactating breasts. Laces adjust the size at the back, while front fastenings allow for quick access when the baby is hungry.

by feeding the baby and letting her take some rest. I have to admit that some men might regard this as an advantage, and not a disadvantage, of breast-feeding.

It would be wrong not to admit these slight difficulties, but the advantages for the baby appear to outweigh them greatly. In some poor parts of the world babies would not survive at all if they were not breast-fed.

Feeding in public. One possible drawback to breast-feeding is that feed times for the baby become less of a social occasion as most women wish to be alone or only with close relatives when they are suckling the baby. A baby can be bottle-fed, of course, when even strangers are present. It is a shame that modern life has banished such an ordinary thing behind closed curtains. Now there are signs that women are becoming less embarrassed about the idea of breast-feeding in front of other people. In fact, it is

In many parts of the world breast-milk is the only food available for babies and mothers go on feeding till the child is about two years old. In the Ivory Coast, as well as other African countries, it is the custom for mothers to carry their babies constantly with them as they continue essential work, and the babies can be fed literally on demand, whenever they are hungry.

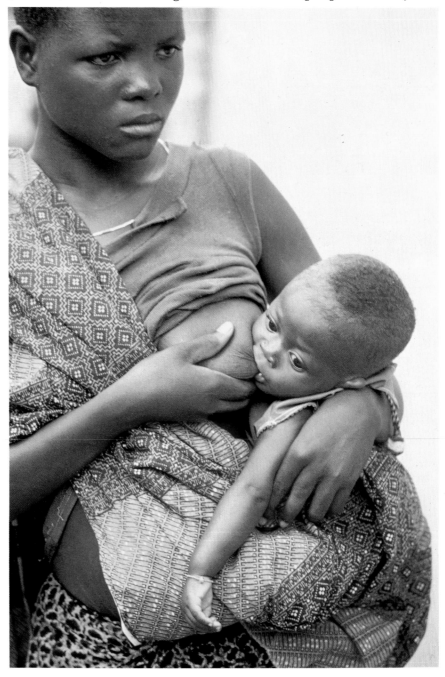

possible to breast-feed a baby in public without exposing the breast to anyone except the baby. I once saw a mother breast-feeding on a bus; she had a scarf over her shoulder which covered the breast and the baby so that he could suckle contentedly. When she had to get off the bus, she took the baby from the breast, slipped her dress up, took the scarf off and gathered up her other children and a pram. The person I was with had not even noticed that she was breast-feeding.

Breast and bottle. Many women think of breast- and bottle-feeding as quite separate alternatives, but, of course, they can be used together very conveniently. During the first few days when the breasts are not producing very much milk the baby may be very hungry and can only be satisfied if some extra milk is given to him from a bottle. It may be convenient for a baby to take the occasional artificial feed if you want to go out for a few hours and leave him with a baby-sitter. Some mothers do not breast-feed because they know that they will have to turn to the bottle after a few weeks to cope with special problems, such as having to return to work. But remember it is still an advantage to the baby and will give him a good start if you are able to breast-feed him for a week or two – even a few days is better than none at all.

Allergies. There is one situation where it now seems important to give the baby breast-milk alone during the first few months. This is when there is a strong history of allergy in your family, producing illnesses such as asthma, eczema or hay-fever. The baby is more likely to develop these allergies if he is given an artificial milk early in life. If he is very hungry it is perfectly

Breast-feeding need not interrupt an evening out with friends or any other social occasion. Choose the clothes you wear carefully – blouses or shirts, dresses with front fastenings, or any fairly loose top will do – and use a special nursing brassiere. These usually unfasten in the front for convenience, and are also designed to support lactating breasts comfortably.

reasonable to give him extra quantities of sugar and water when necessary rather than extra feeds of artificial milk.

Preparation of the breasts in the ante-natal clinic

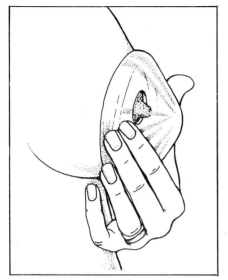

Using the Woolwich shell

You will remember that your breasts were examined on your first visit to the ante-natal clinic. This was to ensure that the breasts are absolutely normal, and to look at the nipples.

Inverted nipples. The nipple is full of blood vessels; when they fill as the result of stimulation of the nipple by the baby's sucking, the nipple becomes larger and longer. Sometimes it does not protrude naturally, but is turned inwards – an inverted nipple – or is flat and round like a button. If this condition of the nipple is noticed during pregnancy, it can be treated quite simply.

The Woolwich shell is constructed like a dome, with a base containing a hole. These shells can be put inside a brassiere so that the hole fits over the nipple and a part of the areola, which is the dark area at the base of the nipple. When they are worn like this during pregnancy, it encourages the nipple to stick out more and then becomes easier for the baby to suck. The shells are quite light and should fit comfortably. It is a good idea to wear them for only part of the day at first and then increase the time to most of the day. They should be kept clean by washing them daily with soap and water.

Care of the breasts during pregnancy

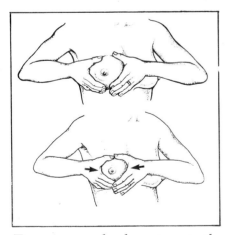

To massage the breast, cup the hands round and gradually work towards the nipple.

All you need to do during pregnancy is to wash the breasts every day carefully with soap and water. The nipple should not be scrubbed, or rubbed vigorously, as this may lead to cracking.

There seems to be some advantage in learning how to massage the breasts and to express the liquid which is produced inside the breast during pregnancy. This is not something that everyone finds pleasant and it is not essential to learn it. However, it may be useful to help empty the breasts when they become too full, three or four days after delivery.

The breast is held by both hands with the thumbs and fore-finger encircling it. The hands are then moved gently forward to massage the breast and ease milk towards the nipple. The thumbs and fingers make a smaller and smaller ring as they approach the nipple. You need to do this several times to be effective. After the birth milk can be expressed by pressing on the areola.

During pregnancy and the first day after delivery, there is a secretion from the breast which is known as colostrum. This is an important substance since it appears to contain many vital anti-bodies. Milk begins to be produced by the breast two or three days after the baby's birth.

Suckling for the first time

It is a good idea for the baby to go to the breast as soon as possible after birth. The stimulation of his sucking on the breast will send a hormone into action to start milk production. It will also help the uterus to contract properly and return to its usual size. If possible, give your baby the first breast-feed while you are still in the labour ward (see page 42); ask the midwife if you may do this. Certainly you should try and feed the baby within about four hours of the birth, unless you have been delivered at night and need good rest until morning.

The breast and the effect of sucking

The correct position of the nipple in the baby's mouth during feeding. Note lips and gums pressing against the areola.

Most of the breast is made up of fat and the glands which produce the milk. From the glands, tubes lead towards the nipple where they end in the small holes through which milk is ejected into the baby's mouth. The milk can collect in a part of the tube beneath the areola; the tube is widened to form a little sac. It is important to realize this as the baby doesn't obtain milk by chewing on the nipple, but needs to press on the areola to empty the sacs. The

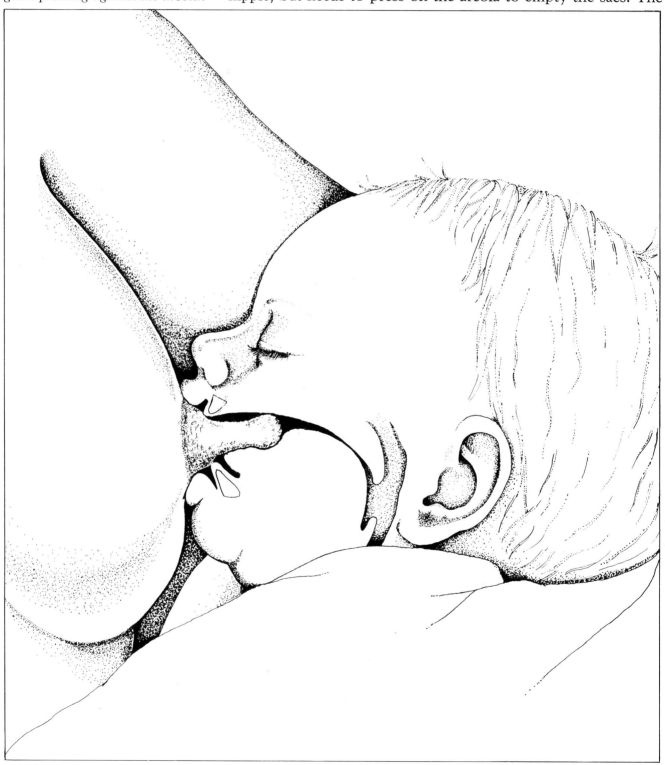

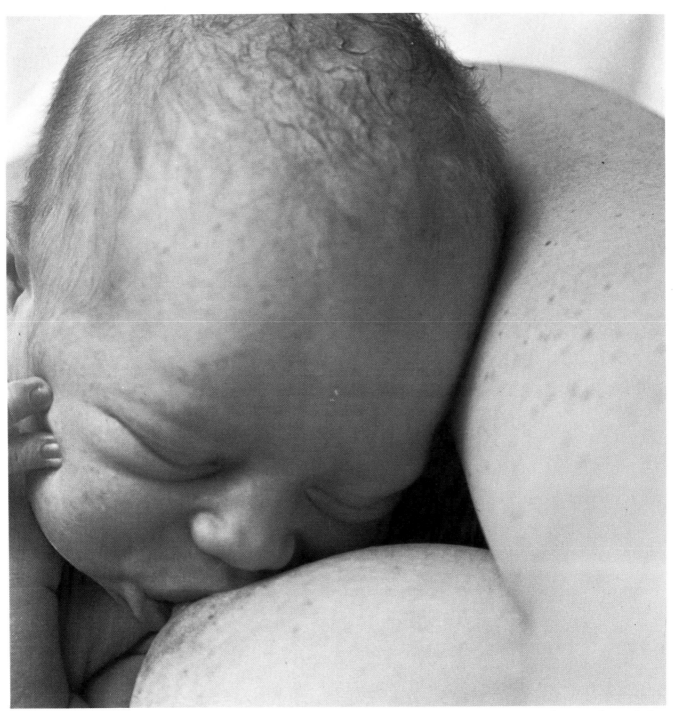

A baby suckling seen from the mother's point of view. The baby's head is cradled comfortably by his mother's arm, keeping his nose well clear of the breast. Towards the end of a feed when they are nearly satisfied they often become sleepy.

diagram shows how the baby's gums press on the areola and the nipple passes well back into the baby's mouth between the tongue and the roof of the mouth. When sucking, the baby empties the milk ducts and rolls the milk through the nipple by squeezing it against the roof of the mouth with his tongue. The milk then squirts into the back of the mouth, ready to be swallowed. Consequently, it is essential that the baby should get a part of the areola as well as the nipple into his mouth.

Giving the feed

Avoid giving the baby any infection when you are feeding him. Always wash your hands before starting a breast-feed. Also make sure that your breast is clean.

The first time you feed, a midwife will help you guide the baby on to the breast and she will also be available for subsequent

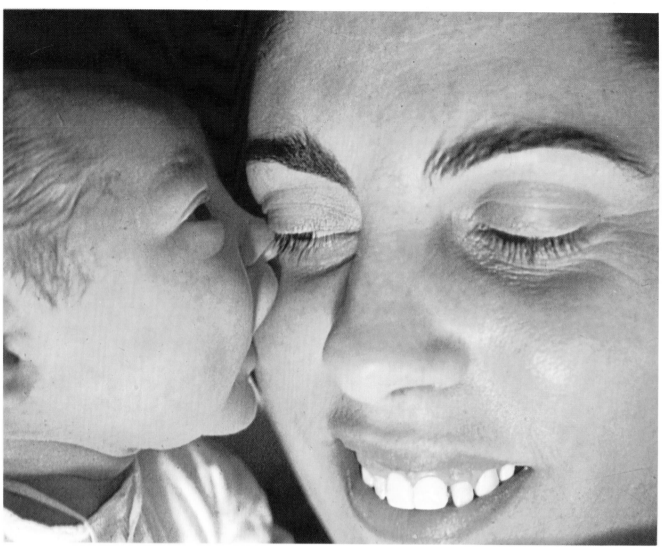

The 'rooting response', which makes a newborn baby turn towards the nipple when hungry can be demonstrated by rubbing any areas such as the cheek against the baby's cheek or mouth. Another way of demonstrating it is to gently stroke the baby's cheek with one finger; the baby will turn to the finger and try to suck it (below).

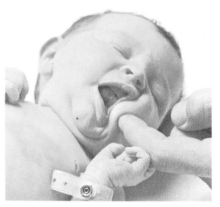

feeds if you have any difficulty. Make sure that you are quite comfortable. Prop yourself up well in bed, or on a chair, with plenty of pillows. Have something comfortable to sit on if you have any stitches or still feel a little sore. When you get home you may find that a low chair without arms, but with a good supporting back, is the best seat for you. You need to cradle the baby in your arms so that you can lower the nipple into his mouth as he looks up towards you. The baby has a reflex, called the 'rooting response', which makes him turn towards the nipple when he is hungry. If you rub the nipple on his cheek he will turn his head towards it and open his mouth to grasp it. This is also helped by expressing a little bit of colostrum on to the baby's lips so that he can taste it. All this is easier if a baby is hungry and ready for a feed.

While feeding, you may need to hold your breast up slightly just above the nipple so that it does not block the baby's nose and hinder his breathing. A comfortable position for the baby is in the crook of your arm and across your abdomen. Another method is to lie on the bed with the baby lying alongside you and your body turned a little towards him.

As soon as the baby has got the nipple well into his mouth and has tasted the colostrum, he usually starts to suck vigorously. It is quite normal for a baby to suck in bursts and then to have a little rest before sucking again. If he stops sucking for a long while you may need to encourage him a little by touching the lower jaw to start the sucking again.

Lengths of feeds. A baby usually sucks for only a short while on the first or second day, but then increases the length of feeds quickly. One cannot lay down a limit for the length of feeds, but most babies can attempt ten minutes on each breast from the third or fourth day of life onwards. They usually suck for shorter periods and less frequently before the third day. In fact, it is common for a baby to empty a breast during the first five minutes he is sucking; there is, therefore, no need to feed for a long time if the baby has sucked well and is obviously contented with the food he has had. He should be taken off the nipple at the end of a feed, because prolonged sucking may cause a cracked nipple.

When the baby finishes a feed he may still want to suck even though his stomach is quite full. This seems to be because sucking is a very enjoyable experience in itself for a baby and will help to keep him content. After a feed you may well see your baby lying quietly in your arms, or in the cot, sucking his fingers happily and peacefully until he eventually falls asleep.

Timing of feeds

Babies often feed quite irregularly. There are some babies who will fit an exact four-hourly regimen, but they are the exceptions and most babies wake up before or after the four hours. It seems that breast-fed babies feed more frequently, about three-hourly, than those fed on artificial milk. You should not leave the baby to cry until you think his next feed-time is due. A baby's cry of hunger changes after about five minutes into a cry of pain; this has been shown by careful recording of crying. A long wait for milk is an unpleasant experience for a baby.

If the baby's cot is next to your bed you will be able to tell when the baby is hungry. This is obviously much easier when you are at home: you can easily have the baby beside you or in the next room, so that you can hear when he cries. In hospital it is not always possible to have the baby beside you for the whole time, but ask if you can have him there. During the first few days you will be able to learn his individual signals for hunger. It takes a little while for you to sort out the different cries a baby makes. The baby's cries, and other hunger signals, alter the amount of milk that you produce. The sound of crying makes your breasts start producing milk, even before the baby has started to suck on the nipple. When he does start to suck the milk flow is increased rapidly and you may find that the other breast leaks some milk.

Demand feeding. Feeding babies when they want to be fed is known as 'demand feeding'. There are good reasons for thinking that it is the most natural method of feeding and will help your breasts to produce the greatest quantity of milk. In many parts of the world babies are carried around by their mothers, often in a sling on the back; they are breast-fed frequently during the day at the least sign of hunger; the baby takes frequent short feeds.

'Demand' feeding is practised quite literally by mothers in many parts of the world, as they carry their babies with them constantly and can put them to the breast at the least sign of hunger.

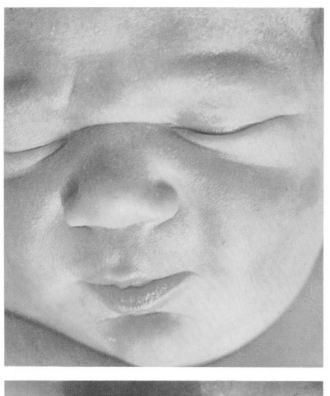

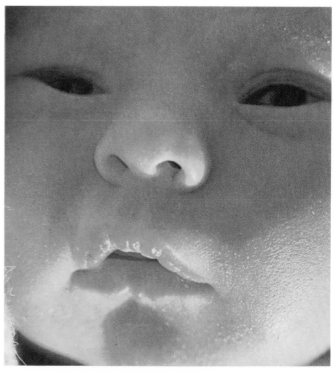

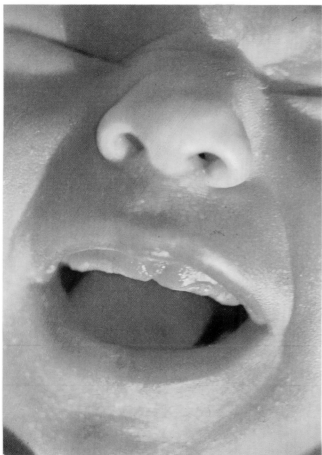

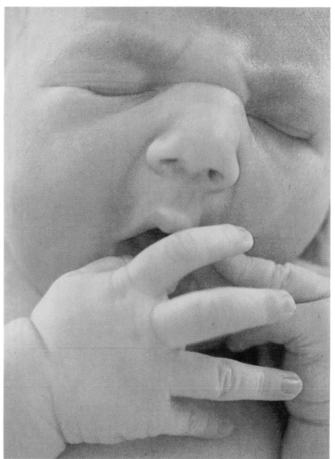

Newborn babies are not static: even when only a few hours old they show many different moods. One of the most active times is when a baby wakes for a feed. First he sleeps – but begins to stir gradually. He wakes properly, but may not cry immediately. Gradually the discomfort of hunger will overcome him and he will start to cry. Crying may alternate with short periods of finger-sucking if his hands come close to his face: a baby cannot voluntarily bring his hands together in front of his face until about three months old. The sucking pads on this baby's lips are normal, not blisters.

This table shows the number of feeds a baby took in the first two weeks of life. Note that the number reaches a peak at the fifth day, when eleven short feeds were given. But by the end of the second week the baby has settled down to a regular routine of six feeds per day.

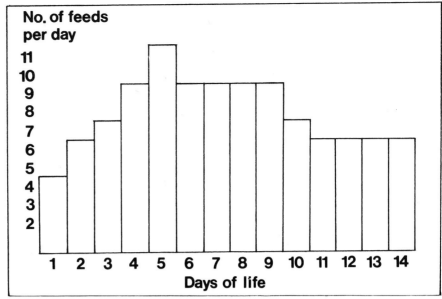

Feeding frequency in the first week. The frequency of feeding varies a lot within the first week. On the first day the baby may feed only once or twice, the feeds then become much more frequent, reaching a peak about the fifth day. After that, the number of times the baby feeds gets less and remains steady from about seven days onward. The chart shows the number of feeds one individual baby took during the first week of life. You will see from the chart the pattern I have just described, the number of feeds rising to a crescendo about the fifth day and then slackening. Your baby will not take exactly the same number of feeds but the pattern is likely to be similar. Try to understand this and don't worry if your baby seems to be feeding very frequently: it is normal and doesn't mean he is not getting sufficient food.

The end of the feed

When you think the baby has had enough time on your breast, he may well have gone off to sleep. However, he may still keep the nipple firmly in his mouth. You can take the baby off the breast by pressing gently on his lower jaw to release the suction.
Wind. When a baby swallows milk, he swallows air as well. As a result of this a bubble of air or 'wind' collects in the stomach, which may be uncomfortably distended. This may cause two things: the baby could be uncomfortable and grizzly after a feed, or could stop feeding because his hunger seems to have gone, although he has not taken enough food. Therefore it is helpful for a baby to belch after a feed, or between one breast and the other. There are several traditional ways of 'winding' a baby; you can sit him up on your lap and rub his back, or you can hold him against your shoulder, with his face away from you, while carrying him around or rocking him until he burps. In many societies the baby is carried around on the mother's back or tucked into a sash at her waist; this has the same effect as 'winding'. When a baby lies down with air trapped in his stomach he can be quite distressed. However, some babies swallow more air than others, so do not be too concerned if your baby does not burp when you try to bring up wind. There is not much point in

continuing for longer than ten minutes. In fact, if he burps after that time it is probably the return of air swallowed while he was sitting up having his back rubbed! The idea of winding a baby is to make him more comfortable, not to insist that he should burp.

Time for a cuddle. Babies need a lot of attention besides keeping them clean and well-fed. Try and put aside a few minutes to hold the baby and cuddle him after a feed. Many mothers cradle babies in their arms and carry them around. Why not use one of the lullabies and baby songs which were used for soothing a baby to sleep. These are genuinely comforting and they help the baby to get used to the sound of your voice. The baby may well not go to sleep immediately after a feed and it is a good time for you and him to be together. To insist on putting him straight back into his cot seems a little unkind and abrupt and you could miss a very useful time to get to know him. But I do not wish to prescribe this sort of thing for every mother and baby, since there are many, many ways of caring for babies; the essential thing is that you should find out what is best for the baby and for you.

Some problems with breast-feeding

Sore nipples may occur at about three to six days after delivery. It seems to be the result of the baby's vigorous sucking. It is interesting to note that it is less common when the baby is fed on demand, presumably because he takes the feed more quickly and hungrily. A common cause of soreness is that the baby is gnawing on the nipple and not on the areola.

The midwife will help you if you have a sore nipple; it may be possible to rest the breast and to feed the baby on the other one for a while. If both nipples are sore, each feed may be given from one breast at a time until the skin is tougher. Sometimes a baby can be bottle-fed until your breasts are comfortable again.

One useful little device is a nipple-shield. This looks like a rubber teat on a plastic base. The base fits on to the areola and the teat fills with milk so that the baby can suck without touching your skin.

Cracked nipples are rather more uncomfortable and can take a little longer to heal. The midwife will be able to give you something to rub on the nipple to prevent infection and you will probably have to rest the breast for a day or so.

Engorgement of the breasts may occur at about three or four days after delivery, because milk is then produced for the first time in large quantities and the baby is not yet old enough to take it all. It is now that the methods of massage and expression which were mentioned earlier in this chapter may help. Get the midwife to help you so you avoid bruising the breast. If your breast shows any sign of becoming swollen and tender, use expression to empty it after a feed, until the baby is sucking vigorously enough to empty it himself. Expression of the breast may also be useful where the baby is not able to suck, if he has been born early, for instance.

Breast pumps can also be used for engorgement. There are two main types: the hand pump has a glass cone which can be placed

'Wind' is an uncomfortable air bubble in the baby's stomach: and needs to be gently eased out by rubbing the baby's back. A baby can either be propped up into a sitting position on the mother's knee or held up against the shoulder. Sometimes you may not even need to rub the baby's back — raising him to a vertical position may be enough to release the air from his stomach.

over the nipple and areola, while suction is applied with a rubber bulb; there is also a more expensive, but very convenient, electric pump which sucks rhythmically and can extract a large quantity of milk very comfortably and simply. It is very useful both for breast engorgement and for the mother of a premature baby to keep her breast producing milk for many weeks.

Inflammation of the breast. If you should notice any particular area of tenderness in the breast you should bring it to the attention of the doctor, particularly if there is redness of the skin over it. He may give treatment to prevent an infection continuing.

Common worries about breast-feeding

Many women are surprised by the appearance of breast-milk. It looks thin and watery when compared with cow's milk, although it is a much better food for a human baby. Do not take your baby off the breast just because the milk does not look rich enough.

Waiting for milk. Waiting for the milk to come can be a very worrying time. During the first four days the baby loses weight and you may think that he or she is never going to get enough from the breast. Remember that it takes many days for large quantities of milk to be produced smoothly from the breast; milk only starts to come in on the third day and it may take a whole week before feeding is going smoothly.

Test weighing. A useful way of checking how much the baby takes is test weighing. The baby can be weighed just before and just after a feed. If he is in the same clothes any weight gain tells you exactly how much milk he has had. It is not necessary to do this at every feed, but your midwife may feel it would be helpful if the baby has not started to gain weight at about six or seven days of age. From about a week of age the baby usually takes around 150 millilitres for each kilogram of body weight during a whole day; this means you must expect an average baby to take about 60 to 100 millilitres at each feed. One millilitre of milk weighs roughly one gram; therefore the baby who gains 100 grams at one feed has taken 100 millilitres of milk. (In Imperial measures one expects a week old baby to take $2\frac{1}{2}$ fluid ounces of milk per pound of body weight per day. This means that a baby takes two to three ounces of milk at each feed from the breast. Test weighing would therefore show a gain of 2 or 3 ounces.)

The baby who does not suck

During the first week a baby may be disinclined to suck. This is especially common if jaundice has made him sleepy. There are many little tricks to stimulate the baby into sucking, such as pushing up gently and rhythmically under the chin. Some babies may cry irritably and will not fix on to the areola. Try to be very patient, even though this may seem very difficult. After a few days spent patiently offering the breast to the baby, feeding usually proceeds very well.

Complementary feeds

These are feeds from the bottle which can be given after a breast-feed if the baby has not obtained enough food. During the first few days, it is only necessary to give the baby water or a dilute solution of sugar since his body is prepared for lack of food. Towards the end of the first week it may be necessary to use complementary feeds of artificial milk, if the breast-supply is increasing very slowly.

Vomiting

Vomiting is very common in babies. They seem to vomit effortlessly, so that it is not quite such a nasty experience as it is for adults. Many bring back a small amount of feed when they are 'winded' – this is usually called posseting. If the baby brings back the whole of a feed repeatedly, you should talk to the doctor.

Food and drugs while breast-feeding

A good, balanced diet is essential if you are to breast-feed and remain healthy. Have a look at the basic principles of diet given on page 88, and try to include nutritious fluids such as milk with your meals. Do not force yourself to drink large quantities of fluid, but allow your thirst to regulate your intake.

Most drugs and medicines which you take are excreted in breast milk, but only in very small amounts. Usually the baby is not affected by these substances, but occasionally your doctor may advise against breast-feeding if you are on a special drug. You must always tell your doctor about any medicines you are taking, if the baby becomes unwell. For example, the baby could develop diarrhoea if you have taken a large dose of laxative. By the way, do not worry about having an occasional glass of wine, beer or spirits. Alcohol will not do the baby any harm in the minute quantity which might be present in breast milk.

How long to go on breast-feeding

You may only be able to breast-feed your baby for a comparatively short while, but remember it is worthwhile feeding the baby even for a week or two. Many mothers ask when is the best time to give up breast-feeding; there can be no simple answer to this because it depends on your feelings, and what the baby wants. For modern life it seems reasonable to feed the baby on breast-milk alone for the first three months and then to introduce other food gradually. You might continue breast-feeding for the first nine months. Even when the baby's teeth have started to come through, he is unlikely to bite on the breast and feeding can proceed quite successfully. Many babies after the age of nine months get a lot of pleasure from a breast feed, and you may wish to continue one or two feeds a day past the first birthday. At this age breast milk is not a complete food for the baby, so it is necessary to give a mixed diet to prevent lack of iron, which can cause anaemia. Iron-rich foods include liver, spinach and egg yolks.

In some parts of the world, breast-feeding is essential for the baby's health because there is no other milk readily available. Many African babies are kept on the breast for an average of two years. This is not necessary in a developed country but demonstrates that it is quite possible to breast-feed for a long time.

Finally, remember that, after the first few days, breast-feeding usually goes very smoothly, without any problems and there is no need to be apprehensive about it.

Bottle feeding

Learning about bottle-feeding

Artificial feeding is a perfectly satisfactory way of feeding a baby. There are many satisfactory baby milks available in the shops; if you follow the instructions carefully, they will give the baby all the food he needs. Even if you are breast-feeding, it is useful to know about bottle milks, because you may need to use the occasional bottle in an emergency.

The midwife should demonstrate how to mix milks and sterilize bottles. Make quite sure that you understand the procedure completely. If you feel a little muddled ask the midwife to demonstrate it again, so you can be absolutely certain that you are able to do it yourself when you get home. If possible, involve your husband in the demonstration. If he understands the procedure you'll be able to ask for his help.

Choosing a milk

You may feel a little confused by the number of brands you see in the shops. There have been several recent changes in baby milks as a result of research, which means that there are now some new milks on the market and manufacturers are producing modifications almost every year in order to improve their products.

Practically all baby milks are made from cow's milk, which is then modified to make it suitable for human babies. There are three main types of baby milks: dried or powdered milk; evaporated milk which has been tinned; prepared milk that can be given to a baby without any modification. You will need to choose the type of milk you want, but it is sometimes helpful to use a combination of them. For instance, you may find it useful to have a few bottles of ready-prepared milk in the store cupboard, for an emergency such as a journey or night out.

There are various things to consider when choosing a milk:

1. The cost. You will need to work out what you can afford, because some milks are more expensive than others. The most expensive milk is not necessarily the best, although it is true that the most recent modifications in milks, to make them safer for babies, have also made them rather more expensive.

2. Powdered or evaporated. Powdered milk has the advantage that you can keep it in a store cupboard safely for some time – it may well be the best milk for you if you live in a hot country. Evaporated milk is very convenient to mix: you only have to add water and stir, but the tin must be used up within 24 hours once it has been opened and must be kept in a refrigerator. By the way, you should not use sweetened condensed milk for your baby, and the same applies to very low fat instant powdered milk – the labels of both types usually warn you not to use them for babies. In the past, most baby milks were produced as half-cream or full-

Bottle-feeding can be just as satisfying for a baby as feeding from the breast. As long as you choose a milk which suits the baby and follow the manufacturer's instructions exactly when making up the feed, all will be well. There are certain things you must be careful about, like sterilization, but it can be a very convenient way of feeding and does mean that both parents can share the task of feeding, especially at night.

cream. This told you how much fat they contained. It is now more common for a brand to be only a full-cream milk. For the average baby it does not matter which milk you choose.

There are some differences in the ways that powdered milk is manufactured. Roller-dried milk is produced on very hot rollers from which the dried milk residue is scraped off; it is often a cheaper milk, but may be more difficult to mix than other dried milk. Spray-dried milk is produced by spraying milk on to a hot surface; it is a finer milk which is easier to mix and there is some suggestion that it is also easier for the baby to digest. Packets of milk include a special scoop for you to use when making up the milk. It is safer and easier to use a scoop which is small and deep rather than wide and shallow.

3. Sugar already included. Some milks have been made by the manufacturers with the correct amount of sugar for the baby. You do not need to do anything more than add water to the powder and give it to the baby. Other milks have less sugar, to allow you to vary the amount in the baby's diet. You may wish to give him more or less sugar, the amount of sugar depending on whether he has loose motions or is constipated. Do not leave sugar out completely to try and make your baby less fat; the milk will not be a complete food if you do. In general, I think it is better to choose a milk which does need extra things, like sugar, added to it. You can then control the formula yourself.

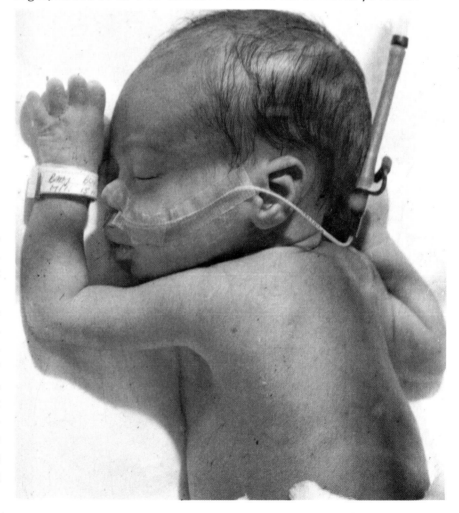

Premature babies are usually fed very small amounts of artificial feed by means of a tube which is passed through one of the nostrils. Because of the very small quantities of milk given at each feed he will generally be given extra vitamins. This is carefully controlled while the baby is in hospital but you may find that you have to continue giving vitamin supplements when the baby is back home with you. The doctor or health visitor will advise you on this.

4. Sodium. Sodium is a part of common salt and is present in human or cow's milk; but there is much more in cow's milk and this can be a problem for a baby. His kidneys may have difficulty in getting rid of it if he is feverish or has diarrhoea. For this reason it is safer to have a milk containing only a little sodium, as near as possible to breast-milk. Unfortunately, the sodium content of milk is not always clearly stated on the outside of the packet or the tin, and when it is, you may not be able to understand it easily. The best plan is to ask the pharmacist about the sodium in the milk and to ask which brand he suggests as the safest. Most of the milks developed recently contain much less sodium.

5. Vitamins. Some milks have added vitamins. If you use one of these milks you will not have to give the baby extra vitamin drops or fruit juice. The only exception is a premature baby; he is likely to take only small quantities of milk and it may need additional vitamins. Your doctor will advise you on this.

Equipment

All the equipment needed for artificial feeding and proper sterilization.

Bottles. Bottles with a wide neck are much easier to use because they can be cleaned so much more easily. They usually come with a plastic cap into which the teat is fitted. These have also solved the fiddly problem of getting a teat on to the top of a narrow-necked bottle. Narrow-necked bottles are in fact becoming increasingly rare. You will need three or four bottles to enable you to make up several feeds at once and then store them in the

refrigerator, making things much easier, specially for night feeds.

Teats. Teats will often be sold with your bottle. They do vary a little in hardness and in the size of the hole. You may sometimes need to enlarge the hole, to allow the baby to suck the milk more easily; this can be done with a needle that has been sterilized by passing it through a flame until it is red-hot and then allowed to cool. If your baby does not suck very vigorously, you could try a longer and softer teat. Experiment to get it right.

Bottle brush. You will need this to clean the bottle thoroughly before it is sterilized. Do not use the brush for any other purpose.

Teaspoon and knife. The teaspoon will be needed for adding sugar and for filling the scoop with milk. The knife is essential for levelling off the scoop before mixing.

Whisk. This may be helpful when mixing a feed.

Measuring jug. You will need this for measuring water or evaporated milk. It can also be used as a container for mixing the milk.

Scoops. A scoop is provided in a packet of powdered milk. The scoop is only suitable for the brand it is supplied with; it must *not* be used for milk of a different brand.

Cleanliness and sterilization

Hypochlorite solution for sterilization can either be in liquid or effervescent tablet form. Make sure the bottles are fully immersed.

Whenever you prepare food for the family, and particularly for the baby, it is essential to have clean hands. This probably seems obvious to you, but it can't be emphasized enough. You should wash your hands with soap in hot water and dry them on a clean dry towel. Unfortunately, it is only too easy to pass on the germs of food poisoning when you are mixing milk, and food poisoning is very dangerous for a small baby. This is particularly likely to

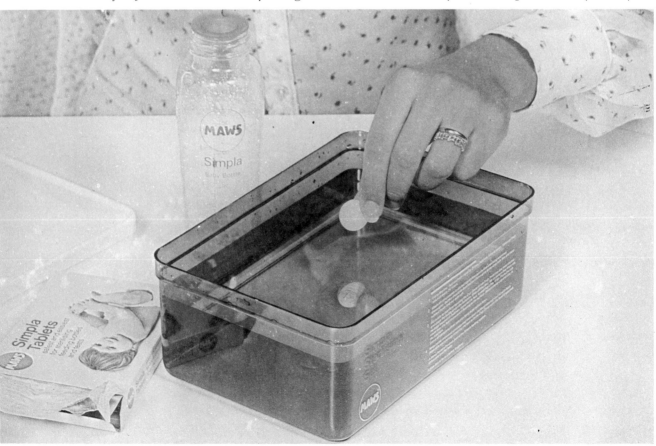

Before sterilization, clean the bottle thoroughly with a bottle brush, and rub the teat inside and out with salt.

happen if you have some diarrhoea and naturally you must then be *specially* careful to wash your hands after going to the lavatory.

You should sterilize the bottles and teats after they have been used for a feed. First of all, clean them thoroughly. If any milk remains inside, the sterilization may not be effective and germs will continue to grow inside the bottle. Wash the bottle carefully and clean off any milk with the brush. Then wash the bottle again. The same should be done with the teats. They may also be rubbed inside and out with salt, and then rinsed.

There are two main methods of sterilization: boiling and hypochlorite solution, using liquid or tablets.

1. Boiling. This is a very effective method of killing germs. The bottles, teats and anything else you need to use, such as the spoon and jug, are *completely* immersed in water which is then brought to the boil. Continue to boil for about five minutes. The saucepan can then be taken off the heat and allowed to cool. If you put the lid on the saucepan, the equipment will be kept sterile until they are needed at the next feed.

2. Hypochlorite solution. This can be bought in liquid form or as effervescent tablets. This is a good method for sterilizing bottles in the home, though it is not so satisfactory for a hospital. You need a large container for the solution; it is best to have a plastic one, but glass or china will do so long as it is not chipped. The hypochlorite solution corrodes metal, so you must not use a container of metal, and you will need plastic spoons. It is particularly important to have all traces of milk removed from the bottle before sterilizing it. The solution is made up according to the manufacturer's instructions and sterilizing is simplicity itself. You immerse all the utensils, making certain that there are no air bubbles left inside them. One place that is easy to forget is the hole of the teat; squirt some of the solution through the teat hole to make certain you have cleared it of bubbles. The utensils must stay in the solution for at least two hours before you use them.

Making up feeds

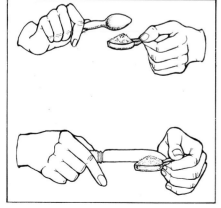

The correct way to fill the scoop: first fill the scoop with a teaspoon, then level it off with a knife.

Please follow the manufacturer's instructions exactly. Several reports have shown that many mothers, as many as 20 per cent, make up feeds incorrectly. Do not be one of them, because it really is very unsafe to make up feeds to the wrong strength. It is particularly dangerous to make feeds too strong, and it is very easy to do this if you are not thinking about it.

Incorrect use of the scoop is the source of many mistakes. It should not be used for taking milk out of the packet; if you do this it is easy to pack powder into the scoop and so add more than you intended. The milk should, ideally, be put into the scoop with another spoon. Then level the scoop off carefully with the back of a knife and again, do not pack it down. Above all, do not add an extra scoop to the water just because you think some more food would be good for the baby, and consult your doctor or health visitor before changing the proportion.

In most cases you add one scoop of powdered milk to 30 millilitres (1 fluid ounce) of water. For this you will want to use

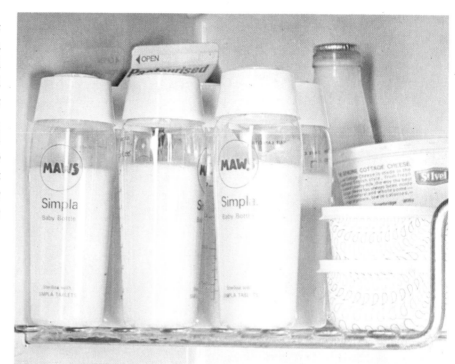

One of the most convenient aspects of artificial feeding is that you can make up several feeds at once and keep them, in closed, sterilized bottles, in the refrigerator. This is particularly useful for night time, while the baby is still on a six-feed routine. Though it is preferable to warm the milk before giving it to the baby, it is usually perfectly acceptable straight from the refrigerator.

After mixing the milk powder into a thick cream, add hot, boiled water to the required strength. Keep the teat, cover and cap on a sterile saucer until you are ready to use them.

boiled water – this does not mean boiling water, but water which has been boiled and has been allowed to cool a little. If you use boiling water you will destroy the vitamin C in the milk. Measure out the milk carefully and put it in a jug, which, like all the utensils that you use, must be sterilized first. Add a little of the warm, boiled water to make a smooth cream with the milk – rather like making custard – and then, add water to make up the milk to the correct volume, stirring well all the time. It is better to use drinking water; the drinking water tap is usually the one in the kitchen. The reason for this is that the water generally comes straight from the main water supply rather than from the reserve tank and is likely to contain less bacteria than water from other taps, which has been standing about in the tank in your roof.

One you have made up the milk, you can use it immediately by pouring it into a bottle, or you can keep it for some time if you cover the jug with a sterilized saucer or cover. You should keep the milk in a cool place, preferably in a refrigerator.

If you make up more than one feed at a time – and this can be useful for journeys, night feeds, baby-sitters etc – you must be very careful to keep the milk free from infection. Keep the jug or full bottles in a refrigerator until the time of the next feed.

If you wish, you can bring cold milk up to a warm temperature by placing a feeding bottle in a jug of hot water for ten minutes. This will heat the milk up to the right temperature for the baby. You can tell that it is all right by shaking some milk on to the back of your hand; if it feels warm, the temperature is correct. It is not necessary to re-warm milk; babies will drink milk happily, even if it comes straight from the refrigerator.

Other methods of making up milk

There are now a number of convenient modern milks available.
Very fine powdered milk is measured into the bottle; warm, previously-boiled water is added and the mixture is shaken in the

Some milks are now fine enough to mix in the bottle.

bottle until it is completely mixed. This is a very convenient way of making up milk with no fuss.

Evaporated milk is very simple to mix; you only have to take 1 measure of the evaporated milk and stir in $2\frac{1}{2}$ measures of water, with some sugar. As the baby grows, the milk can be made more concentrated; follow the instructions on the tin. Once a tin of evaporated milk has been opened, it should be kept in the refrigerator and should never be used after 24 hours. It is always safer to use boiled water for the mixture, but it is more satisfactory to sterilize the milk after making it up. In that case bring the mixture to the boil in a saucepan and stir until it has been boiling gently for three minutes. It will then be sterile and can be allowed to cool, off the heat.

Pre-packed milk is very convenient and if you use it you will not have any preparation to do. It is probably unwise to warm this type of milk before giving it to the baby. If you do warm it you may cause a skin on the surface which could block the teat.

Liquid cow's milk

There are so many good powdered and evaporated milks on the market today that it is hardly necessary to use diluted cow's milk for tiny babies especially as it is rather difficult for them to digest. However, you may need to use it in an emergency and I thought you might like to know the correct formula.

First of all you should be very careful to use milk which is safe and does not have any germs in it. Choose milk that has been pasteurized – this means that it has been heated and cooled sufficiently to kill any dangerous germs. Most milk supplied by the big dairies is pasteurized – unpasteurized milk is rare nowadays. Milk also varies considerably in the amount of cream it contains; it is wise to choose a milk that is not particularly rich in cream or homogenized. Keep it cool and throw it away if it shows any signs of being infected or sour.

When you use ordinary cow's milk for a small baby it will be necessary to dilute it and to add some sugar. Half milk and half water is satisfactory for the first couple of days, then two thirds milk and one third water until five months and undiluted after that. The sugar is added as 1 tsp. for every 3 fl. oz. of feed.

In all cases it is necessary to sterilize the mixture after it has been made up. Do this in the usual way by bringing it to the boil and keeping it there for three minutes. It is probably wise to boil cow's milk until the baby is about six months old. Cow's milk, in its undiluted form, is a standard part of the diet of any baby from six months onwards.

Quantity of food

The baby will tell you how much food he needs, because he will cry if he does not get enough, so rely on him and his hunger. Very roughly, he will take about 150 millilitres per kilo per day ($2\frac{1}{2}$ fluid ounces per pound per day) in about five or six feeds. It is therefore usual for a baby to feed about four hourly, but I must emphasize again that this is often very irregular.

During the first week of life a baby will slowly increase the amount of milk he takes. A newborn baby weighing about 3 kilograms, (about 7 pounds), often takes about 90 millilitres (3 fluid ounces) at each feed by seven days. He will work up to this amount steadily through the first week. You may expect him to take very little on the first day or two, 30 millilitres (1 fluid ounce) on the third day and so on. And remember that babies do vary a lot so your baby probably won't conform *exactly* to this pattern. (See Breast-feeding chart, page 71).

Timing of feeds

Fathers can help with feeding.

If a baby takes about six feeds a day during the first few weeks, they will often be spread out through the day in the following way: an early morning feed at about 6-8 am; a late morning feed before noon; an afternoon feed; an early evening feed; a late night feed just before midnight; and another feed in the middle of the night. Unfortunately, babies usually need a night feed for six or seven weeks, or longer. Perhaps you can get your husband to play his part; the best plan may be to arrange a rota so that neither of you gets very tired. Some people are tempted to get rid of the dreary night feed by giving the baby a heavier meal last thing at night – cereals are often used for that purpose. However, a family doctor has recently shown that this does not work; it seems the baby will stop feeding at night only when he wants to and is not influenced by having a lot of starch which will only make him fat. Stick to milk alone: if the baby seems unsatisfied he will soon indicate that he needs more milk, so ask the doctor or health visitor if it is time to increase the volume of milk at each feed.

The main thing is to feed the baby when he needs it. It is not a good idea to wake the baby if you think it is time for a feed – as has already been mentioned, he will wake when he is hungry and will gradually adjust to longer and longer periods between feeds. Eventually he will develop a fairly normal sleep routine, sleeping through the night with perhaps one or two naps during the day. Milk from bottle or breast is usually given for some time in conjunction with solid food.

Using the bottle

Make sure that you are sitting comfortably and can hold the baby so that you can see his face. It is probably easiest to have baby sitting on your lap supported in the crook of your arm. You can then use the other hand to control the bottle. If the baby is hungry he will open his mouth and take the teat; he will then start sucking vigorously. Be careful not to put the teat too far into his mouth or you may cause him to choke and splutter. It is quite useful to keep a gentle pull on the bottle, as this seems to help the baby suck. If you do not hold the bottle above the horizontal the baby will suck air at the same time as milk. This will fill his stomach; you will have to wind him frequently and he may not take the whole bottle.

Before starting the feed it is useful to shake some drops out of the bottle on to the back of your hand to make certain that the milk will run properly when the baby sucks. If hardly any milk comes through, it might be necessary to enlarge the holes in the

Artificial feeding often produces a lot of 'wind' which can be very uncomfortable for the baby. Don't forget to use the time after a feed as often as you can to cuddle and talk to the baby: it is important for both of you.

teat. Be careful not to make the holes too large, otherwise the milk will pour from the bottle and will make the baby splutter.

The whole feed should take about a quarter of an hour, with a little gap in the middle to sit the baby up and allow him to burp. Wind him again at the end of the feed and then give him a nice cuddle and cooing session before putting him in his cot. Do please remember that this cuddling session after a feed is very important to a baby; it is not a luxury, but something he needs.

Alone with a bottle

Never leave a baby sucking from a propped-up bottle. He may splutter and choke from milk in his throat, though this is unlikely. But more serious is the fact that a baby can easily develop an infection in the middle ear.

Other food & drink

The thirsty baby

Babies can be very thirsty as well as hungry. This is particularly likely if a baby is very hot, for instance in a tropical country or even a centrally-heated flat. You must remember this, because you may interpret a baby's cry as hunger when he is, in fact, only thirsty. One of the main reasons for thirst is artificial milk that has been made up too strong. Remember that cow's milk contains a lot of salt, so it is important to prepare it correctly, (see page 81), following the manufacturer's instructions.

Water

It is a good idea to offer any bottle-fed baby some water during the day. You can do this when he is awake between feeds during the morning or afternoon. You can use boiled drinking water or a dilute solution of orange juice, rose-hip syrup or some other fruit mixture. Do not be surprised if the baby does not take the water. The idea is to *offer* it to him just in case he wants it. He will let you know soon enough.

You should be careful to offer water to any baby who has become unwell. Diarrhoea or fever both cause loss of water from the body. Put him on a dilute solution of fruit juice and dilute his milk for one or two feeds. You can easily do this by adding the usual amount of water to only half the number of scoops of powder. Do not continue with this longer than one or two feeds, unless you are advised to do so by the doctor.

Vitamins

Many artificial milks contain extra vitamins; you will not often need to give supplements. The only real exception to this is a tiny premature baby. The most important vitamins for your baby are D and C. If you are not certain that the milk you are giving the baby contains enough vitamins, or if you are breast-feeding, you can abtain a vitamin mixture from the chemist or from your Child [Family] Health Centre. Ask your doctor or health visitor [clinic sister] if you are in any doubt.

Bear in mind that vitamins can be dangerous for a baby if given in excess. This is true of both vitamins A and D. Aim to give your baby abour 400 units of Vitamin D a day (that is 10 micrograms). This vitamin prevents rickets – a condition causing soft bones which used to be common in childhood. It causes bowing of the legs and swelling at the wrists and ankles.

Vitamin C prevents scurvy which is a condition of bleeding gums, painful bones and anaemia. It is easy to prevent this with fruit juice or vitamin drops. Orange juice or rose-hip syrup are excellent – and safe ways of giving this vitamin; you can give the fruit juice in the baby's daily drink of water. You should start this at about two weeks of age.

Even a breast-fed baby can be simply thirsty at times, and orange juice is a good alternative to water occasionally because of the Vitamin C content, which is essential for all babies.

Fluoride for healthy teeth

If the water in your area does not contain much fluoride it is wise to give supplements of this element. It will protect the baby's growing teeth and will make them resistant to holes, called 'dental caries'. Half a fluoride tablet per day can be started at about two to three weeks of age and continued throughout childhood. These tablets are available at any chemist.

Weaning your baby

A baby does not need anything apart from milk for food during the first three months of life. The very occasional baby is so hungry that he may need some extra food, but the average baby grows very well on milk and easily becomes too fat when given other foods. Recently there was a fashion for giving other food from a very early age, even as early as the first week. This was not satisfactory as it made babies too fat and too thirsty.

There is no real need to give a baby food other than milk, even at the age of three months, if he is contented and is gaining weight satisfactorily. It is reasonable to expect a baby to gain about 200 grams a week (that is, about 6 ounces), so you can leave weaning until the baby is about four months of age. Weaning used to mean stopping breast-feeding and using some other method of feeding. It is a little confusing that the word 'wean' is now also used to mean the gradual introduction of solid foods into a baby's diet, no matter whether the baby was fed on the breast or bottle. When introducing solid food, go very slowly. The various foods are added to the diet one at a time. They are usually given in very small amounts at first, not more than a taste on the end of a teaspoon. If the baby likes the food and does not seem upset by it, then you can continue to use it. You will probably be amused by the first reaction to this entirely new food sensation. If the baby does not like it he will spit it out soon enough, but persevere for a few more times; but if necessary give it a rest and try again a week or two later.

The food should be very soft, as a sort of purée, so that the baby can take a little from a spoon without having to chew or have difficulty in swallowing.

Giving up the bottle

The baby will probably decide when he has enough of the bottle. You may try to give him a cup about seven or eight months of age – the type with a little spout is the easiest to start with. If he enjoys drinking from the cup, he will soon give up the bottle. Do not be surprised, though, if he continues to get comfort from sucking. Many children enjoy a bottle, often filled with diluted fruit juice instead of milk, long in to the second year of life. So long as the fruit juice is not too sweet it should be all right.

Babies may go on sucking from the breast, in some cases into the second year. You must decide the length of time you would like to breast-feed, but do not be surprised if the baby wants to go on longer than you expect.

A balanced diet

Do not forget the basic principles of a good diet. Food consists of proteins, fats, carbohydrates, vitamins, minerals and water. Each

There are many natural, non-processed foods which are nourishing and easy for a young baby to digest. Eggs are particularly useful: soft-boil them and serve the yolks only to start with. As the baby progresses with solid food, introduce mild cheese in the form of cheese sauce made with milk.

of these is very important. You must give your baby a diet which is balanced in them. The different requirements are:

Proteins. These foods are necessary for growth and are present in a number of high-quality foods. They are found in meat, fish, milk, cheese and eggs. There are other types known as secondary proteins, which are very good but not quite as satisfactory as animal proteins. These are present in some fruit and vegetables. The baby gets most of the protein he needs from milk and eggs.

Fats. These are high energy foods. There is, of course, a lot in the creamy part of milk, but also in fatty meat and oily fish.

Carbohydrates. These are common foods and are important because they are cheap and easy to use. The only danger is that they are particularly likely to cause fatness if taken in excess. They are commonly found in sugars, starchy vegetables, such as potatoes, and cereals like wheat, oats and barley.

Vitamins. Vitamin D, to prevent rickets, is found naturally in cod-liver oil, milk and butter. Vitamin C is found in fruit and fresh vegetables. There are a large number of other vitamins, but your baby is very unlikely to run short of them if you give him a diet that contains fruit, meat, vegetables and milk. Milk contains all that is needed before weaning. (See also page 79).

Mineral salts. Iron is needed to prevent anaemia. A premature baby may run short of iron because he is born before proper stores can be laid down in his body. In this case anaemia may be present and iron supplements will be necessary. Some milks are now fortified with iron. Calcium is necessary for good bones – there is a plentiful supply in milk.

Water. Over two-thirds of the human body is made up of water and it is an essential vehicle for the rest of our food. I have already said how important it is for the baby. (See page 87.)

Food for weaning

Opposite: A balanced diet would contain a selection of all these foods, the chief sources of each of the vitamins. 1. Foods rich in Vitamin A. 2. The 'B Complex', a term covering 15 essential substances, including Thiamin, Riboflavin and Niacin, is contained in foods like yeast extract, wholemeal and liver. 3. Fresh fruit and vegetables contain Vitamin C (Ascorbic acid), which cannot be stored in the body and so should be part of the daily diet. 4. Substances rich in Vitamin D should be consumed in the absence of sunshine. 5. Vitamin E is contained in wheat germ and green plants. 6. The leaves of spinach, cauliflower and cabbage – plus liver, soya bean oil and seaweed – are good sources of Vitamin K, which is necessary to maintain one of the clotting factors in blood plasma.

Below: Spoon-feeding a baby can be a time-consuming job to start with. But very soon he will learn how to take food from a spoon and before long will reach out for it in an attempt to feed himself.

Purées. Although cereals are now the commonest foods to start weaning, I think there is a lot to be said for beginning with a fruit purée. Apple purée is quite easy to make and is also available in tins. Peel and core some apples and stew them gently until they are a fine mush, adding sugar until it tastes *just* sweet. Use other fruits as well, like bananas, pears, apricots and peaches.

Egg. This is a very good food for a baby. It is wise to start with the yolk alone – soft-boil the egg and spoon out the runny yolk. Do not add any salt. After a month or so you can give a baby lumps of the white. A whole egg is very nutritious and can be combined easily with milk and sugar to make a custard. Jellies, junkets and cheese are also convenient soft foods for babies.

Cereals. There are now many cereals available for babies. Some, are made from wheat, but others are based on rice. You can mix cereal with milk and then give it to a baby from a spoon. It is a simple and useful food, but avoid giving the baby too much.

Sieved vegetables. In many countries carrots are the favourite weaning food. They certainly look very attractive, but there are many other vegetables which you can cook and use. Potatoes, cauliflower with cheese sauce, turnips, peas and beans, cabbage and brussels sprouts are all satisfactory and help to give the baby the balanced diet he needs.

Meat and fish. One of the earliest foods to use is broth made from bones and meat. This can be given as a sort of soup and often vegetables are cooked in it and then puréed. Meat gravy – the red juice from a roast joint – is an excellent food to start weaning with.

1

2

3

4

5

6

Sieves and blenders. To avoid the bore of hand-sieving, it's worth buying a 'Mouli' food mill, which is basically a metal sieve with a handle and screw attachment which presses food through the fine holes. It is a very cheap kitchen implement and is a simple way of making foods for a baby. You will find it useful for making all your soups and purées.

A blender or liquidizer is one of the most useful and economical items in the kitchen when it comes to baby food. It is possible to produce completely soft foods, suitable for a baby, from food which has been cooked for the rest of the family. Meat and fish can be pounded quickly in to a soft mush. The only essential is to make certain that the food is properly cooked before blending it in order to kill off all the germs. If you have not cooked the food first, then sterilize it by bringing it to the boil for three minutes; afterwards it can be allowed to cool. Almost any meat can be used including beef, chicken and liver. There is a tradition that pork or ham should not be given to a young baby, but I have not been able to find definitive evidence that it is bad. The usual reason given for the unsuitability of pork is that the fibres are too large. If it is cooked really well and then blended, it should be perfectly satisfactory.

Here is a delicious soup you can make for your baby with a blender: in a large saucepan, fry an onion and two celery stalks, finely chopped, in 60gr (2oz) butter, until soft. Stir in 60gr (2oz) flour and gradually add 2 pints chicken stock, stirring constantly. Add a quartered cauliflower and bring to the boil. Reduce the heat to low and simmer for 30 minutes. Remove the pan from the heat and blend the soup until the vegetables form a fine purée. Pour the soup back into the pan, diluting it with a little milk. Bring the soup up to the required temperature, season sparingly and serve at once. This quantity is for four adult servings, so would do for several baby meals. Using the same method, you could vary this recipe by substituting potatoes, carrots scraped and chopped, leeks, broccoli, lentils, spinach, tomatoes, mushrooms or watercress. If the soup is stored in the refrigerator for future use, the milk should only be added shortly before serving.

Tins and jars

Almost every food shop or chemist now has a large number of tins, jars and dried 'instant' foods made for babies. There is no doubt that they are extremely convenient and few mothers would wish to be without some in their store cupboard. They are also reasonably cheap, but in many cases, this may mean that they are full of starch. Look at the label and study the ingredients: it is worth remembering that, by law, manufacturers have to list the ingredients in order of quantity per cent. The main ingredient is listed first, and so on in diminishing proportions. It is worthwhile trying a number of varieties to see if your baby likes the different flavours. You will need to start on the very soft, mushy varieties, but later the baby can move on to the type containing lumps which will give him something to chew on when he has teeth. There are now special foods being produced for toddlers.

Despite the convenience of these foods, I feel there is little doubt that you will be able to give your baby better and cheaper food by cooking it yourself. If you look carefully at the food you need for you and your husband you will find that there is plenty of food that can be blended or sieved for the baby.

Diet from six to twelve months

During the second half of the first year, you can introduce tougher foods slowly. The baby will progress from puréed meat, to meat which has been minced and then cooked. You may not be able to afford the blender but you can buy minced meat at the butcher. Once the baby can hold things properly, rusks can be buttered and given in tiny bits to the baby with a little honey or seedless jam, or your baby may like sandwiches or fingers of bread: introduce savoury spreads, which many babies enjoy, avoiding those with an excess of salt.

If you use food from the rest of the family's diet, you can now cut it up into tiny pieces instead of blending it. The real secret is

From about six to eight months a baby is capable of holding rusks or fingers of toast and feeding himself. This often happens around the time that the first teeth are beginning to grow through and the baby's natural reaction is to chew at anything he has in his hand.

to go slowly and steadily. Always persuade the baby to take new foods but do not force him. Do not be surprised if you have disappointments; babies often turn up their noses at a new taste. Just be patient and try again a few days later.

By the end of the first year the baby should be eating almost the same food as the rest of the family, cut up small.

Fat babies

Watch out that your baby does not become too fat. A fat, 'bouncing' baby is not necessarily a healthy one. You can be suspicious if he gains weight very fast and looks too plump. You need to be particularly careful if your family tends towards obesity. If you think the baby is getting too fat, talk to your doctor. He will be able to tell you if there is anything to worry about and will help you with the baby's diet. You may need to cut down on starches and sweet foods like bread, cereals, flour, potatoes, jam and sugar. On the other hand, do not go to the other extreme and leave the baby hungry. Give him more if he seems to want it, specially of protein foods, fruit and vegetables. But be prepared to throw away food that he does not want.

Cooking hints

When feeding a baby, use a bib with a large surface area.

Once your baby is about nine months old you will probably find that he is showing likes and dislikes in the same way as anybody else. A baby gets bored with the same old meals, day in day out, so try and vary the diet as much as possible.

Breakfast or tea. Boiled or scrambled eggs are always a good idea, with toast or bread fingers when the baby is old enough to chew them. An interesting variation is French toast: fingers of bread dipped in beaten egg and lightly fried.

Lunch or supper. Stewed meat or fish can be blended or sieved with green vegetables and rice or potatoes to make a thick soup. There are endless variations on this – use liver as well, as it is rich in iron. A nourishing vegetable soup can also be made with a few basic items from your vegetable basket: cut up a potato, an onion, a carrot and a turnip or swede and cook gently in about 60gr (2oz) of butter in a closed pan for about 10 minutes. Add a handful or rice, a small tin of tomatoes and about half a pint of stock. Season and cook for about 20 minutes or until the vegetables and rice are soft: then sieve or blend the soup. This is plenty for several baby meals, and makes a delicious soup for adults as well. Another useful basic is cheese sauce: this can be combined with cauliflower, leeks, fish or boiled eggs. Pasta such as ravioli or macaroni is also suitable for babies with mince and tomato sauce.

Sweets and puddings. Purées and fools are always a good idea. Use any fruit in season, though you should generally remove the skins from soft fruit as they are rather indigestible. You can make interesting combinations such as rhubarb and banana, or apple, raisin and honey. Serve with yoghurt, creamed rice, custard, or semolina baked with an added egg and nutmeg grated on top. Old-fashioned steamed puddings or crumbles also go down well: soften them with milk or custard.

Keeping the baby clean

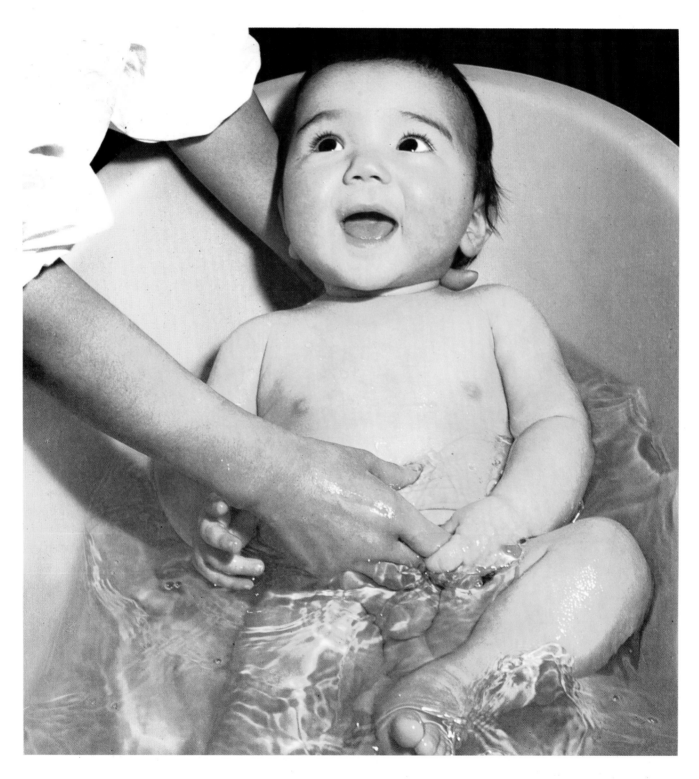

Bathing the baby

Before you leave hospital, the nurses will demonstrate bathing to you. Make sure you thoroughly understand it and if possible, try and get your husband to see the demonstration. He will be a much greater help to you at home if he fully understands the whole business of bathing and changing nappies. If he feels completely at sea he may feel less inclined to help.

Get all the equipment ready before you start the bath:

The bath. Baby baths are usually very simple, and made of plastic. Some types can be put on a stand, others over the family bath, but you will probably find putting it on the floor makes it awkward to lower the baby into the water. In fact, you do not really need a bath and many families use the kitchen sink or a wash basin. This is quite satsifactory as long as you make sure that it is spotlessly clean before you put the baby in it. The family bath is rather too large for a tiny baby, but can be used once the baby is about four months old.

A warm room is essential. You should shut the window and the door to prevent draughts. If you cannot get the room warm to about 15°–20°C (about 60°–70°F) you should bath the baby quickly, so that he does not get cold.

A low chair, comfortable as well as sturdy, for you to sit on.

Soap and a dish to keep it in.

A flannel or soft sponge for washing the baby with.

A towel. Air it in front of the fire or over a radiator.

Clean clothes and nappies. Air these as well and arrange them in order so you can put them on easily. Other useful items are a plastic apron or sheet to protect your clothes, a bucket for dirty clothes and nappies, and a plastic bag for soiled disposable items, such as cotton wool and disposable nappies.

Toilet items. Keep these in a box or a tray. The sort of things you will need will be baby powder, cream for the nappy area and olive oil to rub into the scalp when necessary. You will need plenty of cotton wool and tissues to clean the nappy area, and some twists of cotton wool for the nose – cotton buds on sticks are useful. You can now start to get the bath ready:

1. Fill the bath with hot and cold water together. If you want to be very safe, start by pouring some cold water into the bath followed by hot water, until it is comfortably warm. Test it by

Left: Bathtime can be one of the most enjoyable times of the day for mother and baby. Most babies enjoy the warmth of the bath water, and soon learn to kick and splash vigorously in the water. Above: Many hospitals run classes in baby care, for things like bathing, at their ante-natal clinics. Mothers are shown how to bath their babies during their stay in hospital. Right: Everything you need for bathtime.

putting your elbow in it. You should be very careful not to put hot water into the bath first; you might forget to test it and could scald the baby by putting him in water that is too hot. Accidents can be avoided if you make sure the temperature is around blood heat (38°C or 100°F).

2. Undress the baby. It is probably best to do this on your lap, but some women find it easier on a table, laying the baby on a special mat, towel or blanket. Even if you usually use the table, it is a good idea to have some practice in dressing and undressing the baby on your lap. Then you will not feel flummoxed if you ever have to undress the baby and have nowhere to put him down, on a journey or a visit, for example.

3. Wash the baby's face with clean water and pat it dry. You can prevent him getting cold by keeping him wrapped in a towel while you wash his face and head.

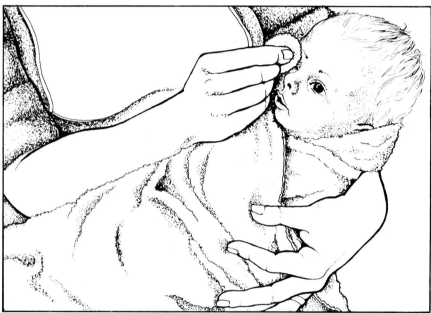

4. Nose, ears and eyes. There is no need to clean the nose unless it looks clogged. If it does appear to be dirty, you can clean it with a cotton wool bud or a twist of cotton wool. You do not need to do anything to the ears, and the eyes can be left alone if they look normal. If there is some discharge from the eyes, so that the lids are stuck together, you can bathe them gently with cotton wool soaked in warm, boiled water. Use enough to clear the eye discharge and allow the eyes to open.

5. Wash the head using a little soap and massage the scalp gently. Rinse away the soap and dry the head. If you notice any scurf on the scalp, use a good baby shampoo to clean it more effectively. When there is cradle-cap – that is, little cakes of yellowish, waxy material on the scalp – rub olive oil into it after the bath. Cradle-cap is very common, and generally disappears after a while as the baby grows older.

Keep a corner of the baby's room or bathroom for all the bath and nappy-changing equipment. If you feel like it, these strictly practical items can be brightened up with pretty cotton holders.

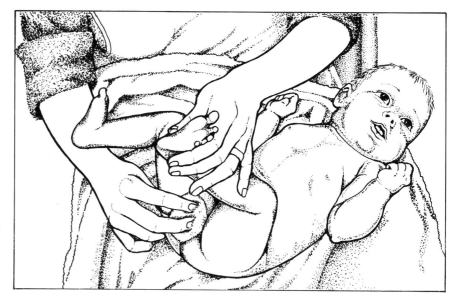

Once the face and head have been cleaned and patted dry, the baby is unwrapped and washed all over with a mild baby soap.

6. Soap the baby all over on your lap by using your hand, a soft flannel or a fine sponge which is only used for the baby.

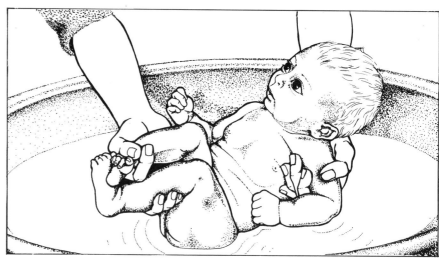

The correct way to hold the baby while lowering him into the water.

7. Lower the baby gently into the bath. Hold him with your left arm under his neck and your hand holding his shoulder, and support his legs and bottom with your right hand.
8. Rinse off all the soap in the bath.

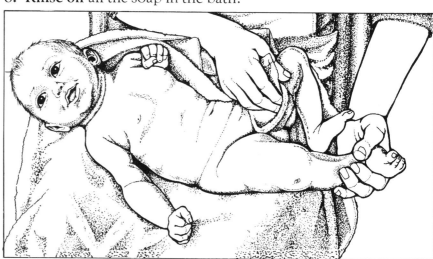

Once the soap is rinsed off and the baby has had a good kick – though not too long in case the water cools too much – he is brought back on to the lap and towelled dry all over.

9. Take the baby out and put him on your lap to pat him dry. Make sure he is completely dry otherwise he may get sores or a

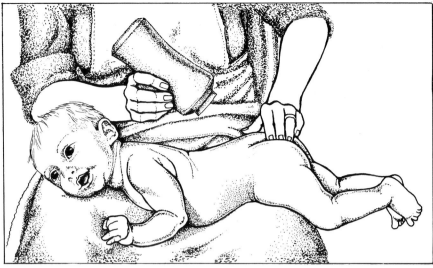

A little powder helps to prevent soreness specially round the neck, under the arms, between the legs, and the bottom. When the baby is very small, it is best to apply powder with your hand, to avoid using too much.

rash. It is best to dry him without rubbing vigorously, because that may break the skin. When you are sure he is dry all over you can put some powder on him, specially in the folds of his skin and some cream on his bottom.

You can choose whatever time of day you like for the bath. The traditional time is in the evening, before the baby is put into the cot for the night. However there is no reason why you should not choose some other time of the day for his regular bath, or a different time for each day.

Nappies: what to use

There is a confusing array of nappies in the shops today. It is wise to look at quite a number of brands before you decide which type of nappy you want for your baby and how you want to clean them. It is a good idea to work out the cost carefully, since you may find that disposable nappies or a nappy service are more expensive than you realized at first.

There is no good reason why you should stick to only one type of nappy. A very sensible plan, for instance, is to use terry towelling nappies for ordinary purposes, but to have a supply of disposable nappies for journeys, emergencies or holidays. Two or three dozen cloth nappies should be enough to make sure you always have a clean supply in the cupboard.

1. Cloth nappies. There are two types generally available:
Terry towelling squares. These are still the most popular washable nappies in Britain and Australia and are very good. They are tough and will last a long time. You can use a nappy liner, preferably a disposable one, in addition.
Shaped nappies. A number of nappies on the market are not made in squares. Some are Y or X-shaped; they may be made of terry towelling or other material. In many ways they are easier to use, particularly if combined with the plastic pants which are designed to fit over them. They do not have much advantage over terry towelling squares, but they may fit your baby better, especially in the first few weeks. It is as well to note that they are usually more expensive than towelling squares.
2. Nappy linings. These are very useful. The baby's skin keeps drier, and the nappy is not as soiled, so it is easier to clean. You

'One-way' disposable nappy liners are very convenient if used in combination with cloth nappies. They have several advantages: they help to keep moisture off the baby's skin, they help to prevent cloth nappies becoming soiled and they can be flushed away down the lavatory without causing a blockage.

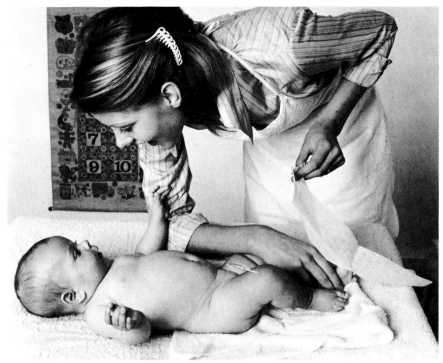

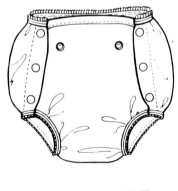

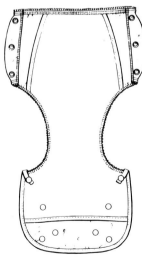

can use ordinary squares of muslin, but the one-way cloth nappies or the disposable nappy liners are more convenient. Some mothers feel that the one-way cloth nappy linings are better for use at night when the nappy is on for the longest period. The disposable nappy liners are very convenient; they are easily disposable and will keep the nappy clean. They are not quite so suitable for long periods because they do begin to disintegrate if they become very damp.

3. Disposable nappies. There are now several disposable nappies available. Some consist of pads of different widths which fit inside plastic pants; others include a plastic backing attached to the nappy itself, which is made of thick, absorbent, fibrous material. These are more expensive but convenient to use. Unfortunately, disposable nappies are rather difficult to get rid of as you should not put the whole thing down the lavatory. Probably the best use for disposable nappies is for emergencies, on holidays or journeys. They are also very useful when you have more than one baby in nappies, such as twins, or a small baby and a toddler who is still in nappies. In this case it is more convenient to use disposable nappies during the day and towelling nappies with linings at night.

4. Plastic pants. Most disposable nappies either are backed with plastic or have a special pair of plastic pants which are made to hold them in place. These usually open flat and have press fasteners or ties. Many mothers also like to use plastic pants to cover terry towelling nappies. There is no doubt that they are convenient and will prevent faeces or urine soaking through to dampen or stain clothes. It is important to have pants which will fit your baby well; you may have to try several brands and sizes before you find one to suit him.

It is unwise to go on using plastic pants if the baby has developed nappy rash. Some types of rash are made worse by plastic pants since water cannot evaporate and the baby's skin is kept moist. If your baby has a rash, do not use plastic pants until it clears up, and discuss the problem with the doctor.

Putting on nappies

There are three good ways of putting on nappies:

1. The simplest is to fold the nappy in half and pin it on either side of the waist. You will need special nappy safety pins for all the methods, which have a hood over the point of the pin to prevent it coming undone and sticking into the baby. Whenever you remove a pin, remember to close it before you put it down.

Nappy-folding, method 2: Right: Lay the baby on the folded nappy, with the fold at about waist level.
Far right: Fold one corner round and tuck it comfortably between the legs.
Centre right: Fold the second corner over neatly so that it is flat and not bulky.
Centre far right: Bring the apex of the triangle up between the legs.
Below right: Pull the apex of the nappy taut and tuck the two other corners under so there are no gaps and the nappy is firm but not too tight.
Below far right: Fasten through all three thicknesses with a nappy pin placed horizontally.

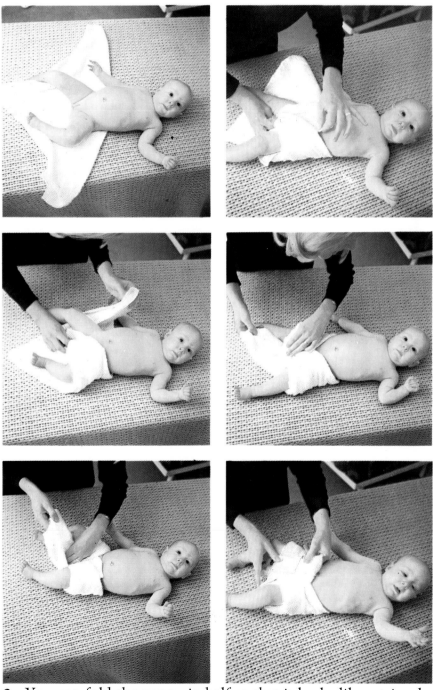

2. You can fold the nappy in half so that it looks like a triangle. The apex of the triangle is brought up through the baby's legs and the other two angles brought round the waist. Only one safety pin is needed, in front of the baby.

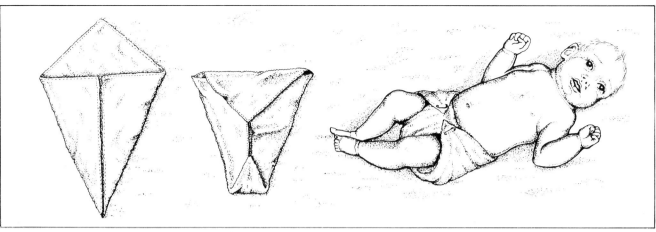

Folding a nappy according to Method 3.

3. This method is slightly more complicated but means the nappy is less bulky round the baby's legs. Place the nappy at an angle so that the corners form a diamond. Fold the left and right corners into the centre, (see diagram) then fold the top corner down over them. The nappy will then form an isosceles triangle shape. Lay the baby on the nappy, bring the apex of the triangle up between the baby's legs and fold the point under neatly in front. Bring the two sides round the baby's tummy and fasten them with two pins on either side.

Changing nappies

Do not let the baby stay in a wet or dirty nappy too long. Change it as soon as it is soiled, because this will help to keep the baby's skin healthy. It is a good idea to change the nappy after every feed. When you have taken it off, clean the skin with soap and water, and dry carefully. It is not essential to apply an ointment or cream to the skin covered by the nappy, but you can use zinc and castor oil cream or vaseline if you wish. If there is any rash use an ointment recommended by the doctor or health visitor.

Throwing disposable nappies away

Do not put them down the lavatory unless they are only nappy liners. You could incinerate them in the garden, but otherwise tie them securely in a plastic bag and put them in the dustbin.

Washing nappies

No one could claim that this is a pleasant task, but it must be done carefully or the baby may get nappy rash.

Wet nappies should be put into a container of cold water to soak. Nappies which have been soiled with faeces should be shaken out over the lavatory to get rid of the faeces, scrubbed under running water, then put in cold water to soak.

Cleaning nappies has become much simpler in recent years with the introduction of special sanitizing products which are marketed under a variety of brand names. Having shaken off most of the faeces over the lavatory, the nappies can be soaked in a chemical solution which cleans them and takes away the smell. Soak them for at least two hours, or longer if possible, in a bucket of the solution made up according to the manufacturer's instructions. Afterwards, rinse them thoroughly several times and allow them to dry. This is a very convenient way to sterilize the nappies and keep them clean and white.

If you do not use this method you will have to find some other way of sterilizing them. A common method is to wash them in very hot soapy water. It is unwise to use detergents as they can sometimes damage a baby's skin – use soap-flakes only. There are some brands which can be used satisfactorily in a washing machine – consult the manufacturer or supplier about this. When the nappies have been washed they should be rinsed in hot, clean water – at least twice – to get rid of the soap. Then boil them for a few minutes in clean water, to sterilize them, and hang them up to dry. It is not necessary to boil the nappies if they are washed in very hot water, such as the hottest wash in a washing machine.

Drying nappies can be very difficult indeed; it is very unpleasant to have racks of nappies cluttering up a small house or flat. A drying cabinet or tumble-dryer is a boon.

Washing nappies is much easier for most people today since there is usually a commercial laundromat in every local shopping precinct. Also, many families have their own washing machine. Do remember that you need to rinse the nappies out carefully before putting them in the washing machine, and use a hot wash.

In some large cities there are special laundering services for nappies. Firms will collect dirty nappies regularly and return them clean and laundered. It is an expensive service, but you may think it worthwhile if you can afford it and want to avoid too much hard work.

Nappies can be inconvenient and expensive, but in the long run it is probably best to have cloth nappies for regular use with nappy liners, plus a supply of disposable nappies for emergencies.

At home with the baby

Getting help at home

You are bound to feel a little nervous when you leave hospital to go home. It is easy to feel frightened when you are all on your own and have to cope with the baby, without the help of nurses who can be called at a moment's notice. However, there will be several people you can call on at home, if necessary. If you leave hospital only a day or two after delivery, the midwife [community nurse] will visit you regularly for a time; you can ask her questions about any problems you have. All new babies in the United Kingdom and Australia are visited by a specially trained nurse, called a health visitor [Baby Health Centre Nurse]; she will call within a few days of your return home. You may find it very helpful to arrange for a member of your family or any close friend who is experienced with babies, to come to stay for a week or so. It is likely that you will feel a little tired and some help around the house will probably do you some good. This is obviously a question which has to be discussed between you and your husband; sometimes grandparents can be an immense help and sometimes they are more hindrance than they are worth. These days, many husbands can take a few days off from work to help around the house during the first week their wives are back at home. Of course, if you have other children, your husband may look after them at home anyway.

Shopping for equipment

Before going home, you should make certain that you have all the equipment you need. Do some careful shopping in the few weeks before the baby arrives, so you do not get caught out. There is a bewildering array of things for the baby on sale, some of which are necessary, some of which are not. A number of specialist baby shops can be found in many towns; there are even chain stores devoted solely to baby equipment. It is well worth taking the time to wander round one of these shops, making a note of the equipment available and their prices. The most important things are listed here.

Clothes for the baby

Opposite: When you come home for the first time with a new baby you can really begin to learn about him and enjoy him.

Babies look much smarter today than they did only a few years ago. Their clothes are much more practical and attractive.

Buy clothes that are made of material which can be easily washed. You will find that synthetic fibres are very useful because they are not only easy to wash but also very hardwearing, and they can be mixed with other materials such as cotton to make them comfortable and pleasant to wear. Make sure they

The most convenient and comfortable garment for any baby, from birth to a year or more: the one-piece stretch towelling suit, with convenient press studs on the inside leg to make nappy-changing simple, and no tiny holes or little ribbons for the baby to get entangled with.

are non-inflammable. In the past, babies used to have many woollen clothes, but this material is much less popular today. However, it is unlikely that you will be able to prevent some fond relative knitting something for the baby. Try as tactfully as possible to persuade her to use a machine-washable yarn, either wool or synthetic fibre. Ultimately it is best to have simple clothes. Tiny bits of clothing, such as mittens and bootees, are a nuisance to put on and fiddly to wash.

You will need about half a dozen vests. It is probably simpler to buy those that do not have to be tied, but choose those that seem most practical for you.

The simplest baby garment is a one-piece suit of stretch material – usually towelling – which will expand as the baby grows. I think the reason babies look so much smarter to-day is that many mothers dress them in these suits. They are often made in bright coloured or striped material, and can be decorated with embroidered or appliqué motifs. They are usually easily washable, with fast colours, and can be used during the day or night. For the small baby, the suit can cover the hands and feet, so avoiding the necessity for mittens and bootees. If you have a reasonable supply of nappies and vests and several of these suits, you should be able to dress your baby extremely well.

The other garments you buy will depend on your personal choice. If you buy a wrapper, it is probably best to have a simple flannelette sheet and not a fancy shawl. You may wish to have a lace shawl for a very special occasion, such as a Christening, but they are not really suitable for everyday use since the baby's toes or fingers could get trapped in the holes. For outdoor wear, in the pram or carry cot, you can buy or make a set of clothes consisting of jacket, bonnet, leggings and probably gloves and boots. These are often made of wool and used to be very popular. In fact, a thick jacket with a hood or bonnet is all that is really necessary, since the baby can be well wrapped-up in blankets if it is really cold.

For night-time wear you can use a one-piece suit, a night-dress or a special sleeping bag which encloses the baby completely.

Do not forget bibs to cover the baby's front; he is bound to dribble or spit out food during the first year or two.

Washing clothes

When you buy clothes, be careful to find out how they should be washed. Many clothes today have a care-label, which will tell you how hot the water should be and other washing instructions. In most cases, you will be able to wash them easily in a washing machine, either at home or in the laundromat. If you do not have a machine, then it is especially wise to have clothes that can be simply washed and dried, and need a minimum of ironing.

The cot

In the first few weeks you can use a small cot. You might want to use a traditional cradle or cot, but be careful with rockers. Once the baby is active enough to turn over or pull himself up, the cradle could be upset, so these cots are only suitable for the first

few weeks. Much better are portable cots. These vary in design: some look like a large sleeping bag with hoops at the side, so that the baby can be carried about very easily; others are just big 'Moses' baskets, lined and with a small mattress; however a carry-cot is probably the most useful design and can be used while the baby is growing. It is usually made of waterproof material and is rectangular in shape; buy one which can be easily cleaned. Many have frames which will convert the cot into a pram, or in to a semi-permanent cot at home. You will probably want to take your baby around with you when you go visiting and, of course, the carry-cot can be put on the back seat of a car. If you do this, buy safety straps to secure the cot so that it will not be thrown off the seat if you have to stop suddenly.

When the baby becomes too big for his sleeping bag or carry-cot, you will need to buy a larger, more permanent cot for the first year or two of his life. A drop-sided wooden cot is probably the best and most durable. You will need one about 120cm (4ft) in length. Make sure that the bars are not too far apart; or the baby may push his head between them and get it stuck; the bars need to be about 7cm (3in) apart. When the baby has grown out of this sort of cot, he will need a small bed. There is no point in keeping a toddler in a cot if he can climb out of it, even if he has not actually grown out of it. He is more likely to fall and hurt himself so he would be better off in an ordinary bed.

Above: A 'Moses' basket can be useful, but not as a permanent cot. Below: A sturdy, drop-sided cot will last for at least the first two years of your baby's life.

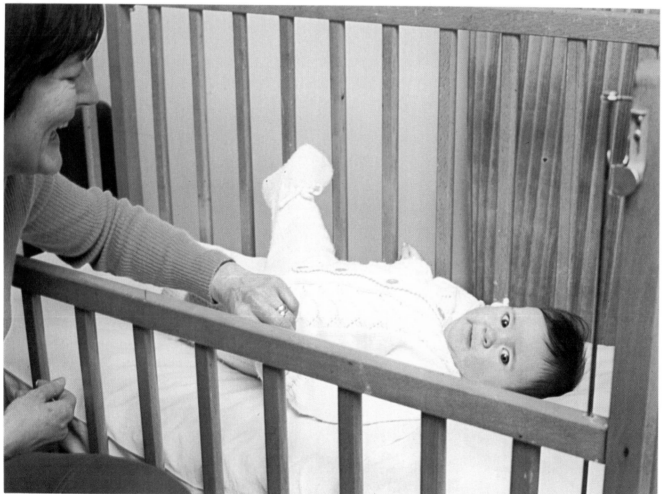

Bedding

Make certain that the cot has a firm mattress covered in water-proof material, which can be easily cleaned if it becomes soiled with faeces or urine. You can use an underblanket to cover the mattress; the baby sleeps between sheets, covered by one or two blankets and an eiderdown. If you have a sleeping bag or a continental quilt (duvet) you will not need these bedclothes.

Adjust the bedding according to the heat of the room. Obviously, if you are able to keep the room very warm you will not need as many bedclothes.

Do not use a pillow. Pillows can be very dangerous, as the baby could turn his face into it and suffocate himself. Although this is very unlikely to happen, it is better to do without a pillow rather than take the risk.

Other furniture

Some people like to use a special table for changing the baby, although it is not really necessary. The table is usually padded and covered with a waterproof, washable material. If you do use one of these, be careful not to let the baby roll off when your back is turned. You can also buy special changing mats, padded and plastic-covered, which can be placed on any available surface, and are useful for bathing and changing.

Have a cupboard, or a chest of drawers, to keep the baby's clothes in. You may be able to use a part of the wardrobe that you use for the rest of the family, but a special one for the baby is very useful. Make sure that it is quite stable so that it will not fall over; when the child is older he may pull on a knob and topple the cupboard on to himself. It would be better to screw it securely to the wall on both sides.

Most babies amass a large number of toys, so you will need somewhere to keep them. You can use a special wooden box on wheels, a collection of cheap storage boxes, or a small low cupboard; any of these the child can use himself later on.

Buy a low chair for yourself, if you have not got one already. You will need this when feeding the baby or when changing and bathing him. The baby will also need a chair with a tray after the first few months when he begins to feed himself. These vary in height; the most important rule is that the chair should be completely steady and will not topple over. Once they can hold their heads up, many small babies, from a few weeks of age, enjoy a simple plastic chair which supports them in a propped up position, so they can look around. These can either be rigid, or flexible so that they bounce pleasantly when the baby moves.

Later on, you may need a playpen; you can then leave the baby to play for short periods and will not be worried that he has crawled a long way or is investigating anything dangerous. Of course, you will not need this until about six months of age. Then you may find it very useful if you have to do some housework in another room or go and answer the door or telephone. However, a baby should not be left for a long time inside a playpen because it is too confining and soon becomes cage-like to the baby.

Top: A plastic-covered mat is useful for bathing and changing. Above: A practical unit for a small room using wire baskets and drawers on rollers for storing all the baby's clothes and equipment.

The pram

Parents often think that a pram is one of the most important things to buy for a new baby. However, many pram designs have been simplified recently so think hard before spending a lot of money on an elaborate baby carriage.

In the first few weeks, the padded sleeping bags with handles are very useful for transporting the baby. Unfortunately, they are not very big, and a baby may grow out of one sooner than you think. The carry-cot is probably the best compromise between a cot and a pram. It converts easily into a pram and it can also be used inside a car or at home.

However you may not be able to resist buying a special pram for the baby. Bear in mind that large baby carriages can be rather cumbersome and only really practical for local use – they

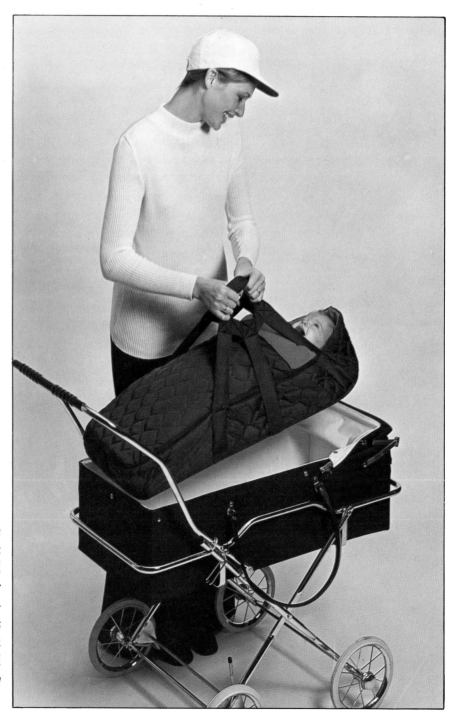

The most practical pram is one like this, consisting of a carry cot which fits snugly into a wheeled frame which can be folded for storing or travelling. Another convenient method of carrying is this sleeping bag with straps and a rigid base. Light to carry, and washable, it is ideal for a tiny baby.

are very inconvenient if you want to go away for a weekend or holiday since they do not take to pieces easily. Whatever type of pram you choose, make sure that it is easy to clean, comfortably sprung, and is provided with safety straps and a brake. Many prams have metal bodies which are lined with an easily cleaned material. Of course, you will need a hood and a waterproof cover to protect the baby against rain and sun. If you are going to put the baby out in the garden buy or make a net to go over the pram so that cats cannot jump into it.

Slings and carriers. Prams are not always the most convenient things when you have to go into a crowded shopping area. They have to be parked outside many shops, so that the baby is left behind while you are shopping, which is not always a good idea.

To keep your baby with you as much as possible, around the house or out walking, a carrying sling or back-pack are very handy. However, back-packs are not suitable for the very young baby who cannot hold his head up properly.

You and your husband may think that a carrying sling is a more practical item than a pram. Some slings are designed so that you can hold the baby comfortably on your hip or across the front of your body, while you are working around the house. They do mean that a young baby can be with you more of the time and you can always keep an eye on him. In many parts of the world it is usual for babies to travel with their mothers, tucked into a band around the waist, or into a sling or bag. There are also baby carriers like rucksacks, which are popular with fathers. These are not suitable for very young babies who have not gained proper control of their neck muscles and cannot hold their heads up. I always worry when I see young babies carried in them, as their heads seem to wobble about the whole time. Make sure you buy one that gives plenty of head support. But certainly for the older baby they are a very practical alternative to a push-chair.

Push-chairs. Many people seem to manage without a pram these days, using only a carry-cot or sling and then a simple push-chair. You could buy a standard collapsible push-chair: there are many variations on the market. But a very useful and popular alternative is the 'baby buggy'; a kind of mobile deckchair: it is slung on a frame that folds to look like a pair of walking sticks on wheels. You can even buy a double one, if you have twins. This type of push-chair is very comfortable for a baby. It is suitable once the baby can hold his head up – from about three months old. However, you will probably have to buy a bigger version as the baby grows. The chair folds easily, which makes it ideal to take on a bus or put in a car. Any folding pushchair is useful for this reason.

A room for the baby

You may be lucky enough to have a separate room in your house or flat which you can use for the baby. But he may have to share a room with his brothers or sisters or you could keep him in your bedroom, if your home is very small. If possible

Opposite: This pushchair is one of the most popular innovations in baby equipment in recent years. Babies find them very comfortable, they are light to push and easy to fold and carry. Right: Light is important in a baby's room, but shade the cot from direct sunlight. Make sure all furnishing fabrics are non-inflammable.

If you are going to keep the baby in your own room, set aside a quiet corner for the cot and equipment. A pretty, unobtrusive cot such as this can actually enhance the decor.

choose a bright and airy room with a window which will get plenty of sun. Try and take him into the open air as much as possible, but it is nice if there is sun in his room as well.

You can ventilate the room by opening the window in summer. But do not leave a window open during the night in the winter, as the room may become much too cold and he might become ill as a result; this is particularly important for the newborn baby.

A room that is never ventilated soon becomes stuffy and unpleasant. The baby will be more comfortable if you can keep the air reasonably fresh and circulating. Never completely seal a room if it contains a solid fuel, gas or paraffin fire for heating.

If you have a room for the baby, you can keep all his equipment in it. Do not forget that children need to be protected against accidents. As he gets older, you will need something to stop him falling from the window – you can use bars, or a safety-catch to prevent the window opening too far. A gate across the top of the stairs will prevent a tumble.

Heating

It is most important that the baby should not be allowed to become either too cold or too hot. In a temperate climate there is always a danger that a newborn baby may become much too cold during the winter. Think carefully about ways of heating your home and, in particular, the baby's room. You will still need a warm room, even if the baby is well wrapped up.

A suitable temperature soon after he arrives home is about 21°C (70°F). If you are lucky enough to have central heating, this is the most convenient and easiest way of keeping your whole house really warm. Oil-filled electric radiators are also effective, though rather expensive to run. As the baby gets older you can reduce the heat in the house; the most important rule is that the baby's room should never become chilled during the night. You should not ideally let the temperature fall below 10°C (45°–50°F) and never as low as 0°C (32°F). A reasonable average temperature after three weeks of age is 15°C (about 60°F).

There are, of course, many other ways of heating a home. You can use solid fuel fires, electric fires, electric convector or fan-heaters, gas fires or paraffin stoves. Any form of heating with a flame or glowing element should be guarded most carefully when there are children around. You need to be particularly careful with paraffin heaters; they can be knocked over and start

If you have a fire with any sort of naked flame make sure you have an efficient guard such as this to protect your baby.

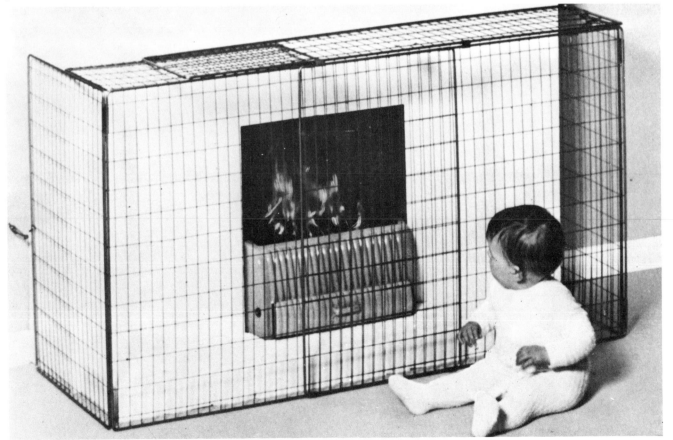

a fire very quickly. If there is a gas fire, the room should be properly ventilated. Ask your local gas board to advise you about this if you are in any doubt. Arrange for the fire to be guarded even when the baby is small, so that you have developed the habit of putting up a guard by the time the baby is starting to crawl or walk. Have a really close-mesh guard, so the baby cannot poke his hand or fingers through, and keep it sufficiently far from the fire so that he cannot get anywhere near really strong heat. The guard should be caged at the top so that a child cannot climb over it. You can use any type of heating to prevent a room becoming chilled at night.

If you live in a hot country, I think it is reasonable to use lighter clothes for the baby. Do not leave the baby in direct sunlight, inside or out. Remember that babies can become too hot as well as too cold. As long as they are protected from drafts and strong sunlight, if it is really hot they will probably only need a single cover.

Decoration of the room

Clean the baby's room thoroughly before his arrival. Do not forget that babies and young children make a lot of mess. If you use high-gloss paint and washable wall-paper, you will easily be able to remove all the dirty marks he makes. Some old paint contains lead and this may be dangerous for the baby. So if your house was built some time ago, strip off all the lead paint and replace it with modern paint.

You will need to cover the floor with something which is easy to clean and comfortable to walk on or kneel on. Wooden floors are not very good because they can cause splinters unless they have been sanded and sealed with polyurethane. If you use rugs make certain that they are the non-slip type, or tack them down, otherwise you might fall when carrying the baby.

Curtains and other soft furnishings should always be of non-inflammable material, like the baby's clothes. There are now many very pretty patterns to choose from which are treated to be flame-resistant.

Toys to play with

Play is very important even to a small baby and is an essential part development. A mobile over the cot can give him something to watch from a very early age, and once he begins to reach out for objects, a set of balls or other toys stretched across the pram or cot can keep him occupied when he is lying awake. Rattles and other toys which can be grasped or squeezed – specially if they make a noise – are suitable for the first year. Once the baby is sitting or crawling he will begin to enjoy toys which move, which encourages him to try and crawl after them if they roll out of his grasp.

Organizing your time

You will probably be very anxious to leave hospital and to get back home. Try not to be in too much of a hurry, but make certain that you have plenty of rest and are able to face the work that you have to do. It may be well worth while staying an extra

A pretty mobile over the cot will give a wakeful baby something interesting to watch.

day or two in hospital to learn about the baby and the best ways of looking after him. You can begin to think about how you are going to organize your time.

Unfortunately, babies are not the regular creatures we often imagine. For instance, the baby will probably not wake every four hours and cry for food, but may wake at intervals of three or five hours. It is also a mistake to think that a baby sleeps the whole time in between his feeds. You may find that he lies awake for long periods, just gazing around, but he may also tend to get upset and miserable. All this means that you will have to be flexible in arranging your day, so that you can feed the baby at an unexpected time and go to him if he is upset and needs attention.

Despite this, you can make some plans about the work for the

Many supermarkets provide special baby carriers attached to conventional trolleys, so that you need not leave your baby in the pram outside. Others have special supervised 'pram parks'.

day. Think out how many feeds the baby will need, if you are bottle-feeding, and then make up three or four feeds. You then have them ready as soon as the baby needs them. When you get on to weaning at four or five months of age you will probably want to blend some of the food that you have used for yourself or the rest of the family. Of course, the baby has to be fitted into your plans for the family's meals. (See page 90.)

Put aside a special time for bathing the baby. Traditionally this is done in the evening, but you could choose any time of the day. The housework and shopping will have to be fitted in, but in fact you will find shopping with a pram relatively simple, specially if you have a shopping basket attached. It is also important for the baby to go out in the fresh air.

One part of the day is liable to be a particular problem for the baby – the evening. (See page 131.) He is much more likely to cry then, between six and ten pm, than at other times of the day. This may well be a time when you have to prepare the evening meal for your husband and you are likely to feel rushed and upset. It might also worry you just at a time when you would like to sit down and put your feet up. If possible, arrange the day so that you have as little to do as possible in the evening, by preparing most of the meal in advance, and persuading your husband to wash up. If your baby should then cry or grizzle, you will be able to attend to him more easily.

Keep a bored baby interested by letting him sit with you in one of these rigid plastic chairs.

Jealousy of the new baby

Either parent can have moments of irrational jealousy when they feel the baby is getting more than his fair share of attention.

The arrival of a new baby upsets a family as well as making it happy. The most obvious jealousy usually comes from an older child (see page 202). You should prepare him carefully and also give him special attention. Of course, your child may not be the only one in the family to feel jealous. Your husband may feel quite upset when the first baby is born; he has been used to receiving all your love and attention and suddenly finds himself displaced by your continual concern for the baby. Try to remember this, because it may help you to understand any grumpiness or moodiness from your husband when the baby has arrived. Do

121

not be so concerned with the baby that you forget to show affection to him.

Similarly, you may feel upset yourself when your husband wants to play with the baby. It is easy to feel that the baby is your personal possession and not the property of both of you. There can be no easy answer to feelings like this except sympathy and understanding. A family has to learn to get used to one another. You and your husband are at least able to talk about these problems, but a young child cannot.

Feelings of aggression

Sometimes you may feel you want to hit your baby if he is being particularly irritating. This is a very common feeling and most people have it at some time in their lives. You should not feel abnormal if this should happen to you but it is not surprising that you should feel frightened by these feelings.

If you are seriously worried that you might harm your baby, you must take advice from your family doctor or health visitor [clinic sister]. Very often they will help you a lot just by talking about the problem. If you need any further help or a check-up for your baby they can arrange it.

Depression and fatigue

A constant complaint and worry for women is that they become very depressed once the baby has arrived. There are probably a multitude of causes for this depression, but part may well be the physical changes which occur in a woman's body after delivery. Depression is often at its worst when the baby is about three or four days old, but it can occur much later, and be quite prolonged. If you become very tired as a result of trying to cope with all the housework and worrying about the baby when you get home, this can make you a bit miserable and depressed.

It may be a small consolation to know that a large number of women feel miserable at this time. You might find, for instance, that trivial things make you cry or that you worry unnecessarily over the minor problems with the baby. Each of us has a different way of coping with depression. Try not to let the chores get on top of you. If you feel too tired to sweep the stairs or make the bed in the morning – don't bother. At this stage it is more important to have a contented baby and a confident mother than a spotless house. On the other hand, you may feel that you can work yourself out of depression, by following a regular routine of jobs so that there is always something to keep your mind off things. In any case don't hesitate to discuss your feelings with the doctors and nurses while you are still in hospital. Talk it over with your husband too and make sure that he understands that depression at this stage is not something that is easy to control. Once he knows this he will probably be more sympathetic and more inclined to help you through the first few weeks at home. Alternatively, lean on a sympathetic friend or relative. If you find yourself becoming intensely depressed after getting home, talk to your family doctor or health visitor about it.

You may feel very depressed when you are at home with the baby. If this happens, don't hesitate to discuss it with your health visitor or doctor.

Most of the time you and your baby will lead a normal, happy life with few worries and a lot of pleasure. However problems do crop up from time to time which are usually very simple to solve. Crying, feeding and sleeping are the commonest sources of worry, especially for first-time mothers.

Common problems with a small baby

You may often feel that there is something wrong with your baby or that he is not acting as he should. In most cases, you will later find that his behaviour is quite normal and that there is nothing to worry about.

Where to go for advice

Your questions can be easily answered by your family doctor, health visitor [community nurse] and doctor at your local Child [Family] Health Centre. At home a health visitor will visit because she is informed of the birth of all babies in her area. She may be attached to your own family doctor or she may work separately, if he does not run a baby clinic. It is a good idea to find out where your local Family Health Centre is and visit it regularly; the staff there will be very useful to you. The nurse can weigh your baby to make certain that he is gaining weight satisfactorily and is neither too thin nor too fat. You can also obtain supplies of vitamins and milk.

The nurse at the centre is specially trained; I expect you will find her advice very helpful. In addition, you may find that a chat to other mothers of small babies will give you added confidence and will reassure you that your baby is normal.

There are two other very important services available at the Family Health Centre: vaccinations can be arranged and a doctor is available to give regular medical check-ups and to see that your baby is developing normally.

Even though you have all that expert knowledge to tap, no doubt you will still have quite a number of questions about your baby that need answering.

Sleeping

After the first week or two a baby sleeps for about 13 to 15 out of 24 hours. As a child grows older the amount of sleep needed will gradually lessen until it is reduced to about eight hours by the time he has grown into an adult. It is easy to be worried that a baby is sleeping too little or too much. In fact, there is an enormous variation from one person to another. Do not be worried by the amount of sleep your baby takes, so long as he is contented. After all, some adults need as little as four or five hours of sleep, while others must have at least eight.

If your baby does not sleep very much, he will probably lie quietly in his cot. But problems can arise if he cries a lot while he is awake; some babies are constantly irritable and upset, and this can be a tremendous nuisance. Watch your baby carefully

Babies generally sleep a great deal, but every baby will have a different sleep pattern with periods of wakefulness which may cut into your own sleep time.

to see if there is anything special that is making him uncomfortable: perhaps he has a nappy rash or some sore place on his skin. Ask your family doctor to look at him if he always seems to be miserable and you feel he is not getting enough sleep; he will examine the baby to make certain he is quite well.

Some babies wake regularly during the evenings or, worse, at night. You and your husband may have to work things out carefully if your baby wakes you a lot during the night. Try not to allow yourself to become worn out by long nights trying to comfort your baby. Perhaps you and your husband can arrange a rota to look after him when he wakes. Your doctor may be able to help with a simple sedative to help the baby to sleep; sometimes a medicine like this can start the baby into a rhythm of sleeping at night. As soon as the baby's pattern of sleep is established, the medicine may be stopped. Many babies have problems with sleeping, so do not feel guilty about it. It is unlikely to be your fault.

Sleep is very interesting. Even in the very earliest days you will notice that the baby has two types of sleep. There is very deep sleep during which his breathing will be slow and regular: he may appear to be very grumpy if you wake him up during this phase. There is also a lighter sleep during which he makes small movements and you can see his eyes moving. Because of this it is often known as 'rapid eye movement', or REM, sleep. This is believed to be the type of sleep during which dreaming occurs, and is very important to researchers into sleep and dreams.

Crying

A baby has many types of cry. The commonest is a signal that he is hungry and wants to be fed, but he may also have a cry to show he is uncomfortable for many different reasons. He may have a wet nappy, be thirsty, too hot or too cold, or have wind.

The baby's signals. The cry is, of course, a signal from the baby to his mother or other people around that he needs attention. It is his part of a conversation with his mother to show his needs. You will soon be able to recognize his individual cries and their meanings; so listen to him carefully.

Teething. Teething can make a baby irritable, but don't assume that it is the only reason for prolonged crying. Some babies are not worried at all by the growth of their first teeth (see page 143), while others do seem to find it troublesome. Avoid 'teething powders' as these can be harmful. If you think your baby is losing sleep from teething, ask your doctor's advice.

Crying is a baby's distress signal and it can indicate a number of different discomforts, apart from hunger.

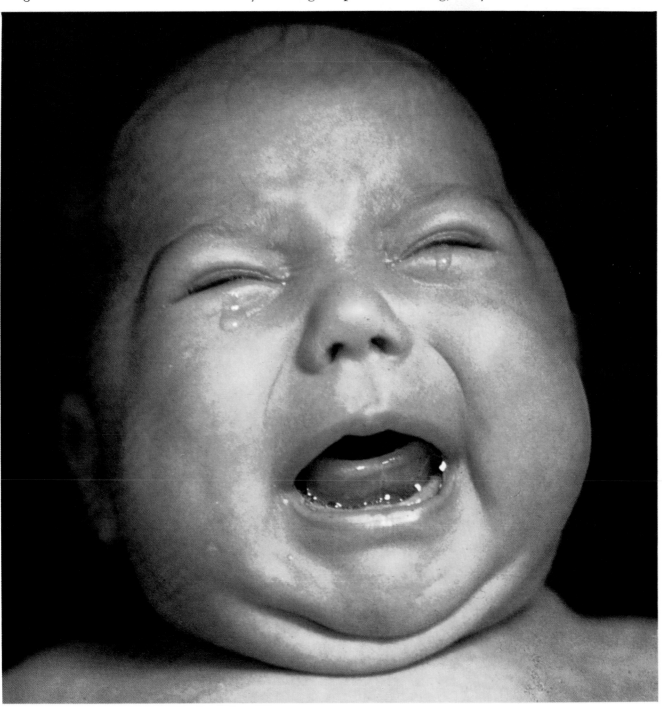

Loneliness overtakes him if his mother leaves the room.

Coping with the problems of indigestion: he swallowed too much air with his feed.

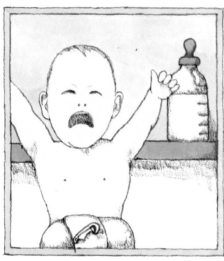

Weaning from breast to bottle may come as an unpleasant surprise – and can take a bit of getting used to.

A sudden bright light startles him.

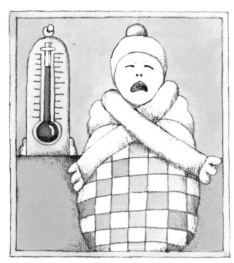

Excessive heat or cold prompt a wail for attention.

Rage: a scream of frustration as toys fall out of reach.

A too-familiar sound, but the baby's cry is his only means of communication. He should not be left to complain alone too long. His demands are usually justified and could be any of the above.

Usually, babies stop crying as soon as they are comfortable again – after a feed or a nappy change, for instance. But babies vary a good deal in the amount they cry, just as they vary in the amount they sleep. It is not yet fully understood why some babies cry more than others, but it is possibly to do with differences in their personalities. The pattern of crying varies during the day and is often at a peak during the evening between about six and ten o'clock. Again, the cause of this is not known, but it occurs even in the first week of life. Many babies will protest when they are put back in the cot or pram to sleep, perhaps after a feed or bath. This is a natural reaction – after all, they have probably had a lot of attention which has now come to an end. Some babies cry when they are tired as well. Do not worry if it lasts for a minute or two – but if it becomes prolonged crying it might be as well to check whether the baby has wind or perhaps needs another nappy change. If you use a dummy for the baby you will probably find that he will cry if he drops it from his mouth. It is a simple matter to replace the dummy and satisfy the baby.

Spoiling or not

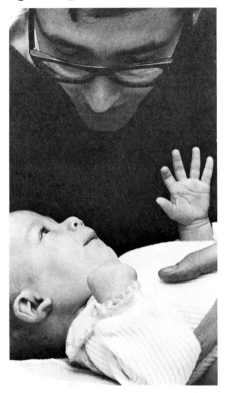

A father can help take some of the strain involved in coping with a fractious baby.

A baby's cry is an insistent call to you for help. You will probably feel that you wish to go to the baby at once, to make him comfortable and to pick him up. Many people feel that it is wrong to pick up a baby who cries, because it will 'spoil' him. It is thought that if you pick him up frequently, he will soon learn that he is on to a good thing and so will cry for attention the whole time. In fact, most women have never paid much attention to this theory and have always picked up and comforted babies when they cried. Mothers often feel rather guilty about this, because their own mothers tell them that they are making it difficult for themselves, but you may well find that your mother did the same thing when she was young and picked you up as well, even though she was told not to!

You will soon learn what is best for you and your baby. After all, you have to live together. Lots of other mothers cannot bear to let their babies cry and want to pick them up.

Attention. Recent research makes us believe that you should pay attention to your baby when he is upset. When some mothers were watched with their crying babies, it was found that those babies who received attention were more content on their first birthday than those that were left to cry miserably. It seems as though women are in fact making a rod for their own backs if they leave the baby to cry, which is quite the opposite of what is often said.

However, the baby who is always crying can be a tremendous nuisance, particularly if he disturbs all the family's sleep. There are several ways you may comfort him. Rocking him in your arms, holding him against you with his head looking over your shoulder, or lying him face down across your knees while you gently pat his neck or back: these are all things which may comfort him. One of the traditional comforters has been rocking. The baby appears to become less miserable when he is rocked at a fast pace: about one rock per second.

In the past, most countries had beautiful lullabies, which were sung while rocking or cuddling a baby, to send him off to sleep. It would be very sad if these songs were lost. Why not learn one and sing it to your baby?

Using a dummy

Sucking seems to be a very pleasant activity for a baby even when his stomach is quite full. A baby may go on sucking

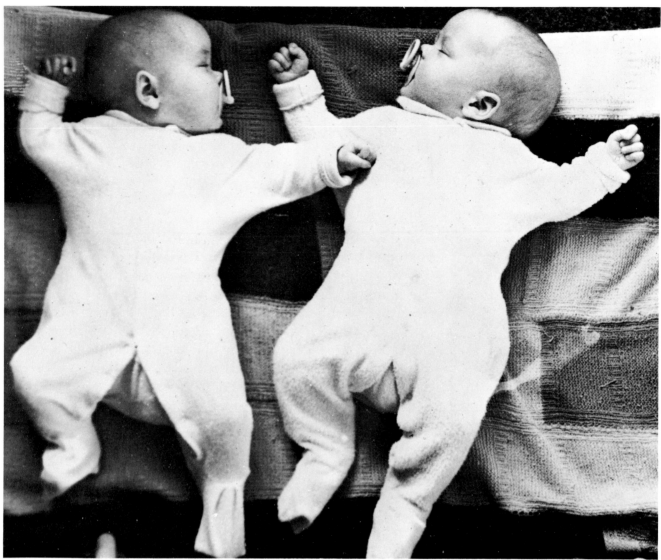

Dummies can be very helpful since babies seem to derive a great deal of pleasure from sucking. They can be particularly useful to the mother of twins, for instance when one baby can be pacified with a dummy while waiting his or her turn to be fed.

contentedly for a while after a feed. Often, you may see him sucking his fist and it seems he gets great enjoyment from it.

It is reasonable to help your baby with a dummy, if he does seem discontented. Some babies are much more contented when they have one of these. So long as they are kept clean, there seems to be very little objection to their use; although many people think they look ugly. However, the baby's appearance is considerably less important than his feelings of well-being. It is as well to keep a dummy sterilized – make a habit of keeping one or two in the sterilizing solution with the feeding bottles.

You may have heard that the use of a dummy leads to prolonged thumb-sucking later. In fact, the evidence suggests that thumb-sucking is less common when a dummy has been used. Babies usually stop using a dummy naturally after a while, spitting it out as soon as you offer it. Don't make your baby continue with the dummy if he obviously doesn't want it.

Never, on any account, fill or coat a dummy with a sugar solution or dip it in a sweet liquid, such as honey or jam, before giving it to the baby. If you do this the baby's teeth will be ruined. (See page 145.)

'Three-month colic'

This diagnosis is often made when a baby cries long and loud after feeds. We cannot be certain that the crying is anything to do with colic, which is a condition of increased and painful contractions of the intestine. It has been thought to be the result of a lot of wind passing through the baby's bowels: 'wind' may cause crying, but it is unlikely to account for all of it. Of course, the baby may be uncomfortable if his stomach is distended with gas after a feed and he is usually more comfortable when he has belched.

If your baby has got a major crying problem and you think it may be colic, talk to your family doctor about it. He will be able to examine the baby to make certain there is no illness causing the crying. You may think his distress is due to stomach pain, if the baby goes red in the face and pulls his knees up while crying. A lot of babies, however, pull up their knees when they cry for any reason. If the doctor thinks the baby has a pain from colic, he may prescribe a medicine to see if this will help. Sometimes, the medicine is immediately effective.

This problem is always worst in the first few months and usually clears up by the time the baby is three months old. As yet, it is not known why it clears up then. It may be that the baby's mind has developed sufficiently for him to take a greater interest in the world and to distract him from his bodily feelings.

Constipation

Many babies have difficulty in passing stools. Constipation means a hard bowel motion, which is passed infrequently. It is more common in babies who are artificially fed; some milks tend to cause it more than others. If your baby has this problem, you will notice that he has to strain hard to pass a motion, which looks like hard pellets. If the baby is bottle-fed, you can often make his stools softer by adding an extra teaspoonful of sugar – particularly brown sugar – to the milk. If this does not make any difference, you can use a very mild laxative such as milk of magnesia (magnesium hydroxide). You can get this from any pharmacist; start with a very small amount, up to half a teaspoonful, once or twice a day and increase it gently until the baby's motions are soft. Never use a stronger laxative for a baby, unless you have asked your doctor.

Sometimes constipation causes a fissure of the anus. This is a small crack caused by passing a hard, large stool. It may be painful and cause some blood in the stool. The doctor will tell you how to treat it; he will probably use a mild laxative, so that the crack can heal and does not reopen.

Regurgitation

Slight regurgitation of feeds is common from the newborn period until about nine months of age. As long as your baby is happy and gains weight, there is no need to worry about this. It seems to get better when a baby takes more solid food and learns to sit up. You may be able to help the problem by thickening feeds; you can do this by adding a small amount of arrowroot mixed to a paste with water and then bringing the

milk to the boil. Make sure that the milk is not too thick to drip through the teat. You can also try propping up the top end of the cot on a book so that the baby lies with his head slightly raised. Do *not* use a pillow for this purpose. If all this fails, your baby will probably be happy to live with the problem until it disappears by itself.

Vomiting

Vomiting must be taken much more seriously. If your baby repeatedly brings up the whole of his feed, you should consult your doctor. This is particularly important if the baby is a boy and brings up every feed so that the milk shoots out of his mouth. This could be due to a condition called pyloric stenosis – a blockage at the end of the stomach which needs special treatment, probably by operation.

Thrush

This is an infection by a fungus. It causes white patches on the tongue and mouth. They can be easily confused with milk curds; you can tell the difference by trying to remove them – curds can be wiped off but thrush is adherent. The baby may have a sore mouth, so that he feeds poorly and may be fretful. Your doctor can give an antibiotic to clear it up.

If your baby has thrush, you must be extremely careful when sterilizing, so that it does not recur after treatment.

Eyes

Babies' eyes are often blue at birth although they may darken after a few months. A baby may not produce any tears for several weeks after birth. Mild infections are very common in the eye; they cause a small amount of yellow discharge, which gums the eyelids together. You can keep the eye clean by bathing it with cold boiled water and clean cottonwool as described in the bath routine on page 98. If the infection continues, the doctor may give you an antibiotic to use.

Repeated sticky eyes can be caused by a blocked tear-duct. Usually, it is wise to be patient with this problem and to

Left: After being fed a baby may often regurgitate a little of the milk while being 'winded'. This is often known as 'possetting'.
Right: In peaceful moments like this many mothers find they enjoy simply watching their sleeping babies.

continue treatment with antibiotic drops or ointment. If it continues as long as nine months, an operation may help to unblock the duct and prevent the infection recurring.

The umbilicus (or navel)

The cord stump, a sort of scab, will fall off by itself. You do not need to do anything except to keep it clean; the hospital may give you a powder or liquid which helps to prevent infection. (See page 54.) When the cord comes off, there may be a small amount of bleeding, but it then heals easily.

Sometimes a polyp forms. It looks like a tiny red button inside the depression of the umbilicus. It may cause a discharge or even a little bit of bleeding. Your doctor can treat it quite simply, by using a little caustic to make it shrivel and disappear.

Hernias

A hernia at the umbilicus is very common indeed. In some parts of Africa, almost every baby has one. It appears as a swelling of the navel, covered by skin; it is much more prominent when the baby cries. If you press on the swelling it flattens easily and you may hear a slight squelching noise as you push it completely flat. This noise comes from the sound of the intestine as it is pushed back into the abdomen. It is an almost harmless condition and gets better by itself. It may take two years or more to heal, but an operation is almost never necessary before the age of three years. I usually only recommend an operation if the hernia is still there at the age of six years. Very occasionally the hernia may become red and inflamed, and impossible to flatten; in this case, you should consult your doctor at once in case an urgent operation is necessary.

These hernias used to be treated by strapping, to hold it flat. For instance a penny was put over the hernia and then strapped down. In fact, it has been shown that the hernia heals slower when strapped in this way. It is therefore not recommended.

Nappy rashes

This is one of the commonest problems in the first few months and probably affects almost every baby at some time or another. There are several types of rash in the nappy area, but the most usual is called ammoniacal dermatitis. When urine is passed into a nappy it meets germs from faeces; some of the substances in urine are then converted into ammonia. You will often recognize the pungent smell of ammonia when you change a nappy which has been on a baby for some time. The ammonia attacks the skin causing redness, spots, or even little ulcers. The redness is usually on the areas which are prominent and is less common in the folds, such as the groin. It can also aggravate soreness on a circumcised penis, caused by chafing on the nappy (see page 53).

Prevention of nappy rash is easier than cure. Try to change the nappy as soon as it becomes wet; this means many times a day, if you are to be certain that the baby does not stay wet for a long time. You may find a one-way nappy liner useful at night (see page 101). Try to keep the nappy area dry and clean. A little acid helps to prevent the formation of ammonia in nappies;

A bad nappy rash such as this should be kept scrupulously clean and as dry as possible. It would probably be treated with a special cream prescribed by a doctor. It is probably a better idea to use cotton wool or a soft flannel, which can be boiled, to clean the area, rather than a sponge.

you could try adding a little vinegar to the water you use for rinsing them.

If there is any sign of redness, apply a baby or barrier cream: those containing silicone are useful. If you do this carefully, you can usually avoid a severe nappy rash. If a spotty nappy rash does appear, do not be too worried; many babies have it and it is not serious. Be particularly careful to change the nappy frequently and apply plenty of cream to prevent the urine reaching the rash. Try and leave the nappy off from time to time as well. If the rash shows any signs of getting worse or does not clear up, you should consult your doctor.

Other rashes. There are other types of rash which can occur in the nappy area. Soreness around the anus is very common in the newborn baby, but less common later. It is usually treated by cream and leaving the baby without nappies. Sometimes thrush causes a lot of small red spots round the anus; this usually occurs at the same time as thrush in the mouth. You should talk to your doctor about this sort of rash, because he may want to prescribe a special ointment.

There is one other type of nappy rash which has become more common in recent years. It affects the whole of the nappy area, even in the creases, unlike ammoniacal dermatitis, and is red, dry and slightly scaly. Sometimes there are little patches of the rash on other parts of the body. We think that it may be more common when plastic pants are used. If your baby has this sort of rash, try leaving off the pants for a while, and talk to the doctor about it.

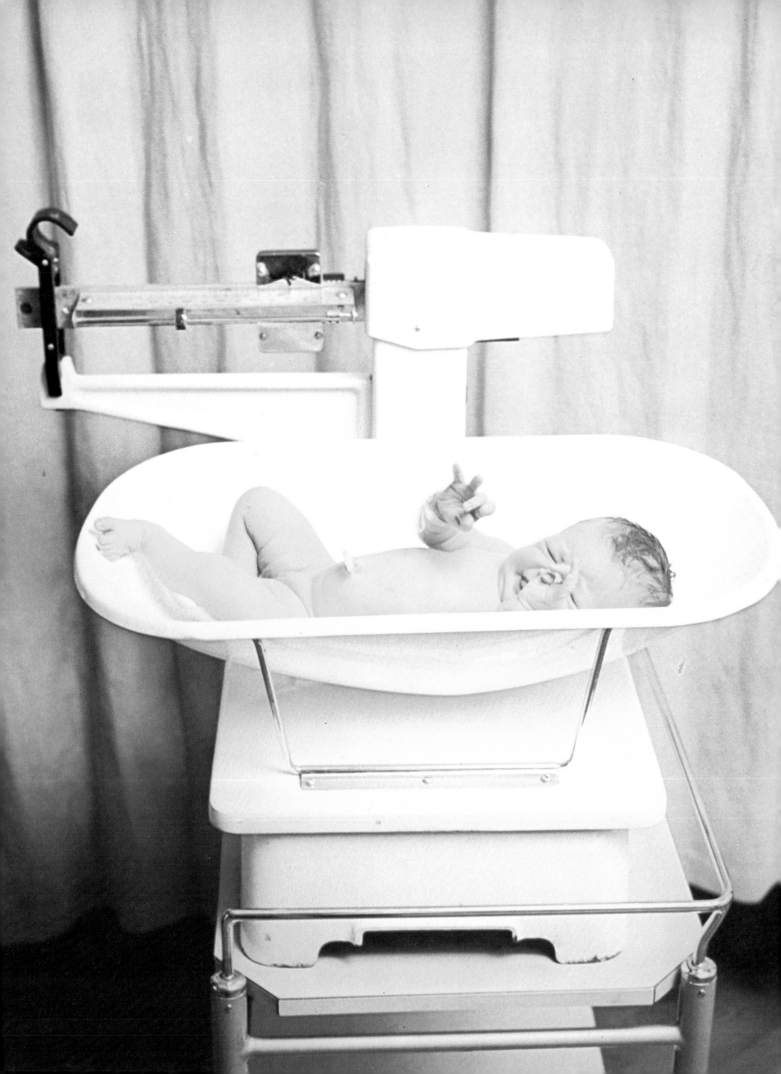

Development in the first twelve months

How the baby grows

A baby grows very rapidly during the first six months of his life and at a rather slower rate during the second six months. An old but useful guide is that a baby doubles his birthweight in the first six months and is three times his birthweight on his first birthday. Of course, this is only a very rough guide and your baby may not follow it exactly.

Babies gain weight very quickly if they are getting fat. You can usually see if a baby is becoming too podgy by just looking at him; you can confirm it by picking up a pinch of skin between your finger and thumb. If the fold looks very thick, he may be too fat. A doctor or health visitor [community nurse] at the Child [Family] Health Centre will advise if he is gaining weight too quickly. He may also gain weight quickly if he is growing very fast. In this case he will be both long and heavy. You only have to worry about a baby whose weight is far more than it ought to be for his length.

It is very useful to follow a baby's growth by weighing him and by measuring his total length. Sometimes babies do not gain weight satisfactorily and fail to thrive. These babies can be discovered at an early stage by several weighings and by plotting the weights on a chart which shows the growth of normal babies. The charts of normal growth for boys and girls are on pages 138 and 140. Use these charts to plot your own baby's growth in the three years of life.

Percentiles

Read this section carefully. If you are to understand growth and not be confused or worried by it, it is essential to understand what the lines on these charts mean. You will notice that each of the lines has a number, such as 3, 25 or 90. These lines are called percentiles. They mean that a certain percentage of normal children have a height or weight below that line. Thus, the 50th percentile is the average since 50 out of every 100 children fall below the line and 50 above. If you take the 3rd percentile, only 3 out of every 100 children will have a height or weight below that line, and 97 above. They are very useful charts since it means you can compare your child with other children. They show how wide the normal range is for children, and also how rapid is growth and weight gain, particularly early in life, and how it slackens off later.

From birth, a baby is weighed and measured regularly and the two results compared to make sure that he is growing steadily and satisfactorily.

137

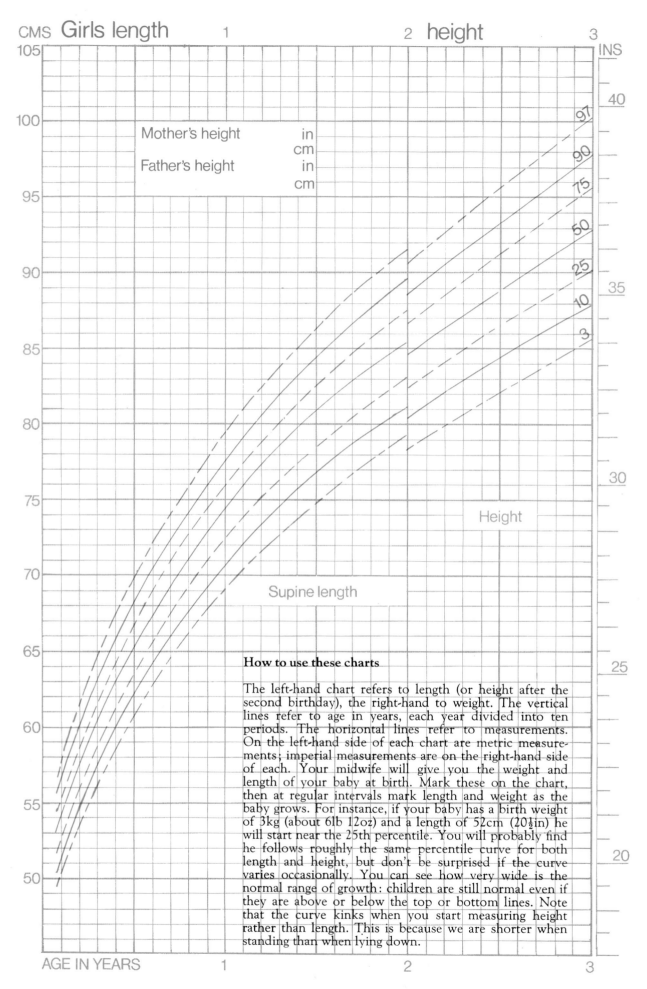

CMS **Girls length**   1   2   height   3

INS

Mother's height   in
                cm
Father's height   in
                cm

97
90
75
50
25
10
3

Height

Supine length

How to use these charts

The left-hand chart refers to length (or height after the second birthday), the right-hand to weight. The vertical lines refer to age in years, each year divided into ten periods. The horizontal lines refer to measurements. On the left-hand side of each chart are metric measurements; imperial measurements are on the right-hand side of each. Your midwife will give you the weight and length of your baby at birth. Mark these on the chart, then at regular intervals mark length and weight as the baby grows. For instance, if your baby has a birth weight of 3kg (about 6lb 12oz) and a length of 52cm (20½in) he will start near the 25th percentile. You will probably find he follows roughly the same percentile curve for both length and height, but don't be surprised if the curve varies occasionally. You can see how very wide is the normal range of growth: children are still normal even if they are above or below the top or bottom lines. Note that the curve kinks when you start measuring height rather than length. This is because we are shorter when standing than when lying down.

AGE IN YEARS   1   2   3   INS

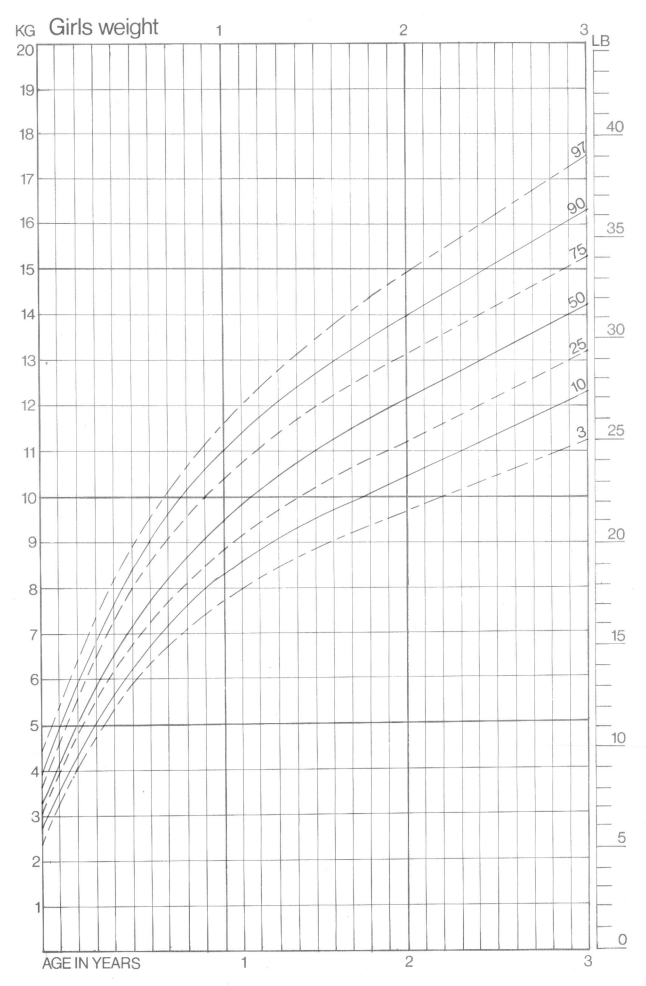

Girls weight

KG

20
19
18
17
16
15
14
13
12
11
10
9
8
7
6
5
4
3
2
1

AGE IN YEARS

1   2   3

LB

40

35

30

25

20

15

10

5

0

97
90
75
50
25
10
3

139

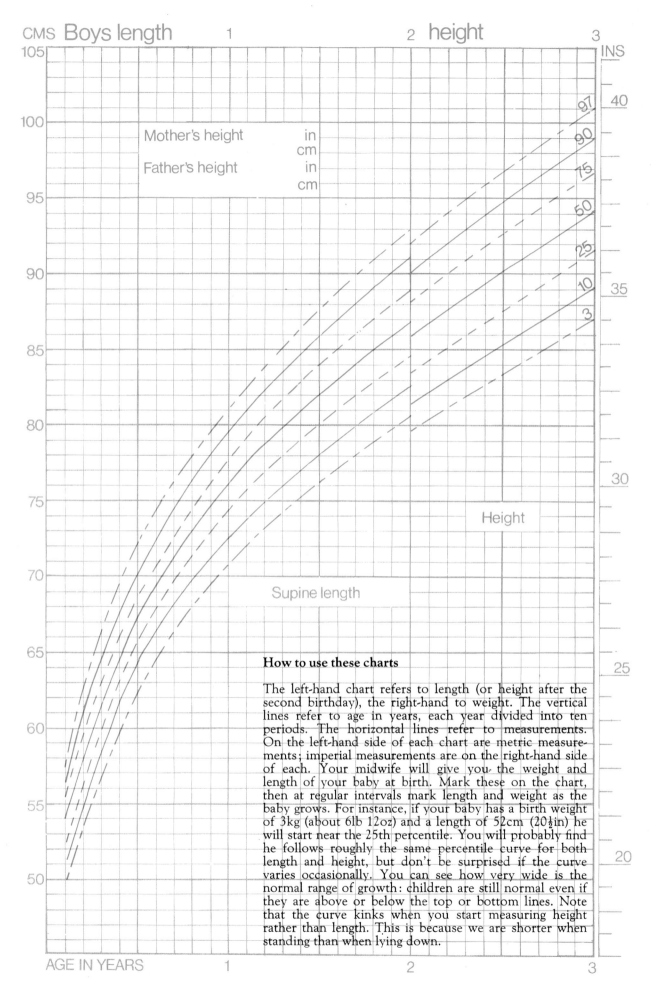

CMS **Boys length** 1 2 **height** 3

INS

Mother's height   in
                     cm
Father's height   in
                     cm

Height

Supine length

How to use these charts

The left-hand chart refers to length (or height after the second birthday), the right-hand to weight. The vertical lines refer to age in years, each year divided into ten periods. The horizontal lines refer to measurements. On the left-hand side of each chart are metric measurements; imperial measurements are on the right-hand side of each. Your midwife will give you the weight and length of your baby at birth. Mark these on the chart, then at regular intervals mark length and weight as the baby grows. For instance, if your baby has a birth weight of 3kg (about 6lb 12oz) and a length of 52cm (20½in) he will start near the 25th percentile. You will probably find he follows roughly the same percentile curve for both length and height, but don't be surprised if the curve varies occasionally. You can see how very wide is the normal range of growth: children are still normal even if they are above or below the top or bottom lines. Note that the curve kinks when you start measuring height rather than length. This is because we are shorter when standing than when lying down.

AGE IN YEARS   1   2   3

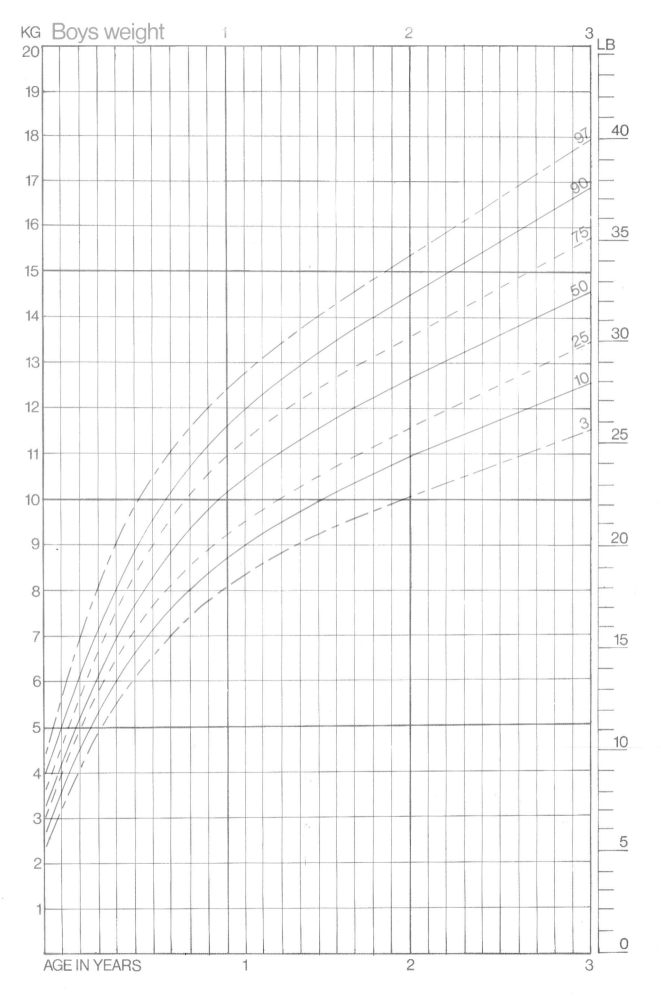

KG Boys weight   LB

AGE IN YEARS

141

Weighing

You must be very careful when weighing and measuring the baby. If you are going to plot the weight on one of these charts, you must remember that the baby should be completely naked otherwise you will include some of the weight of his clothes by mistake. Do not weigh a baby too frequently, because there are bound to be variations from day to day: a baby will weigh a little more after a feed and a little less when he has opened his bowels and passed urine. The health visitor will guide you about the number of times the baby should be weighed. In the past, some people became very concerned with weighing and worried themselves over the fluctuations in weight from day to day. Treat weighing as a useful guide to the progress of your baby and not as the only criterion.

Measuring

Measuring a baby is much more difficult than weighing him. In fact, the only really satisfactory method is to use a special instrument available in some hospitals; the instrument is shaped like a table and has a board at the baby's head, and a movable board can be brought up to the soles of his feet (rather like a foot measuring gauge in a shoe-shop). A gauge shows the exact length of the baby.

You can get a rough idea of a baby's length, if two people measure him between them. The baby should be held fully extended on a table, making sure that his knees are straight and that his head and heels are touching the table. One person can then use a tape measure to find the length from the top of the head to the heels. It is interesting to do this and plot the baby on the graph; you can then watch how he grows. What you will usually find is that a baby grows steadily on or alongside one of the lines on the chart. Always remember that the lines are only a guide. The fact that he may be below the 10th percentile does not mean he is abnormal, but that he belongs to a group of normal babies, 10 out of 100, who grow below that line. Doctors only worry about babies who are very much below the 3rd percentile or very much above the 97th. A baby's growth will, of course, partly depend on the height of the parents. If you are both small, then you must expect the baby to be nearer the bottom end of the normal range. If you have any concern about this, ask the doctor who has other special charts to work out how the baby's size is affected by your own height and weight.

If a baby is running parallel to one of the lines on the chart, this is very good evidence that he is growing normally. However, if he starts crossing lines, particularly if he has crossed two or three lines, there may be some worry that he is getting too fat or not gaining weight properly. Ask the health visitor, if you think this has happened.

Obesity

If your baby is gaining weight faster than the chart suggests is usual, he may be obese. Of course, he could just be a baby who is growing fast as I have already explained. When you have weighed him and compared his weight with the graph, measure him as well. Now compare this length with the graph. If the weight and length are on percentiles very near one another, your baby is well-proportioned and is not too fat. For instance, if the baby has a weight on the 90th percentile and a length on the 75th, these are very near and are quite normal. You should only be concerned if he looks fat and if his weight is on a much higher percentile than his length. For instance, if his length were only on the 25th percentile and his weight on the 97th, it is likely that he is too fat. These are only rough guides and the clinic will help to reassure you that your baby's growth rate is consistent.

If your doctor thinks that the baby is suffering from obesity, you will need to be careful about his diet. Look at the section on feeding (see page 87) and cut down on those foods which contain a lot of starch or sugar. If you do this, your baby has a better chance of being slim when grown up.

Failure to gain weight

This is one of the main reasons for weighing a baby regularly. If the baby is happy, contented and gaining weight steadily, you can be happy about his progress. If his gain slackens, there could be a number of causes. Of course, the baby may not be getting enough food; you and the health visitor can sort this out between you.

Other problems can cause a baby to fail to thrive; for instance, food may not be absorbed from the intestine or there may be an infection present. If a baby loses weight, he should have a medical check-up as soon as you are sure that it is not a temporary weight loss.

Head circumference

Mothers often worry when they see the baby's head being measured. This is done by putting a tape measure around the head to measure the maximum circumference – including the forehead and the back of the head. This measurement is made as a routine at birth, and from time to time during check-ups.

The increase in the head circumference is another useful measure of the baby's growth. However, it is also important because it gives a rough estimate of the brain size. There is a wide variation of the measurements at birth: the 3rd percentile is 30cm (12in) and the 97th, 38cm (15in); some perfectly normal babies have head circumferences outside these figures. At one year the 3rd and 97th percentiles are 44cm ($17\frac{1}{2}$in) and 49cm ($19\frac{1}{2}$in).

Teeth

An occasional baby has teeth when he is born. These are always extra teeth; they fall out and are replaced by normal teeth later on. The first tooth usually comes through, in the front of the mouth, around the age of six months. Like other development, the appearance of teeth is sometimes very late in normal babies. I have seen several quite normal babies who did not have teeth until they were a year old.

The diagrams show the order in which the deciduous or 'milk' teeth appear and the usual age of the baby. The lower central

Your baby's first teeth are a great landmark in his development. Some babies have no trouble at all cutting their first or 'deciduous' teeth; others do suffer some distress. However, beware of diagnosing all your baby's troubles as teething – there could be a more serious cause.

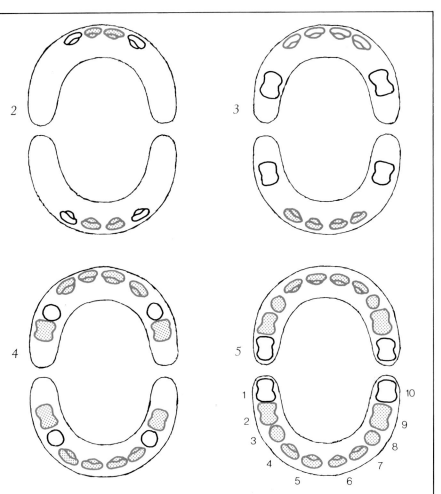

The first, or deciduous, teeth come through in the following order: 1. Central incisors: lower jaw 5-7 months (see below), upper jaw 7-10 months. 2. Lateral incisors: upper jaw 9-11 months, lower jaw 10-12 months. 3. 1st molar: upper jaw 12-14 months, lower jaw 12-16 months. 4. Canines: upper jaw 16-20 months, lower jaw 16-20 months. 5. 2nd molar: lower jaw 20-28 months, upper jaw 20-30 months.

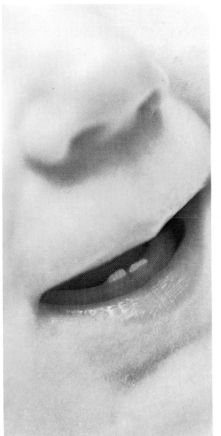

teeth are followed by the upper central teeth (all these are called incisors) and then incisors just to the sides of them, first in the upper jaw and then the lower. After this the teeth known as the molars appear and then the eye-teeth, or canines.

The second teeth do not start coming through until about five or six years of age, and this process continues until adult life.

When a baby starts to develop teeth, he usually enjoys biting things. A teething ring is very useful, as well as hard crusts or rusks. A good diet containing vitamin D and calcium is important if the baby's teeth are to be healthy. Remember to give him fluoride every day, if the water in your area does not contain enough fluoride. The health visitor [doctor] can tell you whether your area has sufficient or if you need to give extra. Give half a fluoride tablet per day from about two weeks old: check with your doctor or health visitor nurse about when to start.

Do be very careful about sweets and sugary things; they can cause so much havoc to teeth. Everybody, including babies, grows a layer of bacteria on their teeth, called plaque, from eating and breathing. The bacteria (germs) on the teeth are not in themselves harmful or abnormal. However when sugar or sticky food containing sugar comes into contact with the bacteria, within $1\frac{1}{2}$ minutes they begin to produce acid which will break down the outer hard enamel coating of the teeth and begin the irreversible process of tooth decay. The usual way of

145

preventing tooth decay is therefore not to eat sugar – you can get as much energy from other sources – and to clean off the acid-producing bacteria by cleaning the teeth correctly.

How your baby develops

One of the major excitements of parenthood is to see your baby develop. You will probably find that the steps or 'milestones' of his progress will be Red Letter Days for you. The first smile or first few steps will be times to remember.

A baby's development is fascinating. You can see the world slowly expanding for him, as he becomes physically able to do things with his limbs and begins to perceive and understand events around him. It is important to watch his progress, because if he is very slow in doing certain things, there may be reason for discussing the problem with your doctor. Very slow development in the first 12 months can mean that a child will be backward later on.

Normal variations of development

Although it is important to watch for any serious delay, one must realize that there is tremendous variation in the rate of development from baby to baby. Very often, you may be told categorically that a baby does such-and-such at a certain time; for instance, it is sometimes said that babies sit up unaided at six months. Of course, you will immediately realize that babies do not start to sit at exactly six months, but within a range of several months – probably between five and eight months. Normal rates of development are set within a *range* of time.

A good example of this is the different ways babies start to walk. Some babies are very clever at getting around by crawling or shuffling on their bottoms. They often start walking much later than usual, but the rest of their development is quite normal. Bottom-shuffling often runs in families – I was a bottom-shuffler and did not walk until I was 22 months old; I often find it useful to explain this to parents who are worried about their baby's development.

Smiling

A baby may start to smile within a few days of birth, but this is unusual; most babies smile at about five weeks of age. First of all, he will start to stare at you intently, particularly while he is feeding; then smiling develops next. When he smiles for the first time, you may not be certain that it is real; but soon he will respond to your smile by producing one of his own. 90 per cent of babies are smiling by the age of seven weeks.

Since this is the first developmental milestone your baby will pass, I thought I should point out here one of the common reasons for babies developing 'late'. If he was born early, you must not expect him to smile at the same time as a baby born at full term. This is because his brain needs to mature sufficiently for him to produce these responses. Thus, if a baby is born six weeks early, it is reasonable to expect him to smile at six plus five weeks – that is, about 11 weeks. Remember this simple rule if your baby is premature, because it may save you a lot of worry.

Sitting

This is the next really major milestone that you will remember in your baby's development. We must be quite clear what we are talking about, because the baby is often said to be sitting when he is actually propped up by all manner of cushions around him. A baby is really only sitting when you can put him on the floor, without any support, and he will not topple over. The average baby does this at six and a half months, but ten per cent of babies are still not sitting at eight months. If your baby was born at full term and is still not sitting at nine months, it would be a good idea to arrange a check-up from your family doctor. The earliest age that babies sit alone without support is just before five months; this shows how wide the normal range is, from under five months to over eight months.

Getting around

Babies have a variety of methods of getting around. Shortly after six months, they can often roll over and may use this to move a short distance. Crawling comes soon after, but is difficult to date because there are so many different types of crawl. First the baby learns to wriggle along on his tummy; then he uses his elbows to pull him forward like a commando.

At about nine or ten months, he can often crawl on his hands and knees. At about a year, when he may already be walking, he can get around on hands and feet – on all fours like a bear.

Some babies have very odd methods of getting around: some drag one leg behind them, others shuffle along on their bottoms.

Walking

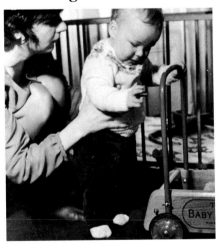

The day a baby first takes a few steps on his own is a great event. It is not surprising therefore that I usually find mothers can remember with ease the age at which it occurs. Often other parts of development, such as smiling and sitting, are only remembered vaguely, but the day of walking can be recalled instantly. Like sitting, there is a very wide range for the age of walking. About 25 per cent of babies are walking at $11\frac{1}{2}$ months and the average is about $12\frac{1}{2}$ months. 90 per cent have walked by $15\frac{1}{2}$ months and 97 per cent by 17 months.

If your baby hasn't walked by 18 months, you should certainly ask the doctor about it. It would be a good idea to ask him earlier if he has been slow in other development as well. If he is very bright, but does not seem to want to walk there is less cause for worry. He will get to his feet when he is ready.

Use of hands

Most babies reach out for things above their cot at between three and four months and 90 per cent of them are doing it by five months. They will usually grasp a rattle when it is given to them at about the same time. You can watch how clever your baby becomes at picking up small objects during the second half of the first year. If you give him a harmless tiny object, such as a raisin, he will probably be able to pick it up between his thumb and first finger at eight and a half months, although some babies are still not able to do this at 11 months. He will be able to hold bricks in his hand and bang them together by the time he is a year.

The fontanelles (or 'soft spots')

Many parents are anxious about their baby's head. The fontanelles or 'soft spots' on the baby's head can seem worrying – specially in the first few months when you can see the scalp pulsating gently, reflecting rhythm of the baby's heartbeat. However, the membrane is very tough and provides adequate protection against all normal pressures and shocks. The segments of the skull gradually close and finally knit together at about 18 months.

Social development

In the next 17 pages there is a pictorial guide to the important stages of development from five weeks to 12 months. Of course, babies develop very differently, but this should give an idea of the time-scale involved. Your own baby may reach a certain stage of development before or after the age given here.

After smiling in response to a smile from you, the baby will produce smiles of his own, in order to make you smile; expect this from about seven to eight weeks, but do not be surprised if it takes a long time, as ten per cent of babies are said to be still not doing it at five months of age.

You will notice a major change in the way a baby greets strangers during his second six months. Whereas a baby of five or six months will smile at anyone, he later learns that his mother and father are different from other people and he will become very shy with strangers. Some babies start this at about six or seven months, and most by nine months and practically all by ten and a half months. When you see this change, you will realize that the baby is finding out about the world and who people are.

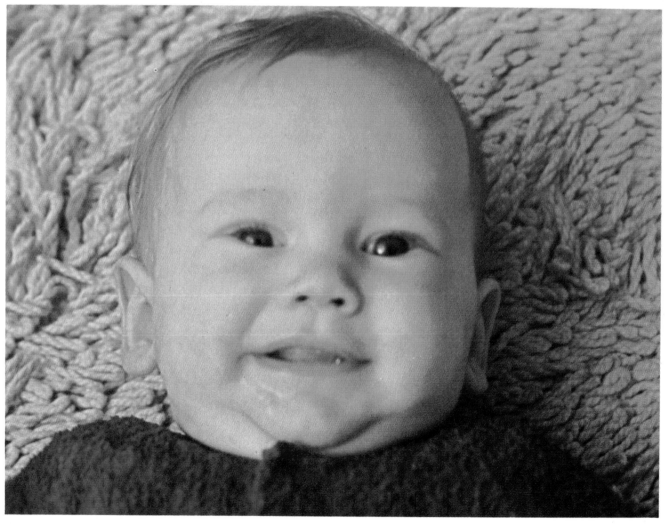

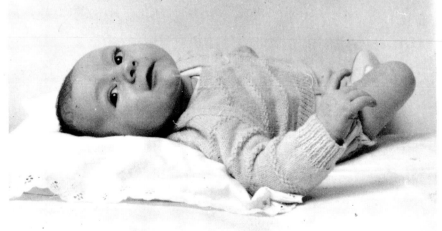

One to two months
At this age a baby may have started to smile (opposite) and looks intently at his mother (above). He can follow a bright object with his eyes (right).

Three months

A baby now smiles spontaneously (*opposite, top*) and will bring his hands together in front of his face (*opposite*). He has much more control over his head (*above*), which was very wobbly before. When lying on his front (*right*), he can lift his head up to look forward.

151

Four months

When pulled up to sitting (*opposite*), the baby can control his head so that it does not drop back. Lying on his front, he can lift his head right up (*opposite, below*), and can support himself on his hands. He grasps a rattle (*right*) and reaches for things hanging above him (*below*).

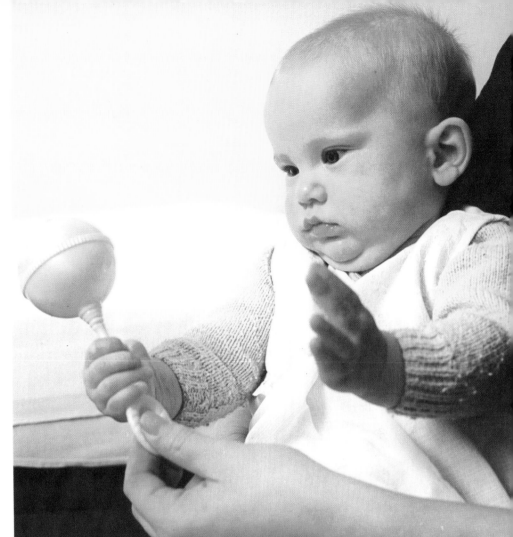

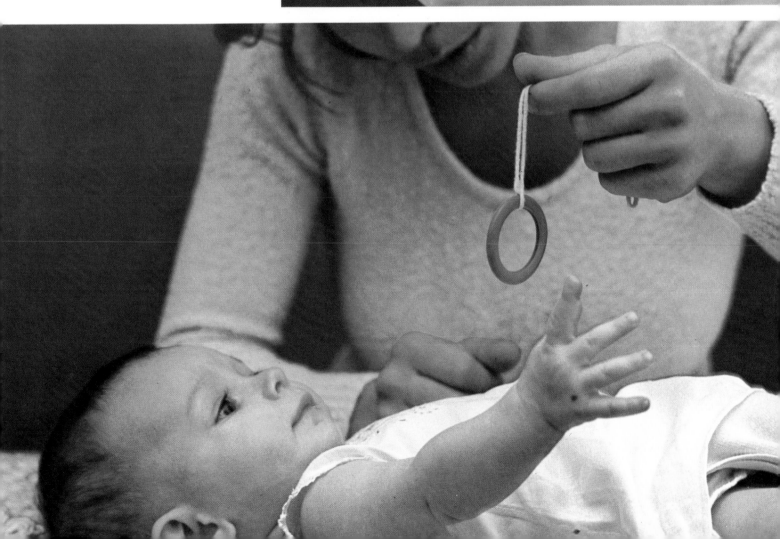

Five months
When the baby is held upright (right) he will support himself on his legs. Opposite: She enjoys sitting with some support.

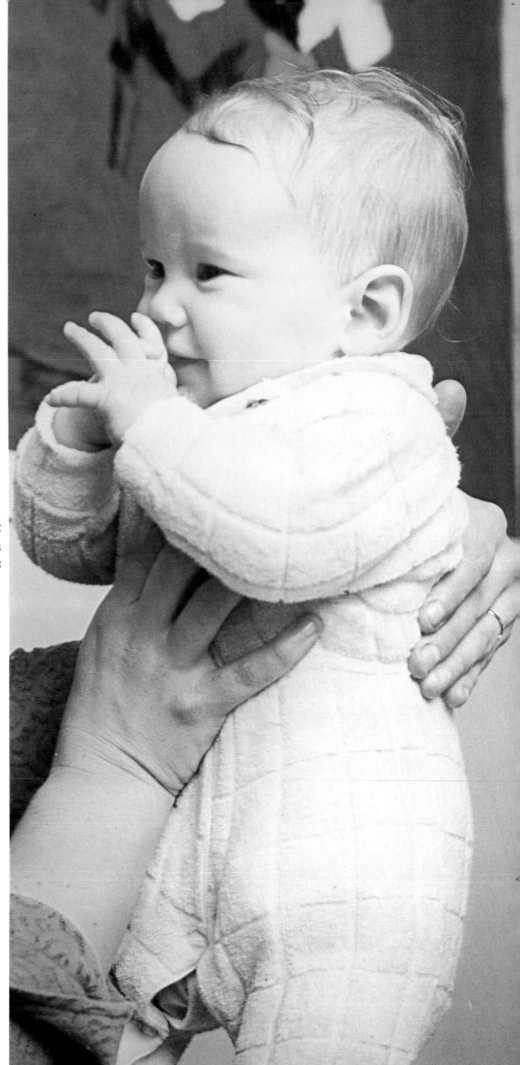

Six to seven months

He starts to sit by himself without any support (*top left*). He often turns to a noise (*left*) and begins to be frightened of strangers (*opposite, top left*). He takes a small toy when it is offered to him (*opposite, top right*). When lying on his front (*opposite, right*) he can wriggle along – some people call this creeping. When lying on his back (*opposite, left*), he often plays with his toes.

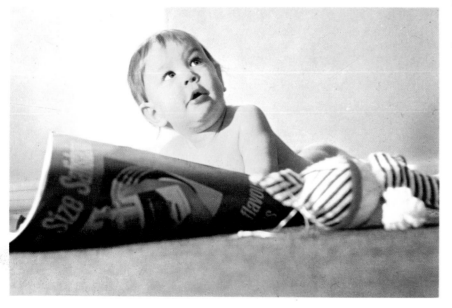

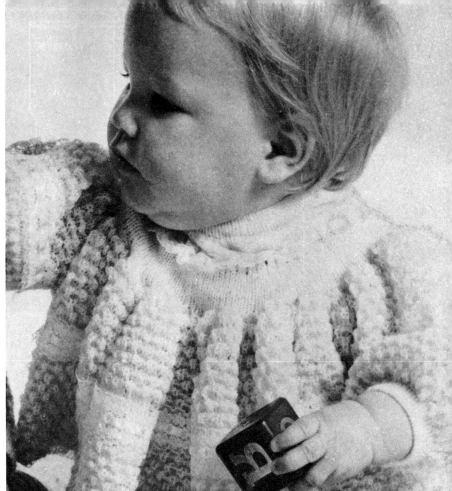

Eight to nine months
He can now sit easily and for some time (left). He makes some attempt at crawling in search of a toy he wants (below). Usually a brick can be held between the thumb and first finger (right). His speech consists of baby or 'Da-da' sounds, but he may start imitating other sounds. He can get himself to a sitting position (below, right).

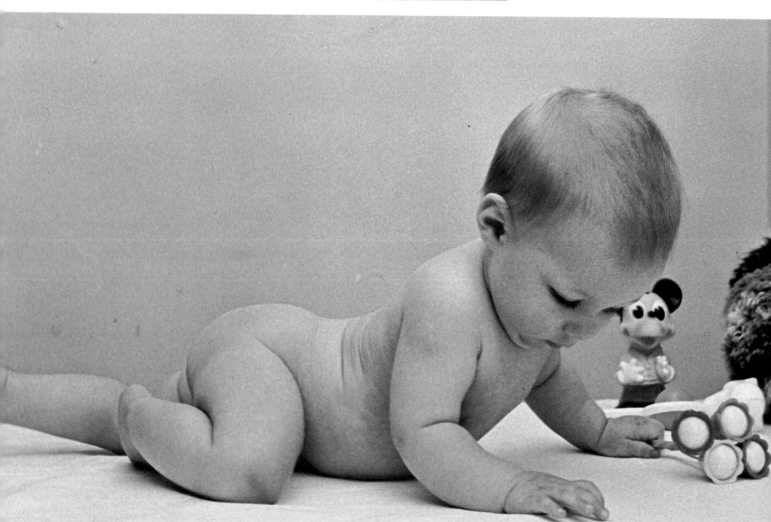

Eight to nine months
He may be able to pull himself up to standing: especially in a cot or playpen (opposite). When put into a standing position (above): he can usually stand while holding on to something. He may even attempt to walk when holding hands like this.

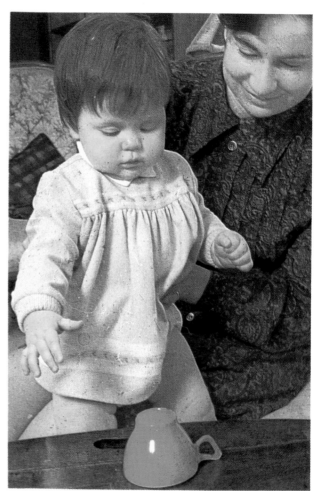

Ten to eleven months

Far left: Her standing has progressed, so that she can stand by herself without any support for a few moments. She has started to walk round the furniture (below, far left). Clapping hands (below) and other simple games (left and right) give her great enjoyment. 'Da-da' has now become a sound attached to her father and she says 'Ma-ma' as well.

Twelve months
Babies are often walking by themselves at this time (*opposite*). A tiny object (*above*), like a raisin or a piece of wool, is held in a fine pincer grip. He can drink from a cup (*right*).

Vision

Babies can see at birth. We know this, because a baby will follow a very big object with his eyes, when it is held in front of him and moved from side to side. Also, if you hold a baby so that a window is to one side of the face, he will usually turn his eyes towards the light. However, newborn babies do not always do this so it is very difficult to test their vision properly.

You can be certain that a baby can see when he responds to your smile when you are not holding him or making any encouraging sounds. An even better test is to flash a bright light into his eyes – for example a torch – at about four or five weeks, while watching to see if he blinks. If, at two or three months, you think your baby cannot see at all, you should report this to the doctor, so that he can reassure you by examining the baby. If he is in doubt he can arrange for a special test and for the baby to be examined by an ophthalmologist (an eye-doctor).

Unfortunately, the young baby can only be examined to see if he has vision or not. Detailed examination to see if he is short or long sighted, and might need glasses, will have to wait until later. There are now excellent vision tests which are used for examining children at three years of age (see page 199).

Hearing

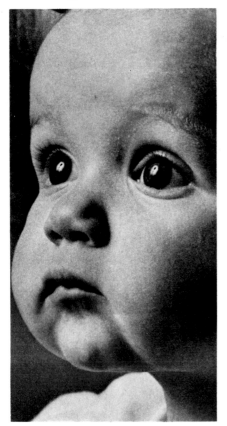

At about eight months, hearing can be tested quite successfully.

A newborn baby can hear, but it is very difficult to test this. It is hoped that some new method of testing hearing in the very young will be developed soon, but at the moment you will have to watch his response to sound as he gets older.

After the first few weeks, a baby will jump or start when a sudden loud noise is made near him. At three to four months, you should be able to convince yourself that he can hear such a noise. If you do not notice any response at all, you should talk to a doctor. A response does not mean that the baby can hear perfectly; further tests are needed later for that.

Tests. One of the most useful tests can be made at about eight months. You, or the doctor, can make a *very* faint noise at one side of the baby's head and he should turn his head towards it. The tester in the clinic will often use a variety of sounds such as a very faint rustling of paper, a spoon rubbing gently on the edge of a cup, or a few words spoken very softly. Towards the end of the first year this test is more difficult as the baby rapidly becomes bored with these noises and may obstinately refuse to turn towards the sounds. Using such a test, one can make certain that the baby has hearing in both ears. It is important that it should be carried out in any baby that has a particular risk of deafness, such as a family history of hereditary deafness, or severe jaundice at birth. Of course, the real test of hearing is whether a baby responds to the human voice. You can make certain of this when he or she produces clear words in imitation of yours. He can only say such words if he has heard them first.

Speech

True speech should not include words such as 'da-da', 'ma-ma' and 'ba-ba' which are used indiscriminately by babies and are present in almost every language. Words only count as real speech when they are used for definite objects and have a definite meaning. A baby usually produces two or three clear words over the same period of time as he learns to walk. Thus about 25 per cent of babies say some words at $11\frac{1}{2}$ months, the average is $12\frac{1}{2}$ months, and 90 per cent have some words by 18 months, certainly by their second birthdays.

Checks on development and growth at the Family Health Centre

Some family doctors run their own developmental clinics. If yours does not, you can always find a Child [Family] Health Centre near you, where there will be a regular clinic. The health visitor who visits you soon after the birth will be able to tell you where it is. The special check-ups they arrange are very important indeed and should not be missed. Often, you will be able to arrange for a check-up to be done at the same time as the baby has a vaccination. In the early days, you will probably want to see the health visitor frequently to be certain that the baby is gaining weight and getting off to a good start.

The best times for the check-up are not yet certain. They vary from area to area and a lot of work is being done to discover the most effective times for examining a baby. In some places you may find your baby has been put on an 'at risk' register. This merely means that you or the baby had some problem during the pregnancy or the newborn period; a careful eye must therefore be kept on the baby and special examinations arranged. Do not be concerned if your baby is on one of these registers; it does not mean that he is abnormal, but merely that he needs special attention. It is reassuring to know that the doctors are watching your baby carefully to pick out any problems he might have.

A plan of examinations might be something like this:

Six weeks. At about this age or at the first visit to the clinic, a full examination of the baby is made. This was already done when the baby was born, but a further examination is an important check and safeguard. It is particularly important for the doctor to examine the baby's heart, because murmurs which could indicate an abnormality may not be present during the first week or two of life and only appear later.

Seven to eight months. The next important examination could take place at about this age, when simple hearing tests can be made to see if the baby reacts to very soft sounds. The doctor can see if he is making normal developmental progress.

14 to 15 months. A third examination might be made now when one would expect the baby to be walking and saying a few clear words.

Three years. Vision can be tested and by this time a child should be speaking sensibly, so a proper check on his hearing can be made.

Five years. All children have a full medical check-up with special hearing and vision tests at five. (See page 199.)

Please remember that this is only one of several possible schemes; there may be a different one in your area. The important thing is to take your baby along for checks when the clinic thinks it necessary. Regular checks will ease your mind and will make certain that a problem is found as soon as possible.

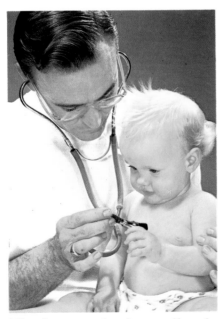

The doctor at the clinic will make sure that a baby is not frightened during his check-up.

Advances in preventive medicine in the past 50 years means that parents can protect their babies from diseases which have previously killed or crippled countless children. It is very important to follow the schedule of vaccination and immunization recommended for your child by your doctor.

Vaccination & immunization

Protecting your child

It is far better to prevent an illness than to treat it. Several of the very serious diseases of childhood, such as poliomyelitis which used to kill or cripple many people, have now almost disappeared because of immunization.

Immunity is the resistance of the body against germs or their poisons (toxins). When a germ enters the body, special substances called antibodies are produced to fight off the infection and to prevent future infections with the same germ. In the same way, antibodies are produced against toxins.

At birth, babies derive a lot of immunity from their mothers, but this gradually wears off during the first few months. It is because of this congenital immunity that measles is very rare in the first six months of life. This early immunity may prevent artificial immunization from evolving properly; the first doses are usually given towards six months when the natural immunity has begun to wear off.

The germs which produce the various diseases are very different, so a different immunization has to be given for each one.

Vaccination

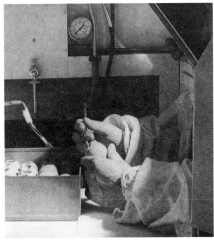

The word 'vaccination' comes from vaccinia, or cow-pox, which was used by Edward Jenner more than 150 years ago to protect a boy against small-pox. He had noticed that milk-maids, who often developed cow-pox on their hands after contact with infected cows, did not develop small-pox which was then very prevalent. The word is now also used for the protection given by any weakened or killed germ.

For many vaccinations it is common to use a live germ, (a bacterium or a virus), which is very like the germ that causes the disease, but is much weaker. Examples of this are vaccinia for small-pox, live poliomyelitis vaccine, rubella vaccine and BCG for tuberculosis. Sometimes killed germs are injected to make the body produce antibodies in just the same way; an example is the killed bacteria used against whooping-cough.

Immunization

Live vaccines are produced in strictly controlled laboratory conditions to avoid contamination. Here live influenza vaccine is being developed in the World Health Organization Laboratories.

The word 'immunization' is used when chemical substances are injected to counter-act the effect of toxins. Examples of illnesses produced by toxins are diphtheria and tetanus (also called 'lock-jaw'); the illness can be prevented by giving the toxin in an altered form, so that it is no longer active.

Vaccination and immunization have been steadily refined over the years; they are now very safe and you should take advantage of them for the future health of your child. It is, of course, true that they have a slight risk, and this is why you will sometimes hear arguments against them. It is important to balance the tiny risk from the immunization against the risk of getting the disease. In some cases, the disease has become rare and it is no longer necessary to give the vaccination to every child routinely. This has happened with small-pox in Britain.

Here are some of the diseases which can be prevented:

Diphtheria

This serious illness has now almost disappeared from Britain. In Australia cases are still seen in children who have not been immunized. In the past, it killed many children by a serious infection of the throat; a tough membrane was formed in the throat and obstructed breathing.

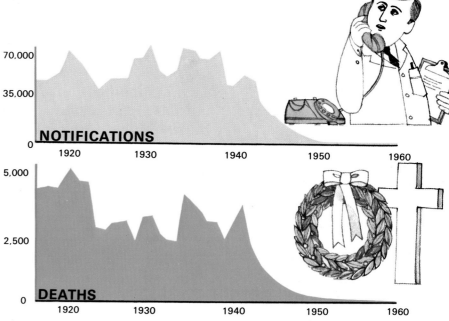

Graphs showing the decline in the number of cases of diphtheria notified, and the number of deaths from the disease, in England and Wales during this century. In the early 1940s a large-scale campaign for immunization was started, and the spectacular success of this is readily seen. Despite the small number of cases seen today, there is still a need to continue immunization.

The germs causing the disease produce a toxin which affects the action of the heart. This was another cause of death during the illness. Complete protection can be given by immunization with an altered toxin from diphtheria; this produces antibodies against the effects of the disease. The use of this immunization in the last thirty or forty years is one of the great success stories of preventive medicine. The injection is given with those against tetanus and whooping cough, three times in the first year of life.

Tetanus

This disease occurs with a dirty wound, especially one contaminated by soil or manure. A germ in the wound produces a toxin which can cause spasms of muscles. The illness is very severe and often leads to death as a result of generalized spasms. Although an injection can be given to a patient when he has had a cut, it is much better to prevent the illness by using tetanus immunization in childhood. It is given with diphtheria immunization in the first year, at school entry and leaving.

Whooping cough (pertussis)

This serious illness causes severe spasms of coughing followed by vomiting. After a spasm of coughing, a sudden breath in may give the characteristic whoop. It causes a very severe, sometimes fatal, illness in babies under a year of age; the immunization is therefore only given during the first year, with tetanus and diphtheria injections.

Whooping cough is a rare disease but it has become more common recently. This is probably because many parents have not had their children innoculated against it. We now think that there is a very slight risk of a severe reaction: however a reaction is more likely to happen in a baby who has had fits or who was seriously ill when a newborn baby. This immunization should not be given if the baby has a fever or is unwell, and you should be careful to report any reaction that occurs after a dose of the vaccine. If the baby should develop a very red arm for several days after the injection or should have a general reaction such as a convulsion or a fever, the doctor will probably not give whooping cough vaccine again.

Should you decide that you do not want your baby to have

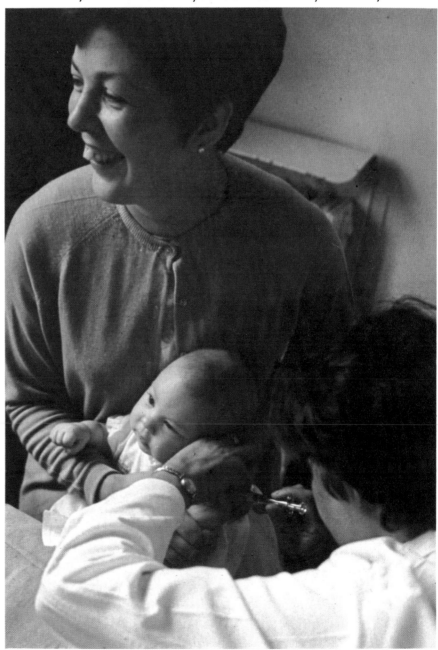

Diphtheria, tetanus and whooping cough (pertussis) are given together in three injections at intervals during the first year of life. The first dose is sometimes given as young as three months, but is usually more effective at about six months. The baby's natural immunity, which is transmitted to him from his mother before birth, may prevent the vaccine 'taking' before then.

whooping cough vaccine or if there is a medical reason for not giving it, do make certain that the baby still has the rest of his immunizations. These can still be given, without whooping cough, and are very safe and important.

Poliomyelitis

This disease is still common in many parts of the world, but has now almost disappeared from Britain and Australia. The virus causes meningitis and a severe paralysis, which is usually permanent. Several vaccines have been produced, but the usual one is a live virus given by mouth; three drops can be given quite simply by spoon or on a lump of sugar. In Britain it is usually given at the same time as the other vaccinations during the first year of life. [In Australia it is usually given in 3 doses commencing at 2 months of age]; further doses can be given at school entry and leaving. It is a safe vaccine and is very important. If you have never been vaccinated against polio, the doctor will give you a dose of the same vaccine that he gives to the baby.

If a case of poliomyelitis should occur in your neighbourhood or if your child is going abroad to a place where poliomyelitis is common, such as Africa and the Indian sub-continent, it would always be wise to give an extra dose of oral polio vaccine.

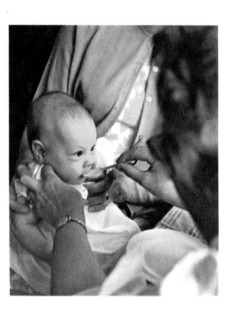

Poliomyelitis vaccine is administered orally. The vaccine is in liquid form; it is given on a spoon to the young baby, an older child might have it on a lump of sugar.

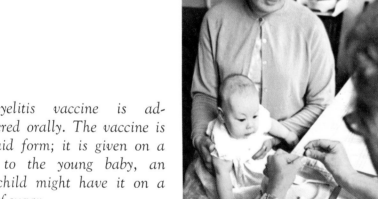

Measles

This disease is controlled by another live vaccine. It is usually given by injection early in the second year. Measles was a very common disease, so almost every baby is protected against it by antibodies transferred from his mother during pregnancy. Many antibodies cross the placenta and so give the baby a stock of resistance to infection for several months – usually the first six months of life. Measles vaccine should not be given to a baby before nine months of age; it will not be effective, because of these antibodies. It is best to leave it till after 15 months.

Sometimes measles vaccination is followed by a fever and a slight rash after a week. These reactions appear to be less common now than when the vaccine was first introduced.

Some children who have serious illnesses should not be given measles vaccine – your doctor will be able to advise you about this. He will probably be cautious in giving it to any child who has had convulsions or is definitely allergic to eggs.

Rubella

This is a very mild illness except during the first three months of pregnancy; the fetus may then be severely damaged by the virus (see page 15). For this reason there is now a campaign to vaccinate girls in their early teens before they get to child-bearing age. It can also be given to a woman immediately after she has had a baby, if she has not had the illness in the past. It should never be given during pregnancy, because it is a live virus and could possibly affect the development of the fetus.
In some countries, like the USA, it is given to all children in the second year of life. A vaccine containing mumps and measles vaccine [MMR] is sometimes used, but not in Britain.

Tuberculosis

This illness is caused by a bacterium and a weak variety of this, known as BCG, is given into the skin as a tiny injection. This is usually done over one of the shoulder blades or on the arm.

This vaccination is often given to a newborn baby where there is a history of tuberculosis infection in a close relative. The injection produces a tiny red lump in the skin and occasionally a little ulcer. The lump appears within one or two weeks and may take quite a while to disappear. In some countries BCG is given to every newborn baby in the first week of life; in Britain and Australia it is only given to selected patients.

At the moment, BCG is given to school children at the age of ten to thirteen years if they did not have it in infancy. The child is usually tested to see if he has ever had tuberculosis. This test

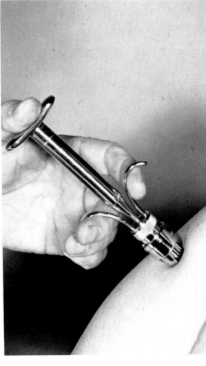

Before BCG is given for tuberculosis, a skin test is made (right) to see if the child has ever contracted the disease. A positive reaction (far right) shows that the child is tuberculin or 'Mantoux' positive and already has immunity to the disease. If there is no reaction, BCG is given.

is done by injecting a substance called tuberculin into the skin. A red lump at the site of the injection, which appears within two days and then fades over about a week, is an indication that infection has occurred sometime in the past. Someone who has this positive reaction to the test is called tuberculin positive or 'Mantoux' positive. If the person is tuberculin negative, he is given BCG which gives him the necessary protection.

You may find that the tuberculin test is made on your child if he has been in contact with tuberculosis or has any worrying illness. When the test is positive in childhood, a course of drugs to prevent tuberculosis is often given. When BCG has been given the test may be positive; for this reason you must always be certain whether your child has had BCG or not; tell the doctor about it, if he is doing a tuberculin test.

Schedule of vaccinations and immunizations in childhood

Opposite are common schemes used at present in most parts of Britain and Australia. Do not forget that the schemes are changed, from time to time, as new vaccines become available and older ones are no longer necessary. For instance, smallpox vaccination used to be routine at 18 months of age, but is now given only when there are special circumstances.

There are several other vaccinations and immunizations which may be used for your baby.

Influenza

This virus illness, which causes a fever and aching of the limbs, often occurs in the winter. The virus of one year is quite different to that of another, so a special vaccine has to be prepared in the year in question. It is usually given in the late autumn.

Some children with a weak heart or chest can become very ill with influenza; your doctor will recommend the injection if he feels it is necessary. Your baby should not have it if you know that he is allergic to eggs.

Smallpox

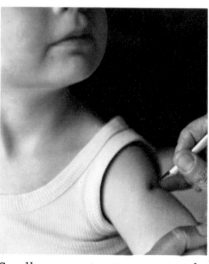

Smallpox vaccination is given by pricking the vaccine gently into the skin.

This disease is now very rare; we hope that it has now disappeared from most of the world. It is of course still very common in some parts, such as India, but is luckily decreasing from year to year. Because it does not occur now, vaccination is no longer recommended for babies as a routine at 18 months. However, the first vaccination against smallpox is safer in childhood than later in life. If you are certain that your baby will go to an area where smallpox might occur, you should explain this to your doctor who can give the vaccination during the second year of life. When you travel to some countries outside Europe, smallpox vaccination is essential and you have to produce a special international certificate to prove that it has been given. It is not essential, under international regulations, to give it to a baby under one year of age, but many countries still require it. It is always wise to check carefully before you go abroad with the baby.

Some people should never be given smallpox vaccination, because they have certain illnesses. Your doctor will be able to

A Vaccine Schedule for Britain

Age	Vaccine	Interval	Notes
During the first year of life	Diphtheria/tetanus/pertussis and oral polio (1st dose)		Pertussis is another name for whooping cough. The first dose for these vaccines is given at about 3 months.
	Diphtheria/tetanus/pertussis and oral polio (2nd dose)	After about 6-8 weeks	
	Diphtheria/tetanus/pertussis and oral polio (3rd dose)	After an interval of about 4-6 months	
During the second year of life	Measles vaccine	Not less than 3 weeks after the last vaccination	Given after 15 months.
At 5 years of age or school entry	Diphtheria/tetanus/oral polio vaccine		Sometimes given earlier to children going to nurseries or nursery schools.
Between 10 and 13 years of age	BCG vaccine		For tuberculin negative children. Now sometimes given at 5 years or at birth for children with a greater risk of tuberculosis.
All girls aged 10 to 13 years	Rubella vaccine	At least 3 weeks between BCG and this vaccination	In some countries this is given during the second year of life.
At 15 to 19 years of age or on leaving school	Polio vaccine and tetanus		

A Vaccine Schedule for Australia

Age	Vaccine	Interval	Notes
During the first year of life	Diphtheria/tetanus/pertussis (1st dose)		Pertussis is another name for whooping cough. Immunization should commence at 8 to 12 weeks of age.
	Diphtheria/tetanus/pertussis (2nd dose)	After about 6-8 weeks	
	Diphtheria/tetanus/pertussis (3rd dose)	After an interval of about 6 to 8 weeks	
	Oral polio (1st dose)		Commencing at 2 months.
	Oral polio (2nd dose)	After about 6-8 weeks	
	Oral polio (3rd dose)	After about 6-8 weeks	
During the second year of life	Measles vaccine	Not less than 3 weeks after the last vaccination	Not given before 12 months old, usually at 15-18 months of age.
At 5 years of age or school entry	Diphtheria/tetanus/oral polio vaccine		Often given earlier, either at 18 months or to children going to nurseries or nursery schools. Tetanus toxoid should be given after any significant laceration or burn. A 'booster' dose is recommended every 10 years.
All girls aged 12 to 14 years	Rubella vaccine		A Rubella HI test is recommended to confirm immunity.
At 15 to 19 years of age or on leaving school	Polio vaccine and tetanus		

advise you about this. Eczema is a common reason for not giving it as the smallpox infection can spread to all parts of the rash. If you or one of the children suffer from eczema, you should keep away from anyone who has recently been vaccinated. The vaccination must never be given in pregnancy.

The infection of vaccinia is introduced by pricking the vaccine gently into the skin. Soon some itching occurs, followed by a blister after about three days; it yellows and dries into a scab after about a week, healing after about two weeks.

Travelling abroad

A map to illustrate the spread of different diseases throughout the world, and how some predominate in certain parts, either as recurring epidemics, or where, unfortunately, difficult environment and lack of medical facilities cause them to be a permanent menace. Modern air transport allows people to move around the world rapidly, sometimes carrying with them the organisms of disease. In 1957 the so-called 'Asian flu' spread to every country from China.

Yellow fever, cholera and smallpox. Injections against these diseases may all be necessary if you have to travel outside Australia or to any place where one of them occurs. Your travel agent will be able to explain which of these injections is necessary; your doctor or the airline can arrange for them to be given. If you have any doubts, ring the embassy or high commission of the country you are visiting, to find out what the regulations are; they vary from time to time, depending on whether or not there is an outbreak of disease. Do please remember to allow plenty of time before going abroad; very often the injections cannot be given together and have to be spaced over several weeks.

Typhoid is another disease for which vaccination is not obligatory but very sensible if you are going to a tropical country.

Poliomyelitis is common in many parts of the world so an extra dose of oral polio vaccine is a very good idea.

Infectious hepatitis is a disease of the liver which occurs commonly in some parts of the tropics and your doctor may wish to give the baby an injection of gamma-globulin; this will protect him against the disease for up to six months.

Malaria. Do not forget that is still a very common disease. It is carried by mosquitoes, which pass it on when they bite. If you know you are taking the baby to a malarial area, it is very

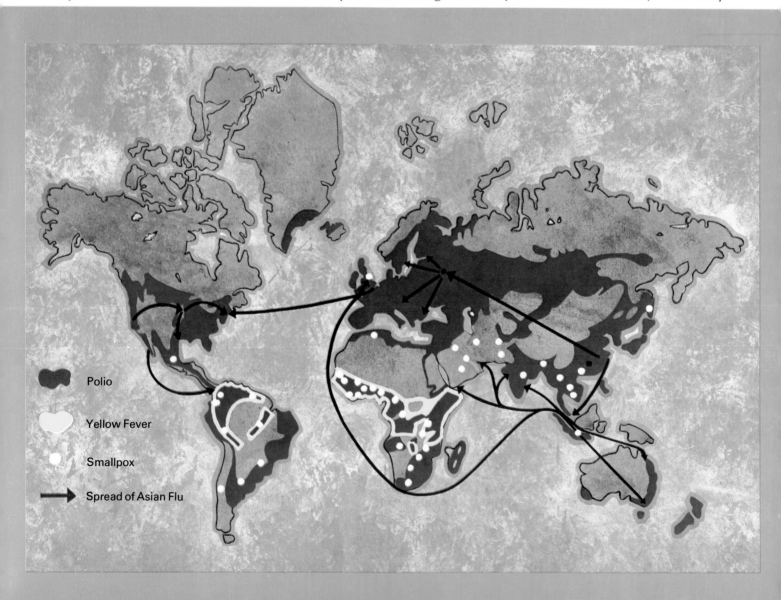

Polio

Yellow Fever

Smallpox

Spread of Asian Flu

Areas in which malaria
transmission occurs
or might occur

Areas in consolidation phase

Areas in which malaria has
disappeared, been eradicated,
or never existed

This map shows the general areas of the world where malaria is endemic, is being controlled and has been eradicated or never existed.

important that you should have drugs to prevent the disease; if you give these drugs regularly, you will be able to prevent malaria even if the baby is bitten by an infected mosquito. Of course, there are other ways of keeping mosquitoes away; for instance, by putting the baby under a mosquito net at night. If you have any doubts about the possibility of malaria in the place you are going to, consult your family doctor who will be able to give you the drugs to prevent the disease.

Gastro-enteritis is a particular problem common in hot countries. You must therefore be double careful about sterilizing bottles before feeding the baby. Be careful never to contaminate his food or allow it to stand around in a hot place, since the germs can grow very quickly; and keep your hands scrupulously clean.

In tropical areas, any damp, swampy locale – especially where water is still and undisturbed – will be a breeding ground for malaria-carrying mosquitoes.

Sue
— 5yrs

Peter
4yrs —

2yrs —
Jane

— 3yrs
John

Transition from baby to child

The early days of a baby's life are interesting, because you can see what his personality is like and how it starts to develop. But the second and third years are even better. Your child will start to communicate with you in words and actions. Each day he will show you more complicated things that he is able to do.

Growth in the second and third years

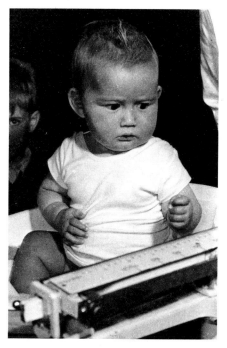

Regular weighing is a good check on growth, but it should be compared to length or height as well.

You can follow his growth and weight gain on the charts we have printed in this book (see page 138). Use them in the same way as you did when he was quite small.

Length or height. You can measure his length by stretching him out on a table, with a tape measure alongside. You will probably need your husband's help to prevent wriggling, which can make the whole thing difficult and inaccurate. After two years or so, you will find it easier to measure his height than his length. Stand your child against a wall, with his heels touching the skirting. Ask him to draw himself up to full height, but make sure his heels are still on the ground. You can then make a mark on the wall, with a pencil, level with the top of his head. It is then easy to measure his height with a tape-measure, and to watch his growth by measuring him regularly.

Weight. Some young children hate being weighed. Never allow them to get very upset and hysterical when they are put on the scales at the clinic. An easy trick is to allow yourself to be weighed on adult scales; you can then be reweighed holding your child. The difference between the two results is his weight. Always do your best to prevent him becoming frightened at the doctor's, or you may have much more trouble at future, more urgent visits.

If you look at the charts you will see that during this period a child grows slower than in his first year, and much slower than in the first few months. Using the chart you can allow for this quite naturally. Some people are concerned that their babies do not grow so fast after the first birthday, but the charts show that this is quite normal.

Development of speech

You will remember that a baby starts by making sounds, which are meaningless, usually of the 'mama' or 'dada' variety. Real words begin at about nine months and are almost always present by twenty months.

Sentences. The next step is sentences. It is important to realize that this means several words strung together to make up a coherent idea. Sometimes words may be compressed together,

Above: Once a small child begins to be able to express himself in words, you will probably find yourself bombarded with questions. Below: By about 18 months most children are getting to their feet.

as in 'it's'. This should count as a single word and not more. Children may start making sentences at about sixteen months. The average is two years, but the range is astonishingly long; it is around three before *all* normal children make sentences.

Mis-pronunciation. When children start to speak they often mis-pronounce words. You will probably notice that your child begins by jabbering away in a language of his own. Sometimes you will be the only person able to understand it and he may get cross with some adults who look at him in blank amazement when he speaks to them. He may find difficulty in pronouncing certain words and consonants; for instance, he may slur or lisp his words. Do not be concerned about difficulties in pronouncing parts of a word, so long as your child is making progress and learning new words rapidly. Children may also have a temporary tendency to speak with hesitations or slight stammering. It is very important that you should treat this naturally when it occurs: it is probably unwise to correct him continually for mistakes in speech. I am glad to hear that stammering seems to be less common nowadays; we do not know why it is rarer, but it may be the result of less pressure on children to speak early and 'correctly'.

You will obviously be anxious to get your child to speak as soon as possible. I suppose that the easiest way for a child to learn is by copying those around him. This means that your encouragement, by just talking to the child, is what he needs, but it is not always helpful to talk to him in his own 'baby language'. From a very early age, you can show a child objects and name them enthusiastically. At first, it does not matter at all whether he repeats the name; he will gradually learn to associate objects with words.

Key points in speech development

Apart from learning to say sentences, your baby will also learn some very important words.

Parts of the body. For instance, you may be able to teach him the names of different parts of his body. Half of normal children are doing this by 17 months of age and only ten per cent are unable to name one part of their body by 23 months. Most families teach very obvious parts of the body to begin with – things such as the nose, eyes, mouth and toes.

Pictures and commands. By two and a half, 90 per cent of children can name simple pictures in a book and are able to follow simple commands – they will get things like cups or spoons when asked.

Plurals and names. In the third year, some important parts of language appear. By two and a half, 50 per cent of children can use the plural of a word and by three, 50 per cent can give their first and last name clearly. By four, 90 per cent know their names.

Delayed speech

If you are concerned that your baby's speech is seriously delayed, that is, he has not learned to say words by about 20 months or is not making sentences after his third birthday, you should speak to your family doctor about it. There are many causes for this, but he will probably want to arrange for a hearing test, to make certain that there is no deafness to sounds in the range of the human voice. For instance, some people are unable to hear very high tones and this may distort the sounds they hear, so making it difficult for them to learn to speak.

You might find that a speech therapist would be able to give you useful advice and to assess your child's speech, if you are concerned that something is seriously wrong. Your doctor will be able to advise if this is necessary. Most speech problems are in fact normal or can be dealt with quite simply.

On the move

You will remember that all normal children are walking by the middle of the second year, unless they have a special method of getting around. After they have learnt to walk, they use this skill to explore the world and find out where things are. This may be trying, as a toddler will be investigating everything.

Up and down stairs

There are many ways in which he may get up and down stairs. He usually starts by crawling upstairs, then learns to walk up holding a banister. Coming down is more difficult; he will probably start by climbing down backwards and it may be some while before he can risk walking down, even with help. He may be able to steady himself against the wall while cautiously taking steps. 50 per cent of children can walk up steps while holding something at 17 months; 90 per cent of them can do it by 22 months.

Walking downstairs is a skill which requires concentration to start with.

182

Right: Ball games begin to be popular at a very early age. There is evidence that these ancient toys have been kicked or thrown by children for thousands of years. Above: Leaping and jumping are fun for an energetic three-year-old.

Ball games

Ball games become very popular by 20 months, when 50 per cent of children can kick a ball forward or throw it well up in to the air. Most children learn to kick a ball reasonably early and nearly all do it by the age of two, but throwing a ball up may be very difficult for some and ten per cent of children still can not do it at three years of age.

Balancing and jumping

During the third year of life, children become much steadier on their feet. For instance, they learn to balance on one foot alone; I find this a very useful test and often ask a child to stand on one foot by copying me while I do it. Most children can manage this for one second during the second year although two to five per cent of them are still not able to do it at three years of age. To balance on one foot for a longer time is only possible a year or so later. Jumping is another enjoyable pastime and most children can do this by the time they are three years old. It is easier for them to jump with their feet close together, so that a jump with the feet spread apart is only possible a little later on. Many agile three-year-olds enjoy jumping and leaping just for the sake of it.

Building with bricks

All children seem to enjoy building with bricks. If painted, make sure it is non-toxic.

More toys for toddlers

A climbing frame is a lasting investment for a family with a garden.

It is great fun to watch children building things with bricks. You can often learn a lot about the way they use their hands and how dexterous or wobbly they are. Around one year, they usually have no inclination to build at all, although they may bang bricks together and can pick up very fine objects in a neat pincer grip. During the first three years, they become increasingly adept at building towers; by 20 months, 50 per cent can build a tower of four bricks, and 90 per cent can by two and a half years. If possible, watch your child doing this with fairly small bricks – those with a side of about 2.5cm (1in) are probably the best. A tower of eight bricks is quite a lot more difficult, although tremendous fun to do. Many can still not do this when they are three. One of the great pleasures of building things is to knock them all down again. At about ten months to a year, many children start a phase when they throw everything to the ground and watch, with great pleasure, while adults pick them up. Of course, if you give the toy back to them it will be thrown down again. As the child gets older, he can use more complicated toys and bricks are used to build other things than towers. Over 50 per cent of children can imitate a bridge made with three bricks by the time they are three years old.

At this stage everything is fascinating to a toddler. The contents of the kitchen cupboard – saucepans, spatulas, wooden spoons, dustpan and brush – all go down well, as they are unbreakable and can be banged very satisfactorily. But other things will be needed as well. Hoops which fit over pegs, shapes to post into

Trains to push, dolls to dress and put to bed, sturdy trucks to ride: all these are the sort of toys that small children enjoy playing with.

special holes, jigsaws with large wooden pieces, all help the child's development as well as being fun to play with. Cars, trains and lorries or any wheeled toy which can be pulled or pushed along are always popular with boys and girls alike, and a simple trolley to push along can give a toddler confidence when he is learning to walk.

Buy toys which are built to last – it is worth paying a little more for well-made wooden, steel or strong plastic toys rather than having to comfort the disappointed owner of a broken toy. Make sure they have no sharp edges or points which could break off, and check that the paint is non-toxic. Many kinds of constructional toys are available apart from conventional wooden bricks, often involving screwing or hammering pieces into place. 'Dressing up', dolls and tea sets are enjoyed by both

Drawing

boys and girls, and all children enjoy playing with a simple dough made from flour, water and salt. If you are lucky enough to have a garden try and construct a small sandpit like a simple, low-sided wooden box – it will occupy a child for hours on a fine day. Keep it covered with a board when not in use to protect it from rain and from cats! If you can afford it, a small climbing frame or slide is a particularly good investment, and you or your husband may be able to construct one yourself. You will probably find that even a very simple climbing frame will be popular with most children up to seven or eight years.

Playing with water is as popular as sand, though you should not leave a small child alone even in the bath (see page 232). A bowl of water in the garden or a small paddling pool for fine days gives a lot of pleasure, and indoors a child will wash up endlessly (see page 184) – but make sure the things are all unbreakable. Bathtime is never a chore if there are boats, ducks, cups or empty plastic bottles to play with.

Before the age of two, most children will not draw definite shapes but scribble with a pencil on a piece of paper. However, by two years of age, 50 per cent of children can imitate a line. The next object they can copy is a circle; 50 per cent of children can do this at two and a half and 90 per cent by three and a half. Be careful that the child does not see you make a circle. You should hide your pencil behind your hand while you are drawing the circle and then ask him to copy it. If he watches you drawing it is an easier test. I was amused the last time I asked a child to do this, because he used his hand to hide his drawing, in exact imitation of me. Other tests like copying a cross or drawing a man are only possible later.

Large wax crayons are probably best for drawing to start with: they don't break if pressure is put on them, they are easy to hold and usually come in a variety of colours.

Painting

Children enjoy expressing themselves in drawing and painting even if they cannot make recognizable shapes. A good supply of wax crayons and a few pots of brightly coloured powder paint, which you can mix up yourself, will keep any two to three year old occupied happily. You will probably find that children of this age will use their hands – and even feet – as much as a paint brush, as they enjoy the feel of paint as much as the look. Finger-painting requires some patience but children enjoy it tremendously: mix up a small amount of ordinary wallpaper glue and pour some on to a table or tray with a plastic laminate surface. Add a sprinkling of dry powder paint and let the child spread the mixture out over the surface with his or her fingers and palms. This is often enough to satisfy them, but slightly older children can make a print by pressing a piece of paper face down on to the patterns they make with the paint and glue mixture. Be prepared for some mess of course, with some protective covering for both the floor and the children: pvc or rubber aprons are best as they can simply be sponged clean. While a small child is painting or drawing remember to tell him the names of the colours so that he begins to learn the difference. You can start doing this as soon as he is beginning to talk, though it will be quite a while before he will get it straight. Only about 50 per cent of children can recognize colours by three years.

Watching television

Children like to watch television, and soon find favourite programmes which they hate to miss.

Television is a very useful way of introducing children to the world outside their homes. In fact most children enjoy it so much that one of the commonest forms of punishment is to prevent a child from watching a favourite programme. Most programmes during the day and early evening are perfectly suitable for children to watch – remember that TV programme planners are very conscious of the fact that they have a large juvenile audience at these times. There is a line of thinking that suggests it is bad for children to be subjected to violence on television; but others say that children should be shown the violence that exists in society. However, only you can decide what you feel is best for your child.

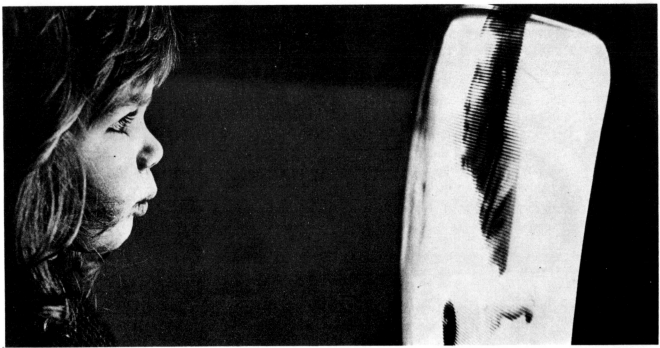

Learning to use a cup and spoon

As a baby, he was dependent on you to give him a bottle and could only cry if he wanted food. He steadily becomes more independent from six months of age; between six and nine months, he may start to put a biscuit to his mouth. During this period also he will drink from a cup, rather than a bottle, when you hold it for him. At first, he may put up his hands to support the bottle or touch the cup when you are feeding him, but very soon after this learns to hold it himself, in order to drink without any help. The average age for this is about a year, but babies can sometimes do it unaided at nine months or may take as long as twenty-one months. During his second year, he will start to use a spoon; at first you will probably find that he makes an awful mess and may even throw food around. A

Using a spoon for the first time may be a hit-and-miss affair, but even so, many babies enjoy the independence of feeding themselves.

plastic sheet, on the floor underneath his chair, may help prevent a lot of mess. The earliest age for using a spoon is about a year but one in ten children still have to be fed at two years. At two most children can ask for food or drink when they want it, and they start to use a fork during the third year. A knife is more difficult to use, so you must expect that to come later.

When children feed themselves

The age at which children learn to feed themselves does vary from one country to another. In some places it is common for children to be fed by adults until the age of two or more; in those places, it is therefore quite normal for a baby to allow everything to be put into his mouth with a spoon. However, if you have the chance, watch a Chinese child learning to eat. Even a three year old can be amazingly clever with chopsticks.

By about two years of age, a small child's use of a spoon becomes really skilful.

Dressing your baby

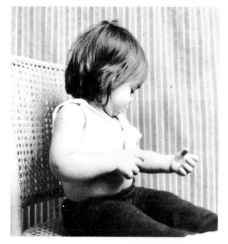

A baby has to be dressed and undressed by you. Soon after the first birthday, he will probably hold up his arms so that you can put it through a sleeve. He will learn to take clothes off earlier than putting them on; this may start with coats or shoes soon after his first birthday and all children can remove them by two years. Hats, socks and gloves are easier, so they may take those off even earlier.

Do not expect them to put on clothes until about 20 months, there are still some who cannot manage at three. The easiest to put on are underpants, socks or shoes. Buttons are difficult, so children do not manage them until about two and a half and many still have difficulty when they are four. You will have to help your child to dress until he is at least three years old; some will need your help even at five.

Top: A small child's attempts at dressing himself are often more well-meaning than effective. Above and right: Bright, hard-wearing dungarees and smocks are practical as well as attractive. It is a good idea to use machine-washable materials.

Clothes for the under-threes

Clothes for the under-threes are very much a matter of personal taste, but there are a few things worth bearing in mind. Small children become grubby very easily so it is practical for them to wear clothes made from machine-washable material. It should, of course, also be non-inflammable, especially for night-clothes. Long trousers or dungarees are very useful, since they can help to avoid too many grazed knees. You could re-inforce the knee area with patches before your child wears them. Simple overalls or smocks can also be used to keep jumpers from getting dirty too quickly. Many children can manage zip fasteners quite early – in any case for your own convenience it is a good idea to avoid having too many buttons to do up and undo. Simple, elastic waist bands for skirts and trousers save a lot of time.

Children's clothes can be expensive and are very often out-grown before they are worn out. As they do not need expert tailoring, you may be able to make them yourself, even if you do not make your own clothes. Alternatively, it can be a great saving to buy or exchange good second-hand clothes, though it is not advisable to let your child wear second-hand shoes.

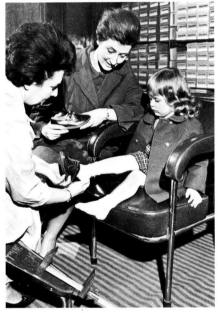

Above: Have new shoes properly fitted. Right: Slip-on or buckle shoes can be managed by a small child.

Feet and shoes

There is no need for a child to wear shoes around the house unless you have splintered wooden floors. His feet will grow and develop well without any artificial support.

In any case, he will not need shoes until he starts to walk. Up to that time, you can keep his feet warm with socks, leggings or a one-piece suit.

Shoes can be made of any material; leather or rubber and canvas are quite satisfactory. Make sure that the shoes do not squeeze or cramp the feet. When they get too small, buy some new ones. Check the width as well as the length.

Learning to live with others

The first step for a baby is to realize who is a stranger and who is not. This happens shortly after six months, when the baby cries if put into a stranger's arms. After getting over the initial shyness, a baby will often learn to play a game with any adult. Favourite games around the time of the first birthday are clapping hands, waving 'bye-bye' or playing 'peep-bo'. Often, a one-year-old will repeatedly go into peals of laughter when these games are played. During the second year, he will probably get bored after a short while and has a bigger repertoire of games. However, he is unlikely to leave you easily before his second birthday; he may cling to you when strangers are around and, if he should feel unhappy or insecure for some reason, may follow you everywhere in the house. This is quite ordinary and is particularly likely to happen when he feels upset or threatened, possibly by the birth of a new baby (see page 202). It may also happen if he has been separated from you for a while, especially when the separation has been unpleasant; it might happen if he has had to go into hospital and you have not been able to stay with him.

One of the first lessons a child has to learn is that something he wants does not automatically become his. To avoid too many battles between toddlers, it's worth trying to divert the attention of both to a totally new interest.

The first time your child is confronted with other children you may find that he or she seems frightened or bewildered. She may cling to you or become upset by small things, but eventually curiosity will probably get the better of her and she will begin to play happily with her peers.

Many children attempt to do many of the ordinary household tasks, and can learn a lot at the same time. Above: Putting away the shopping combines learning the names of the different produce, and also finding their right places in the kitchen. However, don't let a child handle household cleaning items, as most of these are poisonous. Left: Using the dustpan and brush may not be very successful but it does help to develop co-ordination between hand and eye. Far left: Watering the grass may not be very useful but the flow of water is fascinating.

Helping about the house

A child's games are part of education and learning. During the second year, he will start to watch what you are doing around the house and will imitate some of your work. Of course his efforts will probably be pretty useless to you, but it may give you great amusement to watch his attempts at washing up and dusting (see page 184). Between 18 months and two and a half he may begin to help you in simple tasks: for instance, he might put his toys away when asked, help you put away shopping in the kitchen and even bring you his dirty clothes for washing!

Personal hygiene

From about two years, he can wash his own hands, but will probably need help in drying them. You can use his keenness to imitate you to teach him the simple rules of hygiene – whenever he has been to the lavatory, you could help him wash his hands, so that he learns that it is a useful thing to do and will later understand that it prevents infection. Later, at about four years, he will be able to brush his teeth by himself (see page 214).

Playing with other children

While he finds it difficult to separate himself from you, he will not be able to play very effectively with other children. For this reason, most playgroups do not accept children until two or two and a half years. First of all, a child will manage to play near you, but by himself. From about 18 months to two years on he may start to play games with other children; things like hide-and-seek or 'tag'. However, depending on his personality, he may find this difficult or might find the presence of other children frightening. Early in this part of his development you can give him support by just being around, probably chatting with other mothers, so that he knows he can find a safe place if he gets frightened. Later, you will be able to take him to the playgroup or nursery and then leave, because he no longer needs you near him the whole time.

Once children are about two and a half, and start going to playgroup or nursery, they may begin to make friends with others of their own age. If you don't have the opportunity to send them to a nursery even for a few hours a week, it is fun for small children to get together, either in your own home or in a park or playground.

Beginning to think

Children's development is so fascinating that one would often like to know what they are thinking about. It would be interesting to crawl inside a child's mind to find out what his view of the world is. By watching them, you can see how they slowly begin to differentiate between objects and people around them, to get responses from people, and to understand the difference between 'I' and 'you'.

Fantasy friends. It may be a long while before a child can accurately distinguish living and non-living things. Objects are often felt to have some magical power and most children grow up with a vivid fantasy life. For instance, children of three to five often talk to invisible people during the day. Some families have been blessed with an imaginary person who goes with them everywhere.

Transitional objects. One amusing bit of development is the favourite 'comforter' many young children have. It can take many guises, but is frequently a piece of cloth, such as a blanket; it is often something quite cuddly. It means a lot to a child and may

Any favourite toy may become a fantasy friend. For a little girl, a doll may be as real a person as her own mother.

196

Many children become attached to a particular object such as a piece of cloth or blanket, which they will carry with them everywhere and will cuddle when tired or upset. These transitional objects are very important to them.

have a name of its own. It has to go everywhere, particularly to bed, and becomes grubby and smelly. The smell can be very important; you may find that your child will become desperately upset if it is washed. Many families know what a disaster it is if one of these objects is lost. Please remember to take it with your child to hospital, if he has to go there.

These things have been called 'transitional objects'. They seem to provide comfort at the stage in development when separation from the parents is being gradually achieved.

Developmental checks

You can have your child checked in the Child [Family] Health Centre to make certain his development is continuing to be

197

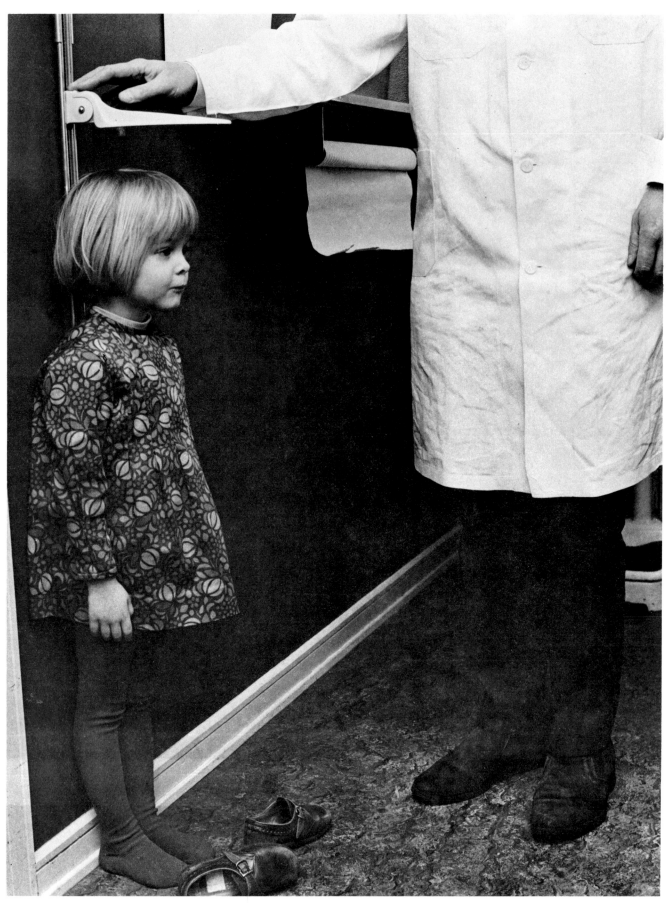

Measuring height becomes much easier after the age of two when a child can stand up properly against a wall. If you are following your child's growth with the percentile charts on pages 138-141, you will notice there is a kink in the curve which allows for the difference between length and height.

normal. The check-ups need not be so frequent as they were in the first year; a yearly one is probably satisfactory.

The doctor will be particularly concerned if your child has not begun to speak at the usual age. This is because it can be the result of deafness. As he gets older, increasingly more sophisticated tests are possible. A very skilled tester can use play to investigate a child's learning; for example, she may ask the child to pick out certain objects among many different ones displayed on a table. A test like this is important because it shows whether a child can understand speech.

From about two and a half years, audiometry can be used. In this test, pure notes are sounded at different degrees of loudness. In Britain and Australia most children are tested with an audiometer when they enter school.

There is now an excellent, accurate test of vision which can be carried out on children around three years old. Even though a child might not know the alphabet at that age, he is able to match letters held up in front of him. The tester holds up smaller and smaller letters to see if a child can match them; he has a card with five or seven letters on them and points to each of them when he sees a similar one. Again, children in Britain and Australia have visual testing when they enter school, or shortly after.

The school entry examination is one of the most important medical examinations. At the age of five, it is possible to test hearing and vision extremely well and it is also a suitable time for a general medical check-up.

Above: This vision test involves showing a child letters and seeing if he can match them to the card in front of him. Here the doctor is showing a child what to do: the test is actually done at a distance of ten feet. Below: Hearing is tested with an audiometer.

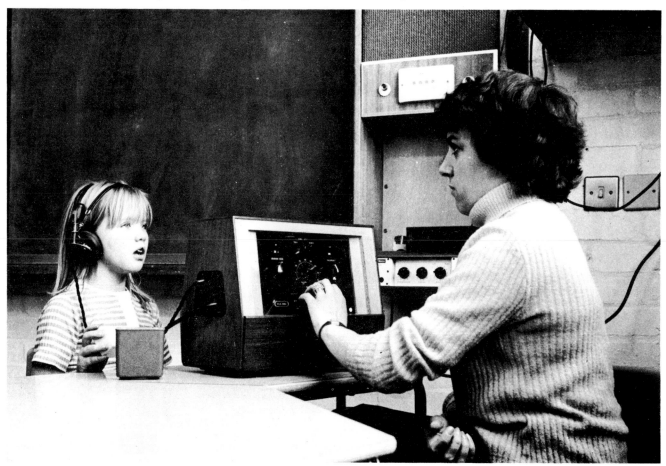

Common problems in early childhood

The growing child and the family

Growing up is a great pleasure, but it can also be a painful time for some families. Learning to live with other people is not always easy and there are bound to be clashes in any family. It is not possible to lay down any rules for the disciplining of children or the correction of behaviour. All of us, adults and children, have very different personalities, so that it will be necessary for you to find out how best to cope with your children depending on their temperaments. You are able to observe and understand them much better than anyone else.

If possible, try to avoid a clash of personalities which grows into a constant battle. Children are good at finding your weak point and can play on it, so that your nerves become really frayed. However, losing your own temper doesn't help.

Father's role

Families are not only a mother and child, but also include fathers, brothers and sisters. It is only too easy to think of your relationship with your child as being most important and to forget the need he has for his father. He usually has a different role from yours in your child's upbringing. Very often, children enjoy rougher, more exciting play with father when he comes home. A typical example is the sort of game which a father plays by lifting a child high above his head and then bringing him down again quickly. Fathers can introduce their children to the more daring aspects of life gradually. Don't leave father out.

Attention seeking

Children are often very difficult to the people they love most. This often seems extraordinary, until one recognizes that difficult behaviour is a way of getting attention. A child, who for any reason needs attention and security, may behave irritatingly. It is very difficult to regard maddening behaviour as an aspect of love, but that is often what it is. Your child would not be behaving like that if he did not care for you; he is trying to attract your attention and to say that you are important to him.

Defiant children

Frustration, anger, fear, pain: any of these can reduce a small child to tears. Luckily, his problems are usually easy to solve.

Some children become defiant very early. As they become more independent they may demonstrate this by being very difficult. It is not an easy problem to solve – the whole family will have to work together to help it. The method you use will depend on your view of discipline. You may find that your child will respond to firm control, but it is also possible that this sort of treatment might make his behaviour worse. You will have to sort this out between you. Children are usually only defiant to

Most children have moments of defiance when what they want to do doesn't coincide with someone else's wishes.

people they know very well and it is sometimes a reflection of how much they value those people. Defiance is just another way of gaining attention. If the child is being defiant about a relatively unimportant matter it is probably best to ignore him rather than have a protracted battle.

Jealousy

The young child may see any of the members of his family as rivals for love and affection. Thus, he may sometimes appear angry when you and your husband kiss. We have learnt how important these feelings of rivalry are in the emotional development of a child from the teachings of Sigmund Freud and other psychoanalysts.

He will not be the only one in the family to feel jealous, but you and your husband can talk about your feelings. A small child cannot explain what he feels and therefore needs a lot of sympathy and understanding. This is bound to happen when a new baby appears (see page 121). All you can do is to prepare him as best as possible. Children know very soon that something is changing in the family; you may therefore notice a change in your child's mood while you are pregnant. It is probably unwise to treat the arrival of a new baby as a secret from your child; you could explain to him simply that the baby is coming. Try to introduce him to the new baby within the first few days. If possible, arrange for him to come and visit you both in hospital; many maternity hospitals now have open visiting for children. It is a nice idea for the child to bring a present for his baby brother or sister; it can

A close family can help an older child accept the arrival of a new baby.

Regression

help him to feel closer to the baby, and more important in himself. However, he may very often go back a step or two in his development – this is called regression.

Any child who is under some strain, particularly during an emotional upset, is likely to go back in development. You may find he becomes very babyish. For instance, he may want a bottle again even though he gave it up a long time ago, or he may demand a cot instead of the bed he has got used to. I can remember one child who actually said 'I want to be a baby again', just after the birth of his brother. You must expect problems with bowels and bladder. Any child who feels upset is likely to wet the bed or have an accident by opening his bowels into his underpants. A child who has got quite used to a pot may need a nappy again for a short while. I think it is important not to regard this as a disastrous set-back, but as a temporary and understandable problem.

He may also become clinging again; perhaps you might manage this by giving him repeated and special cuddles during the day. It might also be nice to set aside a special part of the day for him.

203

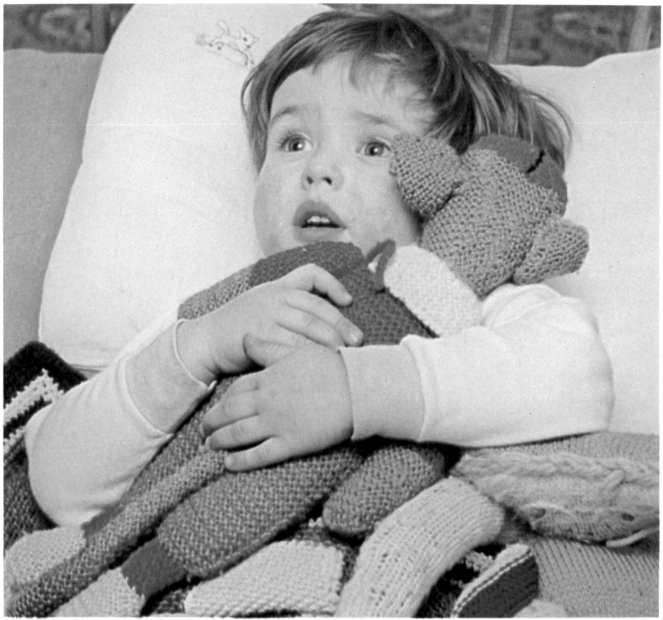

When a small child is upset, he may regress back to a cot instead of a bed or the security of a transitional object or favourite toy.

Temper tantrums

If he feels there is a time when he is the only important person and cannot be interrupted by anyone else, it may help to give him a sense of security.

Some of us are born with a bad temper and others with a good one. Of course, our early life makes a lot of difference, but personality also plays a part. It is very common for children to get very angry when they are frustrated and this anger can turn into a tantrum. A tantrum may also occur after a fright, particularly when it involves pain.

What usually happens is that the child starts to scream and cry. After this he may get himself into such a temper that he actually stops breathing. This is the 'breath-holding' or 'blue' attack that many children have. Because they stop breathing they go blue and may even become unconscious. You will notice that they either go stiff or limp. You may easily find these attacks very frightening, but after a while the child will breath again and you can comfort him. You may be worried that he is having a sort of

204

fit or convulsion; even though the whole thing is so frightening to you, do your best to watch what happens during the attack. If you are able to describe it accurately to the doctor, he will be able to reassure you that the child has not had a convulsion. The characteristic thing is that he cries or gets into a temper before the attack, whereas a convulsion usually comes out of the blue.

A temper tantrum is commonest in the toddler age group. During the attack hold the child in your arms or lie him down; make certain he is turned on one side so that he can breath easily. After the attack, comfort him, because he will be very frightened.

Some children have many such attacks. They can be very embarrassing, especially if they occur in public and you find everyone looking at you rather disapprovingly. There is no simple answer to them. You may learn what things bring them on in your child and can prevent them by avoiding difficult situations. Your embarrassment over a tantrum may cause you to hit the child; this could make the whole thing worse, so try and be patient and understanding.

You know your child best, but watch your reactions carefully so that you don't make a simple quarrel into a major tantrum. If he has a lot of attacks you should consult your doctor; he may prescribe something to help things but this is rarely necessary.

Shows of temper can occur at very awkward moments and jealousy can often set them off. Try to keep calm yourself and you will find it easier to help your child through it.

Children find it difficult to distinguish between dreams and reality. In addition, they may suddenly develop irrational fears at night about familiar objects or sounds.

Night times

All of us dream, and children are no exception. If your child has a nightmare, he may well wake screaming and shouting. When he is like this, he will be very frightened indeed. At his young age, he may not realize the difference between a dream and what really happens in the world. You will need to go to him to comfort him and get him back to sleep. If he can tell you about it, talk it over; this often helps to calm his fears. Nightmares are, of course, more likely to happen when one has had an emotional upset.

Going to bed

I am sure you will realize that all of us vary in the amount of sleep we take. No one can therefore prescribe a certain amount of sleep as necessary for your child. You will be aware of the amount of sleep he takes – this is the right amount for him. There is no need to worry if he only takes six or seven hours of sleep a night, as long as he is healthy and happy. This means that some children go to bed at six or seven in the evening and take a nap during the afternoon, whereas others do not get tired or sleepy until ten or eleven o'clock at night. In Britain, it is usual for parents to value the evening as a quiet time, so the children are put to bed early in the evening, usually after a bath. This is fine if it works, but do not force your child to take more sleep than he needs. It may be

Fathers can be particularly helpful at bedtime, taking over when most mothers feel like putting their feet up for a few minutes, perhaps before cooking the evening meal.

that he will play happily by himself on his bed, until he eventually feels tired and goes off to sleep. In some families, children stay up until they decide they want to go to bed. You and your child will have to work this out between you.

Despite this, most children can be put to bed at six or seven and will sleep happily through the night. A bedtime ritual often helps and is a pleasant time for the whole family. A common idea is to bath the child and then put him to bed. It is very nice if you can read a story then, or perhaps sing a song. Some fathers enjoy this period with their children and get home in time to put them to bed and read to them. Working mothers, too, can make this a special time to share with their children. Do what you think best, but try to make it fun and enjoyable for everyone.

Light sleepers

Some children sleep very lightly and wake many times a night. This can be very trying for you if you find your sleep is very broken. There are various things you can try; these include not giving the child an afternoon rest, so he is more sleepy at night

A light sleeper could be persuaded back to bed with a warm, milky drink.

and so sleeps soundly. A drink of hot, sweet milk before going to bed has been shown to make some people sleep more soundly. If your child has a lot of difficulty with sleeping, talk to your doctor about it. Sometimes, sedatives can be used to help him sleep. They are not a very satisfactory solution if given over a long time and we do not like to give them unless it is absolutely necessary. However, one can sometimes use them for a short period, to get a child into a rhythm of sleep. After this the medicine may be slowly withdrawn and he may sleep more happily.

Food and mealtimes

Mealtimes are another favourite battle ground between children and their parents. Since feeding a child is such an important part of mothering it is easy to be worried if your child does not take enough food. Remember that the amount of food a child takes varies like everything else. Some children grow on a tiny amount of food, while others take much more and grow at the same rate. If another mother says your child is too thin, have a look at hers because he may be too fat. The best guide is to use the charts of height and weight on pages 138 to 141. If you have any doubt about the rate that your child is gaining weight or growing, talk to the doctor or health visitor [Nursing Sister]. I see many children whose parents are very worried about the amount of food they take, but they are growing perfectly normally.

When you have prepared food for a child, it will make you very upset if he refuses it. He will often sense your annoyance immediately; so the grounds for battle are laid. By all means encourage him to eat, but do not force him to eat or make a mealtime into a long drawn out affair. Remember that the eventual aim of encouraging a child to eat is that he will grow up to enjoy food and eat well as an adult. If by arguing with him you put him off a certain type of food forever, you will not have succeeded. My mother cannot bear some food because she was forced to eat it as a child; I am sure her parents had the best intentions, but they had a very negative effect. A common theme underlies most of the methods of dealing with behaviour problems in childhood. If you constantly draw attention to the problem, it is likely to get worse. By ignoring it, if you can, it is likely to get better. We all know how difficult it is to ignore difficult behaviour in a child, but it is still probably the best approach.

Mealtimes can be times of confrontation: a child may use them as a time to assert his or her independence. It is not a good idea to insist that they should finish off everything that is put in front of them.

Cooking for the under-threes

Cooking for a small child can seem a bore especially if he is going through a stage of throwing it about rather than eating it. One way out of this is to make enough extra for the main meal of the day so that you can use some of it for your child the next day. If this involves re-heating meat you should make sure that it is cooked properly and not just warmed through (see page 92). If you have a freezer, you will probably already be aware of the advantage of making more than one meal at a time and freezing the extra for future use.

Salt. It is a good idea to be very sparing with salt when cooking for babies and young children. This is because people who take a lot of salt seem to be prone to high blood pressure later in life. Try not to let him get into the habit of adding salt to his food – which will probably mean avoiding it yourself, since he is likely to copy you.

Sugar. Sugary sweets and biscuits are another area of controversy – most children do eat more sugar than is necessary for them, but it is hard to avoid it altogether. It is a good idea to try and keep sweets just for special occasions, and make sure teeth are cleaned well afterwards. If necessary, try giving your child a piece of fruit he's particularly fond of at other times, rather than a sweet or biscuit.

Toilet training

It is usual for children to take a long while to do away with nappies. You may be startled to hear that 70 per cent of children are still not trained at all at two years of age.

You will probably have your own views on when you would like to start toilet training. Some people start very early, during the first year, but I think this is probably unwise.

Occasionally, you may get your baby to use a pot in an automatic fashion, but a number of children are upset by this persuasion and this may cause problems later on. I do see a number of children with bowel problems – particularly soiled underpants – at four or five years of age, whose toilet training was started very early, at about six months. If you can be relaxed about it, it is probably reasonable to leave any attempt at toilet training until he is nearing his second birthday. From time to time, you might like to put him on a pot after a meal. This is a good time, because the bowels tend to work after food has reached the stomach and he is most likely to pass a stool then. If he does not want to use the pot, do not force him to sit there. But it is a good opportunity to introduce him to the idea of a pot and what its function is. Gradually he will learn to make a sign to you or have a special word, when he wants to pass urine or open his bowels. As soon as he is old enough to tell you this ,you can let him use a pot.

Helpful equipment

There are some special devices which are quite useful. A lavatory seat is frightening and he will probably be much happier if you put a special children's seat over it. There are many types of pot all designed for comfort, and also small chairs under which you can put a pot.

Once children get the hang of it, they will use a pot in the most unlikely locations, but usually preferring to be in the company of someone they know and trust.

Passing stools and urine can be frightening for a child who does not understand his body yet. Do stay with him while he is sitting on the pot and put it in a warm place.

Above all, do not be in too much of a rush to get him toilet trained. There is nothing to be ashamed of, if you are still using nappies after his second birthday. Your reward will come if he has no urine or bowel problems later in life.

Bed-wetting

Bed-wetting is very common in childhood. Most doctors do not feel that any treatment is necessary before the age of five years. There are still a large number of children who are wetting the bed quite often at that age – about one in ten boys, who often take longer to be completely 'dry' than girls.

It is a terrible nuisance, however, and there are some tricks you can use to make life more pleasant. Use sheets that are easily washable, for instance those made of cotton mixed with polyester fabric, and put some absorbent material under the sheet. You may find that newspaper is very useful. Under the absorbent material you can use a rubber sheet, or a sheet of thick polythene.

Persistent bed-wetting. If bed-wetting continues into later childhood, consult your doctor about it. Very often it can be improved

211

in childhood by encouraging him. A good example of this is a star chart which the child keeps himself. He sticks stars on the chart when he has a dry night and is able to show this to his parents and the doctor. The mere act of doing this often produces an increased number of dry nights. Sometimes you may find that giving him less to drink before going to bed or by lifting him to pass urine at about 11 o'clock, or when you go to bed, will help. It seems that children who wet the bed sleep very soundly and they pass urine during the deepest part of sleep. Some effective methods of treating bed-wetting possibly work by altering the depth of sleep during certain parts of the night. Your doctor might like to try some medicine or possibly a special bell; neither of these are really necessary unless bed-wetting is still present at about seven years of age.

If your child has stopped wetting the bed and then suddenly starts again, you should consult your doctor. Of course this often happens if the child is upset, but it can also happen in certain illnesses such as an infection in the urine.

Soiling

Like bed-wetting, a small amount of soiling of the underpants is very common. A lot of children are unable to control their bowels completely and stain their underpants. Others cannot manage to clean themselves properly after opening their bowels. However, if your child passes a whole stool into his underpants, this is something you should consult your doctor about. It is not really abnormal until after the age of three or if it returns when your child has been able to control himself completely. Constant leaking of faeces in the underpants is also a problem which may need the attention of the doctor. It may result after a period of constipation during which the anus has become cracked by the passage of a large stool. The child may then hold the faeces in the rectum because it is painful to pass them; they then leak slowly causing marked staining of the underpants.

Constipation

This can usually be dealt with simply by a change of diet; fruit purée may help to loosen the motions, but an increase of bran in the diet is best. You can add bran to things like mashed potato or stewed fruit, or give it as wholemeal bread. Sometimes a simple laxative such as milk of magnesia may be needed. If it becomes a constant problem, consult your doctor.

Worms

These are very common indeed; one survey showed that one in two schoolchildren had them. Although there are several types, the commonest are called threadworms. They live inside the bowel and you can see them as tiny white 'threads' in a stool. The worms lay eggs which are also present in stools; handwashing is therefore very important after a visit to the lavatory, if the worms are not to be passed on.

You may find the whole idea of worms very upsetting. Luckily they hardly seem to affect children and cause few symptoms, apart from itching round the anus. If you see worms, or if you

Once he is old enough to understand, teach your child to wash his hands after going to the lavatory. The best way is probably by letting him copy you.

are worried about them, ask your doctor. He can give medicine to cure them; if they should come back, it may be necessary for the whole family to be treated.

Washing and hygiene

Make sure a child gets washed thoroughly at least once a day; the best way of doing this is by giving him a bath. Most children need their faces and hands washed several times during the rest of the day, because they get grubby so easily.

Hand-washing. You know that it is important not to transfer germs from the bowel to food. Make certain that children learn early to wash their hands after going to the lavatory. It is a good idea to wash their hands before every meal. Pay careful attention to the finger nails, to make certain they are clean. You should keep them neatly cut, with a pair of fine sharp scissors.

Teething problems

All sorts of problems are put down to teething. Around the time the first teeth are expected, you may notice that the baby likes chewing a teething ring or a hard rusk. He may become more irritable, wake frequently at night and cry more. Doctors are often sceptical when people talk about 'teething', but it does seem likely that some babies are upset when their teeth are coming through (see page 127). If your baby seems upset, have a good look in his mouth in case there is a boil over the erupting tooth. This may be the cause of his pain and might need attention from a dentist. In most cases teeth come through without any difficulty at all. One day you will see the tip of a tooth peeping through his gum and after this it grows without further trouble. It can be dangerous to call an illness 'teething', when it is something more serious. Occasional tragedies have occurred in the past because mothers have made this diagnosis themselves, when there was a more serious underlying condition. If a baby is generally well, is only mildly upset, or drooling from the mouth, there is no need

213

to worry your doctor. What should worry you, and may indicate a serious illness, are: a high fever (38.5°C or 101°F); difficulty in breathing; or the appearance of being generally ill. A lot of crying at the time of teething may be treated by your doctor with a sedative; you should consult him if you are at all worried.

Care of the teeth

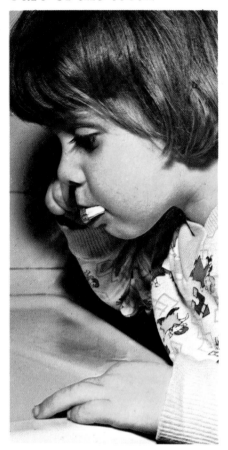

Teeth need to be looked after very carefully. When they first appear, you can wipe them with a little cotton wool or brush them with a soft brush twice a day. As soon as your child is old enough, get him to clean his teeth by himself. It can often be done like a game and he should do it night and morning. Like everything else, good hygiene is learnt more easily if he sees you carrying out the same thing yourself. Brush your teeth in front of him, so that he can learn what to do.

The idea of brushing is to remove small particles of food which lodge between the teeth. If the food stays there, germs may attack the teeth and cause holes (see page 145). The back teeth as well as the front must be cleaned; they should be brushed up and down as well as across the biting surfaces, using tooth paste or powder. It is not particularly easy to brush teeth properly especially for small children; make sure they do not brush across the teeth. Some people find an electric toothbrush much easier to use because the brush has its own up-and-down movement. Never let your child have a sweet or a sugary drink after his teeth have been cleaned at night.

Make sure that your child visits the dentist regularly so that any decay can be repaired in good time. Remember to give fluoride regularly if water in your area does not contain it. You can give it in tablet form or use a toothpaste which contains fluoride. Do your best to cut down the amount of sugar or sweets you give your child. I know this is difficult, but sugar does ruin teeth.

Dummies and thumb sucking

Dentists get worried about thumb sucking after the age of three, because it can lead to severe deformity of the teeth. A child may put his thumb behind the front upper teeth and push against them while he is sucking. His upper teeth will then tend to stick out and this deformity may be difficult to correct later. It does seem that thumb sucking early in life has none of this problem and is therefore quite harmless. If your three-year-old is still sucking his thumb, especially when he is tired, you may try many methods of dissuading him. Encouragement to interest himself in other things is probably the best; punishment may make the whole problem worse. Paradoxically, a recent survey has shown that thumb-sucking children have less tooth decay than others; however, it is believed that this may be because they suck fewer sweet things – a situation which should be avoided anyway.

The use of a dummy as a baby may help to prevent thumb sucking. As you know, sucking seems to be important for young babies and they need to have their fill of it. The dummy may content them or they may wish to suck the breast or bottle long after they are eating solid food for every meal.

214

Nail-biting

This is another very common and annoying habit. It seems to be more common when children are miserable or upset. Giving your child special attention for a while may help to settle the problem. Again, punishment usually makes the whole thing worse. Do your best not to encourage him. Remember that biting your own nails may cause him to copy you.

Rocking and head-banging

A number of toddlers go through a stage of rocking. They can sit for hours, usually in the evening or at night, rocking back and forth rhythmically. Very often, they bang their heads against the cot. It can be very distressing and is usually difficult to stop.

We don't know why children do this. It often happens when they are trying to get off to sleep and may be combined with comforting rituals, like thumb-sucking. Children who are feeling deprived or miserable are much more likely to bang their heads.

First try giving him more attention; he might like to stay up longer in the evening. Perhaps a long cuddle at bedtime, will allow him to drop off to sleep more easily. A talk with your doctor may help; a few days of sleeping medicine may help your child to develop a better sleep rhythm.

If all this fails, it is a problem to be lived with. It will improve as he gets older. Do not worry that he will damage his brain by banging his head.

The genitals

It is common and normal for a boy to touch his penis or a girl part of her vulva while they are babies. Masturbation – that is, deliberate stimulation of the genital area to produce sexual excitement and pleasure – is very rare under three years old; it is much commoner later in childhood and particularly at adolescence, and is of course normal and harmless.

You might feel rather embarrassed if you see your baby touching the genitalia. It is best to remember that he regards it as just another part of his body, except that it may give him greater pleasure to touch it. As he gets older, he will understand that touching his genitalia makes other people embarrassed and so will learn to do it only in private. Do not worry that a boy can harm himself in any way by pulling at his penis. Erections of the penis are very common and may occur several times a day. They are quite normal, even in small babies.

Discipline

No one can lay down any firm rules for discipline. Almost certainly, you will have your own views about the sort of discipline you feel is necessary for a child. It will also depend on his personality; some children are very easy to correct, but the more wilful ones might be difficult. It seems better, if possible, not to hit or slap your child, but if you get very cross you may do this sometimes. Do not feel guilty if this happens, but tell your child that you got angry with him and especially why. Children need to know that other people have feelings of temper, like them.

Perhaps the most important aspect of discipline is the negative one. If you constantly draw attention to a child's faults, he may learn to irritate you by exaggerating those faults. Ignoring bad behaviour does seem to work so long as you explain to the child right at the beginning, that such behaviour is not nice. On the positive side, you will need to constantly explain the reasons for behaving in a pleasant and social way. At first, he will not understand you, so you will have to repeat it many times.

Boredom

Boredom breeds naughtiness and difficulties. If you can interest your baby in all sorts of things, with games and painting, he will have less time to be difficult. It is probably true that he likes a confined realm of living with a fairly set routine. You may need to tell him gently what he can or cannot do. If he is allowed complete freedom it may lead to some confusion in his mind.

Teaching a toddler to take care

Certain things can be very dangerous to children. Fires, for instance, are a hazard; see if you can find your own way of explaining to him how dangerous it is. Suggestions are a sharp 'no' whenever he goes near something dangerous. As he gets older you will be able to explain the reasons more fully to him. Children pick up differences in the tone of a voice very easily, so that you will probably be able to warn him sternly and he will respond. Babies and children are keen to please if you are affectionate and attentive to them. They will soon learn whether you are cross or happy, and can alter their behaviour accordingly.

Physical punishment

If you do decide to use physical punishment, remember not to be too rough. A very slight slap can be very unpleasant to a child and will be enough for most purposes. Think out a plan of discipline and try to be consistent in sticking to it. Very often one sees a child being hit or slapped in the street, more from the mother's embarrassment than for any real need to correct the child. My personal feeling is that it is best to avoid physical punishment. I was never hit by my own parents and I respect them for it.

We have recently learnt that parents do not alter their views about discipline because of the views of doctors or others. I do not expect therefore that you will change your mind because of what I have said. However try not to punish your child by making him unhappy or insecure. For instance, do not use phrases like, 'If you are naughty, mummy won't love you any more', but try to give a general atmosphere of love and concern. Ominous warnings like 'The policeman will come to get you if you are naughty' should also be avoided; later the child may have to turn to the police, for instance, if he is lost, and these earlier threats may deter him.

Discipline is one of the most controversial areas of child-care and it is impossible to make hard and fast rules to suit any family. It is important to work it out between yourselves as a family and try and explain to your child as best you can the reasons for the 'do's and dont's' of your household.

One of the main points of discipline is to help a child grow up as a useful person to others. He will have to live in a world where he depends on other people and in return must be kind, considerate and helpful to them. He will only really believe in these things, if he sees other people around him behaving in the same way. Probably, the best way of bringing up a child is to show him how to live happily with other people; he can then copy you.

Illnesses of childhood

When a child is unwell

An ill child is a great trial to everyone. You may have to stay home from work, he will feel miserable and need lots of comfort.

The commonest illnesses in childhood are infections; a virus infection – which would cause a cold in an adult – may result in severe bronchitis, a high temperature or earache in a child. You must expect him to get quite a lot of these infections when he first begins to mix with other children. Therefore he may develop a lot of colds and snuffles when he first goes to a playgroup, day nursery or child-minder, when his brother or sister first goes to school, or when he first goes to school himself.

When to put a child to bed

He will be the best guide of this. If he feels rotten, he will curl up in bed and remain quiet. There should be no need to force a child to stay in bed; let him get up and run around as soon as he feels well enough. When I was a child, it was a common rule to keep a child in bed for 48 hours after the temperature had come down; I can never understand how I was docile enough to stay in bed. Children these days even get up soon after an operation.

In some special conditions your doctor may feel that your child should stay in bed for quite a while. You will need to occupy him, to prevent him from becoming bored. It is astonishing how much play can go on in the sick bed. Playgroups in hospitals even arrange painting in bed, something that would have horrified Matron in the old days. A thick plastic sheet over the bed will prevent any paint getting on to the sheets. You can arrange for lots of paper and pencils to scribble with. Provide a hard board or tray on which to rest the paper, and once they are old enough, blunt ended scissors and paste for cutting out and sticking shapes. Many games involving puzzles and post-boxes can be carried on for hours either in bed, or perhaps on a chair in the sitting room.

Taking medicine

Luckily, most children's medicines these days are specially prepared to taste nice. Children will quite often actually enjoy them and certainly take them without difficulty. Occasionally, you may need to disguise them by mixing them with another drink. Tablets can often be crushed into a teaspoonful of jam or honey; some brands can be dissolved in water.

Coping with fever

Don't try to keep an ill child in bed if he doesn't want it; he will only become frustrated and fretful, and will get up anyway!

This is the commonest sign of an infection. It may start quite suddenly and go very high, even as far as 40°C (or 104°F). Over that it is serious, and when it is higher than 40.5°C (about 105°F) it is very dangerous. When the temperature goes up, the baby may look very flushed; he sweats when the temperature lowers.

Taking the temperature. You will find it useful to have a clinical thermometer in the house so you can then record the temperature and tell the doctor what it has been. Remember to shake down the thermometer first and allow two minutes before reading the temperature. There are several places for taking the temperature in babies and children. The commonest is under the arm with the bulb of the thermometer in the armpit; the normal temperature is usually said to be up to 37.5°C (99°F), but it gives a lower reading in the armpit and you must not expect it to be above 37°C (about 98.4°F). In older children, the thermometer can be put under the tongue, but young children may not understand this and there is the danger that they may chew it and swallow the glass and mercury. In the young baby, the easiest place to take a temperature is by gently inserting the thermometer into the rectum, usually with the baby lying on his back.

Keeping him cool. When a child gets a fever, make certain that he is not wrapped up too warmly. He will need only light clothes and bedclothes. If you put woolly things on him, his temperature may go up very high, which could be dangerous. When you are worried by a high temperature, you can cool a child by sponging him with tepid water or putting him in a tepid bath. It is important to use tepid water because cold water may decrease the blood flow in the skin and cause the temperature to go even higher.

When to call the doctor. It is difficult to suggest a certain temperature which would always make you call the doctor. Perhaps you should think of this: if the temperature rises above 38.5°C (about 101°F), a reasonable thing might be to ring your doctor

A fever will generally be accompanied by weakness and a child will be much more inclined to stay in bed. Upper respiratory infections are often accompanied by earache, caused by inflammation of the middle ear. If your child is too young to tell you about it, watch to see if he seems to rub his ear frequently. This may be a sign he is in pain. Earache is often very distressing (see page 222) and can disturb a child's sleep.

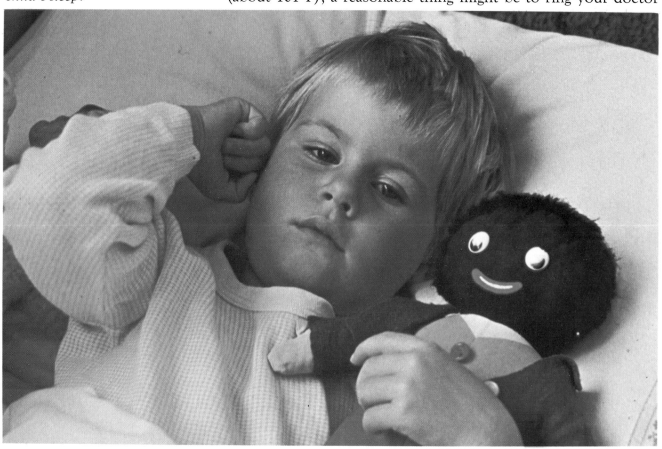

The family doctor will call if you feel that a child's symptoms are serious enough not to allow him out to visit the surgery. Doctors will always try to examine an ill child in a way that will not alarm or upset him.

and discuss the problem with him.

A child is usually more comfortable if you give him a drug to bring his temperature down; it will relieve the headache and misery he often has. Aspirin is a common drug for this, but should never be given to young babies; in the toddler age group, not more than one dose of junior aspirin should be given in a day. It is much safer to use paracetamol; a one to three year old child can be given 250mg, in a mixture or half a tablet, up to three times a day. Under one year, you should speak to your doctor about the dose most suitable for your baby.

Convulsions

These are very common in small children, especially as a result of a sudden rise in temperature. About 1 in 15 children has one at some time, and they are commoner in some families than others. During an attack, a child usually becomes very stiff, is unconscious, stops breathing and is therefore blue, and then his whole body begins to jerk. After a few minutes, the jerking stops, and he passes into a deep sleep. He often wets himself as well.

If your child has one of these attacks, you will probably be very frightened. Do your best not to panic, but watch the attack carefully. The doctor will want to hear about it when he comes. Lie the child down on his side, so that any saliva can dribble out of his mouth. Take off most of his clothes, so that he can cool down. Send a message to the doctor at once.

A convulsion with a temperature does not mean that your child will go on to have epilepsy. Usually, it does not have any after effects at all.

Coughing

A cough can be a very annoying symptom; it often keeps a child awake or causes him to vomit. Of course, it could be a symptom of some illness of the lungs, but is also a common accompaniment of a cold. If your child has a cough and seems otherwise reasonably well, there is no need to go to the doctor, so long as it improves after a day or so.

There are many cough medicines available at the pharmacy for you to use. Very often the best medicine is quite a simple one, like a mixture of honey and warm water. It often seems that a sweet mixture like this helps to soothe an irritating, dry cough.

Vomiting

Children are likely to be sick with any illness, particularly one that causes diarrhoea or pain in the abdomen. Vomiting and tummy pains should be taken quite seriously since they may be the first sign of an illness, such as appendicitis, which would need expert treatment in hospital.

Put your child on a light diet if he is being sick. Sometimes, it is wisest to give only fluids. If you give sweetish fluids, for instance dilute fruit juice, it may help to settle the vomiting. Do not be worried that he is not getting enough food, it is more important to give fluid. He has plenty of food stores in his body, enough to last many days.

Greasy foods are particularly likely to cause vomiting and should always be avoided when he feels sick.

Diarrhoea

An attack of diarrhoea usually means that there is an infection in the bowel. The stools may often contain slime, be very smelly, and might be a little bloody. In a small baby, diarrhoea can lead to lack of water very quickly. This is called dehydration and could be very serious. You should offer him water or diluted milk (quarter or half strength) to drink quite often. If the diarrhoea is watery, or if the baby looks really ill, consult your doctor.

Very strong sugar solutions or milk can make diarrhoea worse. Rely on very weak fruit juice or water for an older child.

Earache

This is usually caused by inflammation in the middle ear, behind the drum. It can cause very severe pain in the ear, a high temperature and will lead to a runny ear if the drum bursts. You may notice that your child is rubbing one ear if he is in pain; mention this to the doctor when he comes. He will be able to look at the drum, which would be red if inflammation were present. These days, ear trouble is much less common because middle ear infection can be cleared up quickly with antibiotics.

Croup

This is very common in the toddler. It is caused by the same germ that gives laryngitis to an adult; in this infection, a person loses his voice or becomes very hoarse. A child develops a harsh, barking sort of cough, is hoarse, and has difficulty breathing in. There is a crowing noise whenever he breathes in. The illness can be very worrying; if it is more than mild, he may have to go into hospital. He may well be better in a moist atmosphere; so you could run a hot bath and put his cot into the bathroom. In hospital, a mist tent is often used to allow him to get better quickly.

Bronchitis

This usually causes wheezing, accompanied by difficulty in breathing out; it may be very severe in the young baby. Some children are prone to many attacks of wheezing, which may lead one to suspect that he has asthma.

In most cases an attack of bronchitis or wheezing can be dealt with at home. The family doctor can give medicine to prevent an infection or to release the spasm of the small passages in the lungs. It may take a while to clear completely.

Allergies

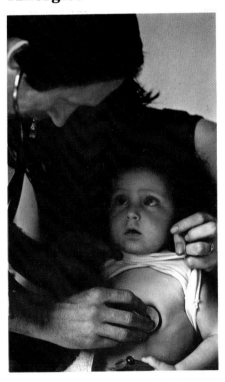

Some families have many more allergic problems than others. They can take many forms but the usual ones are: asthma, eczema and hay fever.

Asthma. This takes the form of repeated attacks of wheezing. The first time it happens, bronchitis is usually blamed, but then it returns. The small tubes in the lungs (bronchioles) suddenly clamp down and this causes wheezing and difficulty in breathing out. An attack can result from an infection, an allergy, or result from an emotional upset. It is treated with medicine to relax the bronchioles. Later, powder or spray which can be inhaled is very useful. You will need to discuss your child carefully with your family doctor if he seems to suffer from asthma. He may wish to organize a number of tests.

It has recently been shown that some people are often allergic to house dust. If your child wheezes, keep him out of the room when you are doing the housework especially when making the beds. Vacuum his mattress regularly. It may help to enclose his mattress in plastic sheeting; use foam pillows. Allergy to house dust is worse when a room is damp, so arrange to keep his bedroom as dry as possible.

Eczema. This is the common rash which affects many parts of the body. It occurs on the face, the scalp, over the trunk and particularly in front of the elbows and behind the knees. Its main problem is that it causes intense itching, so that the baby scratches furiously. It tends to get better during childhood, but modern ointments and creams can help it a lot.

Hay fever. This usually occurs in older children and adults. The sufferers are allergic to pollen. They develop a running nose, sneezing, and red eyes during the spring or summer. There are drugs which alleviate some of the symptoms, but they sometimes have unpleasant side effects. Your doctor will advise you.

Tonsillitis

The tonsils are found at the back of the mouth on each side. If you look in your child's mouth you will see the little round irregular growth on each side of the palate at the back of the tongue. They become very large in childhood; sometimes so large that they may frighten you. However, they are only a problem when infected: this is called tonsillitis. The tonsils become very red, painful and swollen. The child finds it difficult to swallow and has a very high temperature. You may notice that glands in the neck become swollen; they are trying to prevent the infection spreading to other parts of the body.

These days, tonsillitis can be treated fairly easily with an antibiotic, such as penicillin. When tonsillitis comes back frequently, it can sometimes be prevented by taking the tonsils out – tonsillectomy. This is very rarely necessary under the age of three.

Adenoids. The adenoids are small tonsils at the back of the nose. They can block the nose (causing snoring) and can cause many ear infections. They are often removed when the tonsils are taken out – the operation called adenoidectomy.

Scarlet fever. The germ that causes tonsillitis, called the streptococcus, can cause other problems. Sometimes it produces a bright red rash which is called scarlet fever. This illness used to be very severe 150 years ago but is now quite mild; the rash peels within a week. An inflammation of the kidneys, known as nephritis may also follow tonsillitis, but is prevented if a proper course of antibiotics is given.

Other common infectious diseases

Between the moment when someone is exposed to an infection and the time the illness appears is called the incubation period.

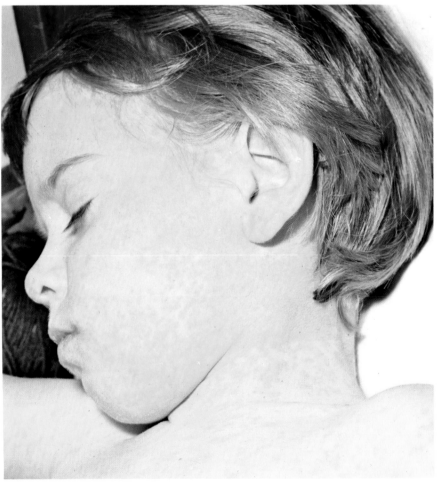

Measles can be a serious illness in young children and can have unpleasant complications. After four days of symptoms similar to a heavy cold or 'flu, spots appear in the mouth. A blotchy rash then spreads over the body, beginning usually behind the ears, and gradually fading after a week.

224

During this time there are no signs of illness, but towards the moment when the illness appears the person is infectious. We usually get an infection from another person through the air; the germs are breathed out in droplets of water from the lungs. Sometimes, infection is spread by direct contact; the best example of this are the germs of gastro-enteritis carried on hands and passed into food.

Measles

This is caused by a virus and the incubation period is about ten to fourteen days. At the end of that time, the child appears to have a severe cold, with a runny nose, a cough, red eyes and a temperature. This lasts for about four days, at the end of which some spots appear on the inside of the mouth, and then a red blotchy rash spreads all over the body. The rash usually begins behind the ears, then covers the face and spreads on to the trunk and limbs; it fades slowly over a week and changes from a dull red colour to a browny red. The child is often quite ill, but there is no need to nurse him in the dark unless he wants it.

Measles is a world-wide illness but can now be prevented by vaccination (see page 172).

Chickenpox (varicella)

The incubation period is between 12 and 20 days and the child is infectious for two days before the rash appears. It is one of the mildest of the infectious diseases in childhood. The rash usually appears on the trunk, the face and then on the limbs. It begins as

A throat examination is usually done with the aid of a special torch. A doctor will find evidence of many different illness by examining the mouth and throat, so it is part of a routine which often includes listening to the chest, checking the pulse and taking the temperature.

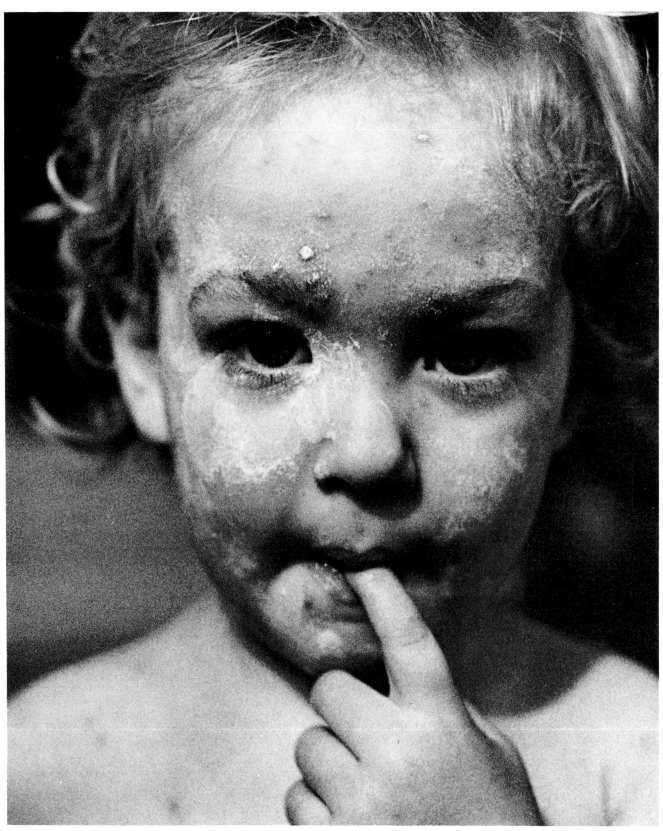

Chicken pox isn't usually serious: but the spots can be irritating. Calamine lotion can help to alleviate the itching.

red spots which develop into tiny blisters; they become scabs and fall off after several days. The rash comes out in crops; it can be rather itchy and scars may result if the lesions are scratched severely. You can use calamine lotion to relieve the itching.

German measles (rubella)

This is a very mild illness in childhood and has an incubation period between 14 and 21 days. It is of course dangerous for women in pregnancy because of the damage it causes the unborn child (see page 15). The illness consists of a slight fever, some enlarged glands at the back of the neck, and a rash of fine pink spots which lasts a few days.

Mumps

The incubation period here is quite long – about 17 to 21 days. The illness consists of swelling of some glands around the back of jaw on one or both sides. Usually there is some pain behind the jaw and then the swelling appears. After a few days the glands go down and there are usually no further problems.

Whooping cough (pertussis)

This disease appears gradually; the incubation period is about one to two weeks. At first a child appears to have a severe cold or sometimes bronchitis. The cough becomes more severe, especially at night and has a characteristic type of paroxysm. The child has a sudden burst or coughing – repeated short coughs, 20 or 30 times – and then draws in his breath making a characteristic whooping noise. Very frequently he vomits after coughing. The whooping stage lasts a week or two and then gradually disappears, but a cough may persist for many weeks.

It is a very serious illness in very young babies and can lead to damage of the lungs. Killed bacteria are used for the vaccination to prevent the illness (see page 170). It can also be caused by a virus; it may therefore occur in a child who has had a complete course of vaccination.

Urinary infection

A germ may easily get into the bladder or kidneys; this causes a high temperature, abdominal pain and vomiting. Older children may complain of pain when passing urine, may start to wet their beds again, or may pass urine very frequently. Sometimes the urine smells rather strong, but this does not always happen.

It is commoner in girls than boys, except during the first week of life. The only secure way of proving the infection is to take a clean specimen of urine; it can be examined under the microscope and the germs can be grown in the laboratory. If an infection is found, it can be treated quite simply by a course of antibiotics. It is necessary to take further specimens of urine later on, in case the infection returns.

Appendicitis

This is an inflammation that occurs in the tiny appendix at the beginning of the large bowel. The infection may break through the wall of the appendix and spread quickly and widely inside the abdomen – it is therefore a very dangerous condition. Unfortunately, it can be very difficult to diagnose in a young child. The most important symptoms are abdominal pain and vomiting. The doctor will find tenderness when he touches the abdomen; it is almost always on the right side and very low down.

If you are worried about abdominal pain in your child, particularly if he vomits and is a little constipated, you should ask your doctor to see him. Never give him a laxative in this situation; it could make the condition a lot worse.

Accidents & their prevention

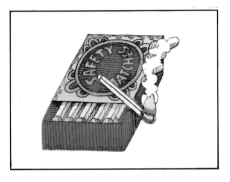

Unfortunately, many children die or are injured by accidents every year. They now are the leading case of death in children over the age of one year. As homes become more complicated and have more electrical gadgets, and as roads contain more cars and lorries, we may expect accidents to continue. Everyone should take accident prevention very seriously; we must do our best to make children's lives as safe as possible. Look around your house and try to correct anything you see which could be dangerous.

Falls and head injuries

These cause only a small number of deaths, but they can be a great problem. Heavy furniture should be very secure, so that it cannot topple on to your child. Anything used by him must be very stable; a high chair is a good example of something which could fall over. Recently the high chair has been replaced by a lower, more stable chair.

Children are very adept at climbing up to windows. If there is any danger of a child falling out, you should put up bars to protect him. A young, crawling child could easily get to the top of the stairs and then tumble down them. There are plenty of practical gates you can fit at the top of a flight of stairs.

Do be careful not to let a child fall from a high bed or table on to a hard surface, such as a stone or concrete floor. If you have a high cot, put up the side of the cot before leaving it to fetch something. A baby can easily roll off on to the floor. Be especially careful if you have one of the new changing tables for babies; never leave a baby by himself on the table.

Whenever you take the baby out in the pram or push-chair, make sure he is strapped in firmly, especially if you are leaving the pram unattended for a few minutes. Once a baby can pull himself up it is only too easy for him to topple out of a pram which could lead to a nasty head injury.

Head injuries If your baby or child has a knock on the head you should watch his progress carefully. If he appears limp or drowsy immediately after the injury take him straight to the doctor or casualty department of the nearest hospital. Keep him warm and loosen his clothing, in case he is suffering from shock. If he seems to be all right at first, you should still watch him carefully for 24 hours. If he becomes drowsy suddenly, apart from going to sleep in the ordinary way at bedtime, faints, or begins to vomit, again you should take him at once to your doctor or casualty department. If there is a deep wound you should expect

Accidents can happen unpredictably (above), but there are ways to prevent them. Playgrounds are fun, (left) but don't let small children go unaccompanied.

him to have stitches to make the lesion heal properly.

Nosebleeds. Some children are more prone to nosebleeds than others, though any child can have one as a result of a fall or bump. The classic way to stop it is to get the child to bite on a cork and then bend the head over a bowl and let the nose drip until it stops. The important thing is to get him to breathe through his mouth. You can also pinch the nose till the bleeding stops, since most of the bleeding occurs low down in the nose.

Eye injuries

It is always safest to have an eye injury attended to by a doctor. However, if a harmful liquid gets into the eye, flush it immediately with clean water. Specks should be removed at once, whether by drawing the upper lid down and away, allowing tears to wash out the eye, or by a sterile eye bath. If this is ineffective go to a hospital casualty department.

Road accidents

These are only a minor cause of death under one year, but cause many deaths and injuries to children over that age.

Inside the car. If you put a carry cot in the car, arrange for it to be carefully strapped to the back seat. It must not fly off if you have to brake suddenly or bump into another car. Of course, you should always use a seat-belt when you are in a car; it will prevent your head hitting the windscreen and your knees hitting the dashboard. Never allow a small child to sit in your lap in a car. It is very easy to forget this and allow them on your lap for very short journeys; it is dangerous as they may fly out of your hands and through the windscreen if the car should stop suddenly. Make it a firm rule that all children

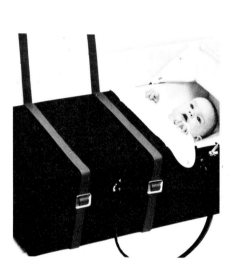

Seat belts and safety chairs for children can help to avoid serious injury in some road accidents. If you know your children are safely strapped in, it can make a car journey less nerve-racking.

When driving a car, watch out for children behind parked cars or lorries. Above all don't let your children play in a street, especially where heavy lorries park – they have been known to run over a child retrieving a ball like this from behind the back wheels.

always travel in the back seat.

There are now some very good children's seats with a full harness. They can be anchored securely to the body of the car and fit on the back seat. Use one that has passed the British or Australian Standard. Make certain that the car doors have a special 'child-proof' catch on them; they should shut firmly, so they cannot fly open while you are travelling.

Out in the road. Many children get run over because they are allowed to play in an open street. A young child should be accompanied when he goes out and particularly if he has to cross a road. Even at a very early age, you should help your child to understand the rules for crossing a road. Children should be taught to cross at a zebra crossing or where there is a person on duty to control the traffic. Teach them the rules of the road (Green Cross Code in Britain) as soon as you can.

If you are driving, be very careful to watch out for children. They often run into the road from between parked cars; unless you are driving slowly, you will not have time to brake. Be especially careful when you reverse a car out of a garage; you must make certain that there are no children playing in the drive or road. Quite a number of children die because a car is reversed on to them.

Railways

Railway tracks are dangerous places for children. Unless there is adequate fencing, they can easily stray down on to the track. A train may knock them down or they can be electrocuted on an electric rail. If your house is next to a railway, make certain that the fencing is secure and the children cannot get near the tracks.

Drowning

Small children can drown even in a shallow pond. If you have an ornamental pond in the garden or nearby make certain that it is fenced off or only allow them there with a responsible person. Don't leave a child alone in the bath.

Quite small children or babies enjoy being taken to a swimming pool Of course, you will need to be with them, but if you enjoy swimming you may like to teach your child to swim from quite an early age. Give them inflatable arm bands rather than rubber rings for buoyancy. Do not force your child to go in the pool if he is frightened.

Burns and scalds

Unhappily, these cause many deaths in childhood and lots of admissions to hospital. Even quite a small burn may mean several weeks in hospital, with much misery and upset. Do your best to make your home as safe as you can.

Burns. A child's clothing can easily catch fire; only buy clothes that are made of fireproof material. If there isn't a special label, always ask if a material is safe when you buy something. Other

fittings in his bedroom, such as the curtains, should also be made of safe material (see page 118). The most dangerous clothes are often those made for a special occasion, such as a frilly party dress. Many children have been severely burnt when showing off a party dress in front of the fire.

Any open fire should be carefully guarded from young children (see page 117). It is important to have a guard which children cannot put their hands through and which is a reasonable distance from the fire. The best guards are box-shaped and enclose the fire completely; they have a guard at the top so that children cannot climb over on to the fire. Fix guards to the wall securely, because some children are fascinated by fire and will do all they can to get the guard away.

You will need to help your child to understand how dangerous fire is. Talk to him sternly if he plays with matches; it is anyway a good idea to keep matches well out of his reach. Similarly, be very careful if you use a night light or candle in his bedroom.

Some paraffin stoves are very unsafe if they are knocked over. The modern makes are safer and have automatic extinguishing mechanisms which close if the fire is knocked over. But make sure yours has passed the British [Australian] standard. If possible, avoid using a paraffin stove at all as a method of heating. Of course, you may find this difficult as it is often much cheaper than any other form.

If a child's clothes catch alight, catch hold of him quickly and lie him down. If he runs around, his clothes will flame up more and the burns may be more severe. Cover him with any heavy cloth at hand, something like a coat or a rug, to put the flames out. You may have to roll on him yourself to prevent air getting to the flames; this will extinguish them. The burnt area can be treated immediately by putting it in cold water for ten minutes or until the pain ceases. Cover the burn with a sterile covering to prevent it becoming infected. A freshly laundered handkerchief is a suitable sterile dressing. Do not try to remove clothes if the child has been seriously burnt, but get medical help at once.

Scalds. These are even commoner than burns and can occur when even a simple cup of tea is spilt over a child. Be very careful when you are cooking on a stove. The handles of saucepans should be turned inwards. If they stick out over the front, a child can easily pull the handles and pour boiling water or fat over himself.

A tea or coffee pot is very unsafe if it is on a tablecloth. A common accident occurs when a child pulls the tablecloth and hot water from the teapot or teacups tips over him. It is wiser not to use a tablecloth when there is a small child around. Make certain the pot and cups are near the centre of the table, and that the table itself is steady.

When you draw a bath, always add cold water at the same time as hot. I have seen several bath scalds after a child jumped into a bath of hot water, before cold water was added.

Scalds are always worse where hot water soaks into the child's clothing and is held against the skin. If hot water has been splashed

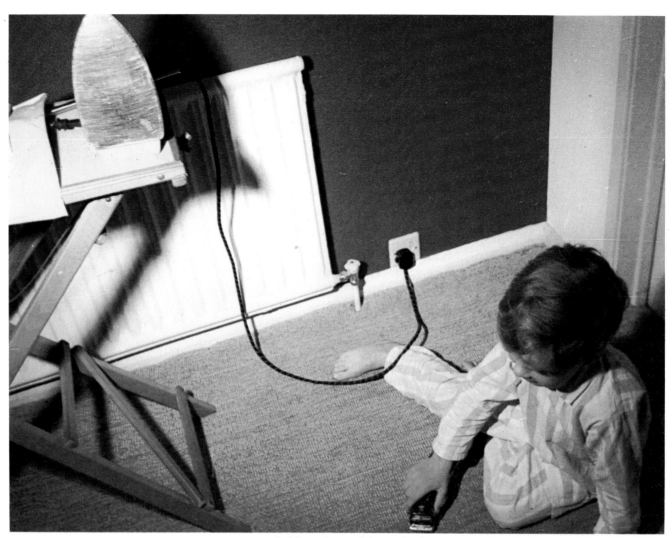

on a child, take off his clothes as quickly as possible and then immerse the scalded area in cold water. You should take him to see a doctor, unless the scald was very mild indeed.

Fireworks

These are dangerous and should be kept well away from children. Never allow a young child to play with fireworks. It is much safer to arrange a display for them; it should be entirely controlled by the adults. The children can then watch and enjoy the bangs and lights, without being burnt by them. Every year on November 5th too many children are admitted to hospital with burns.

Electricity

Modern homes run much more efficiently because of the easy availability of electricity. We use all sorts of gadgets in our homes, but this means that there are many more plugs and electrical apparatus which can be a danger to children.

Make certain that you have safe electric wiring throughout the house, so that your child cannot put his fingers into the sockets of plugs or pull loose wires and electrocute himself. If possible, plugs should be high up on the wall and out of any child's reach. Make certain that the electrical circuits are installed competently and that all wires are joined up properly and carefully.

A connecting plug on a wire for an electric kettle or iron is a particular danger. If it is not connected to the appliance, but left

Left: Electric irons are particularly dangerous, if left unattended, propped up in this way on an ironing board. A child may either touch the hot-plate or knock the iron off the board on to himself. Right: Electric flexes are also dangerous – a child may accidently trip over one, causing it to break and perhaps cause a short circuit. Plugs are often irresistible to a toddler – make sure they aren't accessible to little fingers by having them fitted out of reach or hidden behind heavy furniture, and, if possible use special 'dummy plugs' to cover the sockets when not in use.

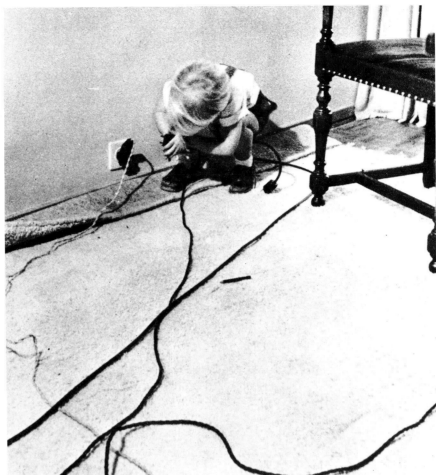

dangling with the electric current still on, a child may put it in his mouth and get severe electric burns of the tongue and lips.

Electric fires should be very carefully guarded indeed. Horrible burns can occur across the palm of the hand if a child puts his hand through a guard and grasps the electric element. The electric current causes his hand to clench and he is unable to release it.

An iron is also very dangerous if left unattended. A child may not realize that it is hot and can easily get burnt badly by touching the hot-plate when the iron is switched on.

Asphxyia

A child may die from suffocation when not enough oxygen can get into his lungs. A pillow is dangerous and unnecessary for a baby. It is possible for him to turn face down into it and therefore not get enough oxygen. This occurs rarely, but is a sufficient reason for not using a pillow in a cot or pram.

Sometimes a baby may choke on food. Milk may get into the lungs instead of going down the gullet. You should never leave a baby propped up with a bottle, because this could be dangerous (see page 85). Older children can sometimes inhale a small object, especially a tiny toy; try not to let him play with objects which are small enough to get right into his mouth. Some foods are particularly dangerous; the worse culprit is a peanut. This is easily inhaled and can cause quite severe damage to the lungs.

To remove an object lodged in the throat, bend the child forward and pat him vigorously on the back. If it is a large object, such as a piece of meat or apple, you may be able to reach into

235

his mouth and pull it out with your fingers. If he stops breathing, try mouth-to-mouth respiration – a useful technique which your local St John's Ambulance Brigade would be able to teach you.

Never allow a child to play with a plastic bag. If he gets it over his head, it will stick close to the face so that he cannot breathe. Throw away plastic bags when you have finished with them, or keep them in a very safe place.

An old refrigerator can be very dangerous. Never leave it on some waste ground unless the door has been taken off. A number of children have died after climbing inside old refrigerators to hide from others; they find themselves shut in and die from lack of air. All waste grounds, building sites, demolition areas, old quarries, etc., can be dangerous. Make sure your child does not have the opportunity to wander into one alone, and warn older children of the dangers.

Foreign objects in the nose and ears

Don't poke at an object stuck in a small child's ear unless you are sure you can remove it very easily. It could be dangerous if it was pushed down into the ear. If you are in any doubt at all, take your child to the nearest casualty department.

Objects stuck up nostrils are slightly easier to cope with: if the child is old enough you can either get him to blow his nose or possibly remove the object with a pair of tweezers. However, a small child or baby may breathe in hard instead of blowing out which could lodge the object in more firmly. Again it is better to go to a doctor or casualty department if there is any difficulty in removing it yourself.

Cot death

I have included this here because it is often confused with an accident. Some babies in the first year die suddenly; they are found dead in their cots, even though they were perfectly well only an hour or two before. Sometimes, they have signs of a slight cold. We do not know the cause of these tragedies and they are a great worry to doctors because they cannot be explained.

In some cases a definite cause for the death is found, an illness such as pneumonia, heart disease or meningitis. In most cases, however, no cause can be found on post mortem examination. It seems likely that they could be due to a sudden and serious virus illness which does not leave any trace in the body. Doctors hope that more will be found out about this cause of death and ways of preventing it.

Poisoning

Many children have to be admitted to hospital because they have swallowed some drugs or a chemical. Usually, they are given some medicine to make them vomit or have their stomachs washed out. Some babies die as a result of poisoning. It is a serious problem and you should do what you can to keep all chemicals out of the way of children. This is becoming increasingly difficult, because of the number of things usually kept around a home.

Drugs. Many drugs today look like sweets; this is particularly true of iron tablets, which often look like the common chocolate

sweets covered with brightly covered sugar. The drug manufactureres have done their best to make medicines and drugs palatable for people, but they are therefore more attractive to children. Drugs should always be kept out of the way of children. You should have a medicine cabinet, with a lock, placed high up on a wall. Try to remember that all medicines should be locked away in this cabinet and keep the key separate.

Unfortunately children are very inquisitive and may devise all sorts of schemes, like putting one chair on top of another to reach cupboards out of reach. Consequently you should keep all tablets in a child-proof bottle. Tablets which are packed individually, in 'blister' packs, may be safer; each tablet is in a bubble of plastic, which has to be broken before a tablet is taken. It is then much more difficult for a child to take a large number of tablets, because each one has to be taken separately, instead of a handful out of a bottle.

There are several common medicines which are extremely dangerous to children, and these include aspirin and iron. Sometimes medicine given to one child may be dangerous to another. An example of this is the anti-depressant, imipramine (Tofranil) which is often used for the treatment of bed-wetting in an older child. When taken in large doses by a toddler it can be fatal.

If you think your child has taken a large dose of drugs, do not hesitate, call the hospital or family doctor at once.

Other poisons. There are many chemicals in your house. Quite a serious one is bleach, which is often kept in an unlocked cupboard, which should be locked away as medicines are. Never put any chemical in another bottle, but keep them in the original container or in a special bottle made for poisons. Sometimes children have died because they took a drink from a 'pop' bottle, not realizing it was used for a chemical such as paraffin or weedkiller. Do not attempt to make your child vomit after consuming a poisonous substance, especially petrol-based products, since vomiting could be positively harmful. Leave it to a doctor to decide whether to induce vomiting or not, depending on the type of poison which has been taken. The important thing is to seek urgent medical help.

Sunburn

Small children are quite susceptible to sunburn. Take it easy in the first few days of a summer holiday in the sun. Half an hour at a time is probably enough. Keep small babies completely out of direct sun. Remember that the redness of sunburn often doesn't appear until long after the damage is done. Bad sunburn can result in vomiting and fever. If this happens, consult a doctor. Keep sunburned areas completely covered until the redness goes.

Animals

A small baby is pretty defenceless against a dog. Even if you feel your dog is trustworthy, it is as well to avoid a situation where a dog and a baby are left alone together. The most docile pet can snap or scratch if provoked, so try and explain to a child that pets need gentle treatment.

Leaving your child

The working mother

Many people feel that women should devote their lives to the care of young children and should therefore not leave them with other people. I do not believe that this is a practical idea in the modern world; it might not be the right thing for lots of families. Many women feel that they are able to care for their children better if they have some time away from them; this is particularly true for women with special qualifications, who might feel irritated at home if they were unable to use their special skills. If you can, try to be with your children a lot; if you feel able to look after them yourself up to school age, that would be very nice. If at all possible, arrange your life so that you can be with them during special moments of upset, for instance when they are ill.

Who should care for your child?

There are very good reasons for believing that children become very disturbed if they do not have their mother with them, or someone to take the regular place of the mother, during early childhood, up to about four years. This does not mean that you have to be with them the whole time, but it is important for them to be left in the care of somebody they know and in whom they have confidence.

Sometimes this is possible within a family; you may have an aunt or mother who will be able to care for your child regularly while you are at work. Otherwise, you might find someone who would look after your child in your home, or in her house. Try to introduce the child to her on one or two occasions, before you leave him with her.

Unfortunately, those in most need of child-minders, the women who have to work to earn money for the family, often find it most difficult to find a satisfactory person. Everyone should press continually for proper arrangements in society to give women as much freedom as possible and to make certain that children are looked after safely and happily. Some day-nurseries are provided at factories, offices or colleges, where mothers can then visit their babies several times a day, during breaks from work. Unfortunately this sort of arrangement is still very rare.

However, whatever arrangement you finally choose, don't let your child be looked after by a series of different people, as this can cause a lot of insecurity and upset.

If you're going out to work, it's a help to leave the children with someone they know and you trust. A close relative, like the children's grandmother, can often fulfil these requirements ideally, and will probably be only too glad to make herself useful in this way.

How your baby reacts

When you leave your baby with someone else, he will probably cry. This is bound to make you feel upset and guilty. You will feel happier if you know that your child has been left with somebody he knows. Very probably you will hear that after you leave, within a minute or two he quietens down and is able to play happily and contentedly. Make a special fuss of him when you come home; his father will do the same thing, when he returns from work. This sort of thing can usually be worked out within the family. Each family is different and some have their own excellent ways of running their lives. It might be that your family works more easily if father looks after the children, and you go out to work. However you arrange it, as long as there is a certain amount of continuity your child will be secure and happy.

Clinging children

If a child has been separated for a while, you will probably find that he is very clinging. We know that this is particularly common if a child has been in hospital. He may want to go with you everywhere in the house or might hang on to a part of your clothes; in some cases, I have known this clinging to be such a problem that the mother cannot even have a bath or go to the lavatory by herself. Your baby or child will need your special sympathy and cuddling at a time like that.

Going to hospital

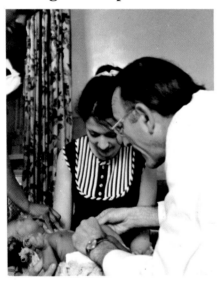

Between about six months and four years of age, a child may be very upset by an admission to hospital. This is usually much worse if a familiar person is unable to accompany him. It will be best for you to go into hospital with him, but it could be your husband, or a relative, instead. The problem is that nurses cannot be with him throughout the day, because of all the work that has to be done. In addition, there are always different nurses on at night – a time when he might be most upset.

If you know that your child is going to hospital explain it to him, even if he is very young. If he is under four, try to find a hospital where you can stay with him. There are now many children's units with bedrooms for mothers. The staff will understand that you are the best nurse for him; you know how to dress, feed and care for him. They can then concentrate on the technical aspects of nursing and leave his ordinary care to you. If you cannot stay with him, arrange to visit him as much as possible.

Babysitting

When the baby is small, choose your babysitter carefully – a close relative such as your mother or sister is probably best. At any rate, it is probably as well to ask someone you trust and who already knows the baby. In the first two or three months you might take the baby with you in his carry cot when you visit someone else's home. But it can also be a marvellous treat for you to leave the baby with someone, so that you can go shopping or to the cinema with a friend. Choose a time when the baby is likely to be most content. Later on, you can find people willing to babysit regularly for a small fee, or even for nothing. If you don't have a relative or neighbour who can babysit, try the girls at a local school or college. There are also many babysitting agencies, which, though not particularly cheap, can be very useful if you want to go out at short notice. Always leave a telephone number

Day nurseries usually cater for quite small babies as well as toddlers and small children, and will have a staff of trained nursery nurses to look after them professionally.

where you can be contacted and the number of your family doctor. It is a nice gesture to provide some refreshments.

Going back to work

You will need to organize proper care for your child on a regular basis.

Care outside the home

Day nurseries. There are private and state-run nurseries but even the private ones often have waiting lists, if they have a good reputation. If you are lucky enough to get a place, go and talk to the matron or supervisor, look carefully at the place, the qualifications of the staff, and ask about the number of staff. Above all, look at the other babies and children there; if they seem happy you can be sure that the staff are doing a good job. Good buildings and new equipment are not always important; remember that fascinating toys can be made from cardboard boxes, paper cups and straws!

The local authority will have a list of state-run or private nurseries in your area. If you know of a nursery which they do not have on their books, do not send your baby there. Talk to your health visitor or the social worker in charge of day nurseries to help you make a choice. They will know the best ones.

Child-minders. In Britain and Australia day nurseries and child-minders are covered by law. The latter must be registered with the local authority, if she looks after one or more children under 5 to whom she is not related, for reward, and for more than two hours per day. There are many 'illegal' child-minders who would probably be acceptable if they were inspected,

241

A good registered child-minder will try to make the life of the children in her care as homely as possible, organizing birthday parties and other activities that a working mother might not always have the time to provide.

but who simply don't know that they ought to register. If you come across someone in this situation, suggest that they contact their local social services office as soon as possible – the penalties for illegal child-minding are quite severe.

If you decide to use a child-minder, first make sure that she is registered. Talk to her about your baby and get to know her before you leave him in her care. See if there are toys and interesting things for the children to do. You must discuss things like feeding and meals, so you know the baby is getting a good diet. It is probably best if the house or flat has access to a garden so that the children are not house-bound the whole time. You may wish to spend time there at first; you can see how she manages your baby. Remember, that like day nurseries, the social services department will have taken many things into account when registering a child-minder: such as the space available, toilet facilities, equipment, fire regulations and, of course, the suitability of the child-minder herself. If you are in any doubt, talk to your health visitor or social services department.

Care in the home

You may know someone locally – a close friend, relative or neighbour – who can come to your home daily to look after the baby while you are out. Alternatively, you could have someone living in, if you have a spare room.

Nursery nurses. Fully trained nursery or mothercraft nurses are expensive, whether they live in or not; but they undoubtedly are useful and entirely trustworthy, especially with a small baby. A professional woman who does not want to interrupt her career for too long would probably find a nursery nurse ideal. Unless the nursery nurse prefers to be self-employed, you will be

A sympathetic nursery nurse or mother's help can add a lot of fun to a small child's life perhaps by having a bit more time to take him to the park or playground, read stories and help with games and toys.

responsible for her Worker's Compensation Insurance.

Mother's helps. Many girls, especially straight from school, like to work as 'mother's helps'. For some it is a good way of filling in a year between school and college. Others could work as a mother's help while studying at night school. Either way, it is a sort of halfway house between the trained nanny and the 'au pair' – it is a full-time job and you would be responsible for tax and insurance, and also full board. Define exactly what her job will be, and make sure you both agree about her spare time. It is fair to give her all weekends free, unless you come to a special arrangement to give her free time during the week.

Other help. Unlike European countries, it is unusual to have an 'au pair' girl arrangement in Australia though occasionally 'amahs' are available from Southeast Asian countries. Amahs, though paid, are usually more part of the family unit than other domestic helpers.

Most families who need help, and can afford it, will use one of three categories of helper – the trained mothercraft nurse, the part-time neighbourhood woman or the living-in single mother. As already mentioned, mothercraft nurses can be employed on a living-in or living-out basis. They are available to help mothers with their new babies and to help with other children. Mothercraft nurses are expensive and most families will need to find some other source of help.

The most available type of help is usually from someone in the neighbourhood, often a more mature woman, who wants several hours work a day. These women really act like the English 'nanny' though most have had no formal training. Like mothercraft nurses, they will help with your new baby or with the other children, and if you are lucky may even do light domestic chores. An advertisement in a local paper is more likely to be productive than one in a national paper.

Single mothers, either pregnant or with a small family, are often available as living-in domestic help but most want a longer period of employment than the other two categories. If you have enough room in your home to accommodate a mother with a family, this is the least expensive and most useful way of getting domestic help.

Playgroups and nursery schools

At two to two and a half years, a child can often enjoy playing with other children. Up to that time, his games have been solitary or have only involved you. At first, he may be shy and unsociable with other children, but learning to live with them is an important part of his education. If you have given him lots of attention and cuddling as a baby, he will probably feel secure enough to explore the world and its inhabitants. Do not force him to mix with others if he is unhappy. At first, you must go with him when he attends a playgroup. Try one morning or afternoon to start with; you can increase it to two or three times a week later. Most playgroups have an arrangement whereby mothers come and help for one session per week or fortnight anyway.

Ask your health visitor if she knows a group near you. You may need to enter your child's name early, because many groups have waiting lists. If there is no group near you the easiest thing may be to start one of your own with some other mothers. Nursery school is an essential – though not always available – bridge between home and full-time school. Children normally start at about three years of age.

One of the most enjoyable activities at playgroups and nursery schools is finger-painting (see page 187). Most children are fascinated by the feel of the paint and the patterns they can create with their fingers.

Postscript

I thought it would be best to end with this little postscript. I am always worried when I write anything about children and their problems in case I describe a sort of perfect world full of rules which should not be broken. You know your baby much better than I do; you will soon learn what he wants and what will make life easiest for your husband and you.

No one can hope to be the perfect mother all the time. You will sometimes feel tired and irritable. If you snap at your child and seem grumpy, do not feel guilty. This is a normal part of life and your child needs to understand it.

Be as patient as you possibly can be; this will make life easier for everyone. It is a mistake, though, to think that you can always be a model of good temper. With good food, cleanliness and love, children can grow up without experiencing many of the problems I have described in this book.

Index

246

Picture credits